THE EVERYTHING®
Healthy Cooking
for Parties Book

Dear Reader,

I love throwing parties. I've had parties for everything from a surprise fortieth birthday party for fifty to an intimate dinner for two. The comfort of my guests always comes first, and you'll learn some of my secrets for a successful party that you can enjoy too.

When my husband was little, his parents entertained frequently. He and his brother and sister loved to steal samples of the foods as their mother prepared them. A favorite was the cut-up fresh vegetables with dill dip; my mother-in-law couldn't stop them eating it! However, they were never treated to this favorite snack at other times. Perhaps it was the factor of sneaking a treat that added flavor to the recipe.

While I was browsing through the Internet and my cookbooks for party foods, I was really appalled at the nutrition statistics. The best recipes have enormous amounts of fat and sodium and not much in the way of nutrient density. By working with a sophisticated nutrition program, I was able to cut the fat and sodium and increase the nutritional density of the foods in this book. The exception is low-carb foods; those are almost always high-fat. But that's the nature of foods low in carbohydrates.

I hope you enjoy these recipes and tips on hosting the perfect party. Choose recipes from this book, then sit back and have a wonderful time.

Linda Larsen

Welcome to the EVERYTHING® Series!

These handy, accessible books give you all you need to tackle a difficult project, gain a new hobby, comprehend a fascinating topic, prepare for an exam, or even brush up on something you learned back in school but have since forgotten.

You can choose to read an *Everything*® book from cover to cover or just pick out the information you want from our four useful boxes: e-questions, e-facts, e-alerts, e-ssentials. We give you everything you need to know on the subject, but throw in a lot of fun stuff along the way, too.

We now have more than 400 *Everything*® books in print, spanning such wide-ranging categories as weddings, pregnancy, cooking, music instruction, foreign language, crafts, pets, New Age, and so much more. When you're done reading them all, you can finally say you know *Everything*®!

QUESTION?
Answers to
common questions

FACTS
Important snippets
of information

ALERTS!
Urgent
warnings

ESSENTIALS
Quick
handy tips

PUBLISHER Karen Cooper

DIRECTOR OF INNOVATION Paula Munier

MANAGING EDITOR, EVERYTHING SERIES Lisa Laing

COPY CHIEF Casey Ebert

ACQUISITIONS EDITOR Katie McDonough

DEVELOPMENT EDITOR Elizabeth Kassab

EDITORIAL ASSISTANT Hillary Thompson

THE EVERYTHING® HEALTHY COOKING *for* Parties BOOK

Delicious, guilt-free foods all
your guests will love

Linda Larsen, BS in Food Science and Nutrition

JG PRESS

An Everything® Series Book.
Everything® and everything.com® are registered trademarks of F+W Media, Inc.

Published by World Publications Group, Inc.
140 Laurel Street, East Bridgewater, MA 02333
www.wrldpub.com

ISBN 10: 1-57215-763-1
ISBN 13: 978-1-57215-763-7

Printed and bound in China

10   9   8   7   6   5   4   3   2   1

Library of Congress Cataloging-in-Publication Data
is available from the publisher.

This publication is designed to provide accurate and authoritative information with regard to the subject matter covered. It is sold with the understanding that the publisher is not engaged in rendering legal, accounting, or other professional advice. If legal advice or other expert assistance is required, the services of a competent professional person should be sought.
—From a *Declaration of Principles* jointly adopted by a Committee of the American Bar Association and a Committee of Publishers and Associations

Many of the designations used by manufacturers and sellers to distinguish their products are claimed as trademarks. Where those designations appear in this book and Adams Media was aware of a trademark claim, the designations have been printed with initial capital letters.

Dedication

To my mother, Marlene, who taught me how to be the perfect hostess.

Acknowledgments

My thanks to everyone I ever entertained, either in my home or at potluck parties and parties that I catered. To my dear husband, Doug, of course, who is the best kitchen assistant ever. To my agent, Barb Doyen, for her help and support. And to my family, who is always there for me.

Contents

Introduction

When you think of party food, you automatically think of rich, gooey desserts, entrées full of fat and flavor, and breads and vegetable side dishes slathered with butter and cheese. When entertaining, you always want to serve your best and most flavorful recipes because your main goal is the comfort, happiness, and well-being of your guests.

But there are lots of things you can do to prepare and serve healthy food, not only to your family, but also at a party. The changes don't have to be drastic, and the food will be delicious because you're using fresh, whole foods and more homemade products.

Parties come with built-in reasons to celebrate. Whether you're giving a surprise bridal shower or a milestone birthday party, a holiday gathering or a party to celebrate a job success or promotion, these celebrations are easy to pull together. But serving healthy food at these events is another matter. Most of the so-called best recipes you'll find in books, online, or from friends and family load on the fat, calories, and simple carbohydrates with little thought to health.

The emphasis in this book is on nutrient-dense foods. *Nutrient-dense* means that a food provides a lot of vitamins, minerals, fiber, and micronutrients for the calories it contains. Junk food and snack foods, candy bars, cakes, and white bread are generally considered empty-calorie foods. That means they provide very few nutrients for the calories.

Small changes will make a big difference: throw some carrots into a beef daube, add sweet potatoes to your favorite creamy potato recipe, grate carrots into spaghetti sauce, and serve an apricot sauce over a chocolate ice cream dessert. It's not difficult to work more produce into your diet; it just takes a little thought and imagination.

Here's another tip: don't try to make a brand new recipe for a party. You understandably want to serve something special, but do try a new recipe a few days or weeks before the party. Make sure you understand how to safely prepare it, that it tastes good to you and your family, and that it's within your skill level as a cook and baker.

One of the most important secrets to a good party is to relax. Humans are animals, after all, and we can sense the mood and tension in a room. If the host is worried and anxious, the party is never going to get into full swing. The most important rule is to have fun and enjoy yourself, no matter what. If something burns or a recipe doesn't turn out as planned, don't let that spoil your evening. Shrug it off and order pizza. The point of a party is to get friends and family together, enjoy each other's company, and have fun.

Chapter 1

Throw a Healthy Party!

So you're having a party! That alone is cause for celebration. Reasons for hosting parties include birthdays, notable accomplishments, anniversaries, weddings, and holidays. But a celebration is not a reason to throw caution to the winds and your diet out the window. There are things you can do to ensure that you feed your family and guests healthy, hearty food that is so good no one will guess it is good for them. And the best news is that this food will still be delicious and fit for a celebration.

What's Healthy?

Debate has raged for years about what constitutes a healthy diet. Fad diets have come and gone, miracle foods are discovered and discarded, and the American population continues to gain weight. Scientists and nutritionists are slowly reaching a consensus about healthy foods: whole, fresh foods, simply prepared, with little or no artificial ingredients. First, we have to understand what our bodies need for good health.

Daily Calorie and Nutrient Requirements

Nutrient	Children Under 11*	Women Under 50	Women Over 50	Men
Calories	900–2,200 kcal	2,000 kcal	2,000 kcal or fewer	2,700 kcal
Fat	35 grams	65 grams	65 grams	88 grams
Protein	40 grams	50 grams	50 grams	63 grams
Carbohydrates	150 grams	304 grams	304 grams	410 grams
Sodium	1,500 mg	2,000 mg	1,500 mg	2,000 mg
Fiber	26 grams	30 grams	30 grams	30 grams
Calcium	1,300 mg	1,000 mg	1,200 mg	1,000 mg
Vitamin A	2500 IU	2333 IU	2333 IU	3000 IU
Vitamin C	25 mg	40 mg	40 mg	40 mg
Iron	15 mg	18 mg	8 mg	8 mg

*Nutrition for children varies depending on age. These are average amounts. Children are evaluated by adult requirements when they are eleven years old.

Did you know that heart disease was an uncommon illness in the American population until the advent of processed foods? As hydrogenated fats, lots of sodium, fast food, junk food, and fake ingredients have worked their way into our diets, heart disease rates have skyrocketed, and heart disease is now the number one health problem in the country.

Diets have come and gone for years; the diet industry is a billion-dollar industry. If diets worked, there wouldn't be so much money spent on them every year! The solution is to eat a varied diet in moderation, exercise daily, and enjoy life without stressing about everything you put into your mouth.

Nutrient Dense

The nutrients your body needs are those that it cannot make itself: fats, carbohydrates, protein, vitamins, and minerals. These include minerals like iron, calcium, potassium, and sodium and vitamins A, C, B, D, and E. A nutrient-dense food is one that provides a good amount of these nutrients for the amount of calories it contains. By focusing on foods high in vitamins and minerals, you will automatically be eating the healthiest diet.

JESTION?

What about supplements?
Supplements can be a good addition to a diet, but they are no cure for a poor diet. The recommended daily amount for vitamins is considered a minimum necessary to stave off disease, not the amount needed for best health.

One way to automatically include nutrient-dense foods in your diet is to build a colorful plate. Include many fruits and vegetables that have a deep color: deep oranges, reds, blues, yellows, and greens. In general, the more colorful a food and the deeper the color, the higher its vitamin and mineral content.

Empty-calorie foods were briefly mentioned in the Introduction. These are foods that are the opposite of nutrient dense. Candy bars, French fries, soda pop, unenriched white bread, white pasta, and snack foods all provide very little nutrition for the calories provided. Reducing these foods in your diet is a must.

Nutrient-dense foods should be the mainstay of your diet. That includes fruits, vegetables, whole grains, fish, and low-fat dairy products. You can, of course, include some empty-calorie foods, but they should be the exception, not the rule.

Build a Colorful Plate

The simplest change you can make is just to build a colorful plate; that is, include more fruits and vegetables in all recipes in your diet. Most Americans do not eat the recommended six to eleven servings of fruits and vegetables a day; in fact, only about 10 percent of us do. Making a conscious effort to add more of these healthy foods to your diet will result in positive changes in your health.

When you arrange your dinner plate, half of the space should be taken up by fruits and vegetables. Another fourth can be filled with some type of protein, and the final fourth filled with whole grains like breads, brown rice, legumes, and whole wheat pasta. Follow this basic rule with a smaller plate and your diet will automatically be healthier.

Factors in a Healthy Diet

A healthy diet is defined as one that provides the nutrients your body needs, including calories, fat, protein, carbohydrates, vitamins, minerals, and fiber. There is a constant debate in medical literature about the level of vitamins and minerals we need for good health versus the minimum amount necessary to prevent nutritional diseases like scurvy. Megadoses of vitamins, especially the fat-soluble vitamins, aren't safe. It's best to get most of your nutrients from whole foods.

Low Fat

In general, Americans consume too much fat. The American Heart Association recommends that no more than 25 to 35 percent of our calories come from fat. But many people consume 40 to 50 percent of their calories from fat. Just reducing the amount of fat we eat is a good start toward a healthy diet.

But it's not as simple as that. We shouldn't be afraid of good fats—those fats that can actually have a positive impact on our health. Olive oil, nuts, avocados, butter, fatty fish, and flaxseed are examples of good fats that we should include in our diets. Don't be afraid of saturated fats in butter and palm and coconut oils. Those fats were unfairly lumped together with trans fat in early health studies in the 1950s and blamed for increases in heart disease. We now know that moderate consumption of these fats is actually healthy. Butter contains vitamins and minerals, and the saturated fat in palm fruit and coconut oils is immediately burned for energy. Coconut oil also has antifungal and antibacterial properties.

Essential fatty acids are fats that your body needs to survive and thrive. The two main essential fatty acid families are omega-3 and omega-6. The ideal proportion is a 1:2 ratio, but the actual ratio that our diets provide is more like 1:20. Omega-3 fatty acids are found in flaxseed, fatty fish, and nuts. Omega-6 fatty acids are found in cooking oils, snack foods, fast foods, and margarines. Consuming whole foods and natural foods while reducing foods that don't provide much nutrition will automatically help put this ratio into balance.

Trans fat is one food that is, quite simply, bad for you in any amount. It's included in everything from solid shortening to peanut butter. Using trans fat–free products is one step on the road to a healthy diet.

JESTION?

Can a diet be too low in fat?

Yes, it can. Your body needs fat to help transport the fat-soluble vitamins, A, D, and E. If you don't eat enough fat, your skin and hair will become dry, and you may become malnourished. A diet that is very low in fat is also unpalatable. Children, especially, should not be fed a very low-fat diet because fat is necessary for growth and development.

What about artificial fats? There are many snack foods and junk foods made with fake fat, but that doesn't mean that you can load up on these foods and feel virtuous. These foods do not provide many nutrients, even with a reduced calorie load. And fake fats have unpleasant side effects. It's also possible to become deficient in the fat-soluble vitamins when you consume fake fats instead of healthy fats.

In the end, keeping yourself healthy is a balancing act. Don't be afraid of good fats, but eat them in moderation. If you build a colorful plate and eat in moderation, your diet will automatically become healthier.

Low Sodium

Americans eat too much salt. It's difficult to cut down on sodium because it's naturally present in so many foods. We run into trouble when we consume too many processed foods, which are universally high in sodium. Too much sodium can increase the risk of high blood pressure and heart disease. We need some sodium in our diets every day, but not two to three times what is necessary.

Concentrate on basing your diet on whole foods, not processed foods. Not only will this reduce the amount of sodium in your diet, but there are many micronutrients that scientists don't even know about that are found in whole foods. Many of these are lost in processing. It's better to eat a whole baked potato than fast-food French fries.

Television chefs pile on the salt, often adding salt to every layer in a dish. Adults should consume no more than 2,000 mg of sodium per day—that's a little less than 1 teaspoon. It may take a little while for your taste buds to adjust to less salt, but once they do you'll find that most processed foods and restaurant food tastes too salty.

Low Calorie

It's a fact that Americans consume more calories than they need. The trick is to offer food that is not too high in calories but that still satisfies not only nutritional requirements but hunger. Moderation is key. If you offer a few higher-calorie foods, be sure to include lower-calorie choices so your guests can pick the foods they want to eat.

Follow the USDA food pyramid for recommended servings of each food group and for serving sizes. With the advent of super-sized portions, we have become used to eating two and three times a standard portion in one sitting.

It's okay to indulge from time to time; in fact, if you don't, the odds are good that you'll go on an eating binge that could last for days, if not months. Satisfy your sweet tooth by choosing foods that are still healthy. Strawberries dipped in dark chocolate, for instance, are not only delicious but offer a good amount of vitamin C from the strawberries and polyphenols from the chocolate.

Single-Serving Portion Sizes

Type of Food	Amount	What It Looks Like
Meat	3–4 ounces	deck of cards
Vegetable	½ cup	tennis ball
Fruit	1 medium, or ½ cup	tennis ball
Greens	2 cups	2 fists
Bread	1 slice	audio cassette tape
Cheese	1 ounce	2 dominoes
Pasta	½ cup	cupped palm
Chips	1 ounce	cupped palm
Butter	1 teaspoon	thumbnail
Ice cream	½ cup	½ baseball

High Fiber

Fiber is an essential nutrient. Fiber comes from plants. It is not digested by the body; it passes through. This may sound strange, but it's essential to good health. If you don't eat enough fiber, your digestive system will have a difficult time processing foods. A high-fiber diet can help reduce the risk of disease, especially heart disease and cancer. This type of diet can help lower cholesterol levels and control blood sugar, making it easier to manage diabetes.

There are two kinds of fiber: soluble and insoluble. Soluble fiber dissolves in water and forms a gel in your digestive system. It is found in foods like oatmeal, fruit, and legumes. Insoluble fiber is not digested and is found in foods like oat bran, nuts, and vegetables (particularly dark green, leafy vegetables).

Nutritionists are now studying a new type of fiber, called resistant starch, in addition to soluble and insoluble fiber. This fiber is found in legumes, rice, pasta, and potatoes and may be a critical partner in the fight against heart disease. It encourages metabolism of fats over carbohydrates and helps signal a sense of fullness.

Foods high in fiber also help you feel full sooner, and they help you stay full for a longer period of time. High-fiber foods are usually nutrient-dense foods, providing good amounts of vitamins, minerals, and phytonutrients like antioxidants and polyphenols that are important to good health. High-fiber foods include:

- All-bran cereal
- Brussels sprouts
- Corn and other vegetables
- Peas
- Apple with skin
- Pears and other fruits
- Legumes
- Seeds and nuts
- Oatmeal
- Kale
- Lentils

If you include more high-fiber foods in your diet you will automatically get more nutrients in your diet. But it's best to add these foods slowly. Don't suddenly go from two servings of fruits and vegetables one day to eleven the next. Your body needs time to adjust to the change.

Low Carb

The low-carb diet originated with Dr. Atkins, who believed that it was carbohydrates, not fat, that was the enemy. Because your brain needs glucose, a carbohydrate, to function, if you restrict carbohydrate intake, your body will make carbs from protein and fat. This throws your body into a state called ketosis, and you will lose weight.

While there are people who still follow this type of diet, it isn't the healthiest choice. Any diet that restricts entire classes of food is not a sensible plan that can be followed for a lifetime. One of the tricks of the diet is that you will get sick of eating high-fat, high-protein foods and will eat less, thus restricting your caloric intake. But this plan is low in fiber and can be low in essential vitamins and minerals, especially vitamin C.

JESTION?

Can you eat low-carb and low-fat?
Think of food like a balloon made up of calories, divided into three sections: fat, carbohydrates, and protein. If you take away one of the sections, one or both of the others have to expand. Most low-carb diets are high in fat, just because you have to eat something! Look for good natural fats in a low-carb diet, including olive oil, nuts, and, yes, butter.

If you or a guest at your party has diabetes or must severely reduce sugar intake, sugar substitutes like Splenda will work in most baked goods. They are substituted in a 1:1 ratio. But unless you fall into this category, sugar substitutes aren't the best choice for good health. There is a lot of controversy about the long-term health effects of these artificial ingredients. And again, sugar substitutes aren't a whole food; they are extensively processed.

The National Academy of Sciences recommends a diet with at least 120 grams of carbohydrates a day. The USDA recommends 300 grams of carbs for a healthy diet—about 60 percent of total calories. Compare that to the Atkins diet, which recommends 20 grams of carbs per day.

A better plan is to restrict simple carbohydrates, sometimes called bad carbs. Simple carbohydrates are short-chain monosaccharides like glucose, sucrose, and fructose, along with short-chain carbohydrates like those found in white flour. These carbs give you a quick burst of energy, but then you will crash and feel hungry and tired. Concentrate on adding complex carbohydrates, like whole grains, legumes, vegetables, and fruits, to your diet. This is not only less restrictive, but it is a healthier diet with more variety. It's an eating plan you can stick with for life.

Kids' Health and Food

Children need good nutrition during their early years so they can grow up strong and healthy. In the past thirty years, the child obesity rate has more than doubled. Kids are eating too much fast food, too many empty calories, and not enough nutritious food. In addition, their lifestyle is much too sedentary.

What can you do? The best way to teach kids how to eat well is to eat well yourself. Let them see you enjoying fruits and vegetables, eating whole grain foods, and indulging in empty calories and fast foods just once in a while. You are their most powerful role model.

Introducing Food

Scientists have estimated that it takes up to fifteen introductions for a child to even try a new food. They are born with a strong preference for sweet flavors, which makes breast milk desirable. Sour and bitter foods are naturally unpalatable to them, but this changes as they grow older.

ALERT!

Most parents have a story about struggling to get their kids to eat healthy foods. Bitter foods like Brussels sprouts, broccoli, and dark, leafy greens are unpalatable for kids because their taste buds are so sensitive. Don't force these foods; that will only solidify their hatred for them. Offer them once in a while, enjoy them yourself, and just be patient.

You can resort to hiding healthy foods in foods your children like to eat. This can be a way to get more nutrition in their diets, but eventually you will have to come clean. Don't tell them after the fact that there are carrots in the spaghetti sauce or cauliflower in the macaroni and cheese; that will build a feeling of distrust. But get them involved in the preparation of these foods. If you start young, they won't look twice at these more unusual additions.

Get Kids Involved

Other ways to encourage healthy eating include getting your children involved in food selection and preparation, giving them a small garden spot so they can grow sweet foods like tomatoes and peas, and giving them lots of options. Kids can wash vegetables and fruit and measure ingredients for making breads and soups. Older children can be taught how to peel and chop fruits and vegetables.

Healthy Cooking Techniques and Tips

Using whole foods—in other words, foods that have not been processed—is the best way to naturally and easily upgrade your diet. Restrict processed foods that have long ingredient lists, use ingredients you can't pronounce, and have high amounts of sodium and fat. Avoid foods that have fat or sugar as one of the first five ingredients in the ingredient list.

Most recipes are quite tolerant; that is, you can change proportions and amounts, and they will still work if you substitute ingredients. Baking recipes, like those for breads, cakes, and cookies, are less forgiving, but cooking recipes, like those for soups, main dishes, and salads, can be significantly changed.

Reduce the Fat

In most recipes, even those for baked goods, you can start by reducing the fat by about one-third. Use less fat for sautéing vegetables to start a soup or main dish, and reduce the fat in your favorite cake recipe. If this lower-fat version is acceptable to you, reduce the fat to one-third of the original amount. You really can't go beyond this restriction without compromising quality. Also, use good fats like butter and olive oil instead of solid shortening or margarine. The foods will taste better and will be better for you. Trim any visible fat from meats and discard it. Meat has enough intramuscular fat that trimming off fat from the exterior isn't going to affect the flavor.

Reduce the Sugar

You can cut the sugar in most baked goods by about one-third. If the product is still acceptable to you, cut it by half. But you really can't go beyond that amount; sugar is necessary not only for the structure of baked goods but for flavor, moistness, and browning.

In cooking, reduce the sugar by half. You can also substitute other forms of sugar; honey or maple syrup are good choices. Sugar substitutes can be used, but as with any artificial food, use them judiciously unless you are feeding someone who is diabetic.

Cut the Salt

You can easily cut the amount of salt in half for just about any recipe without greatly affecting the flavor. Our taste buds are accustomed to too much salt; just think about fast food French fries that are coated in it. With less salt, the other flavors of the food can shine through. Increasing other flavors also helps. Add citrus juice, fresh herbs, spices, hot peppers, and other flavorful ingredients to mitigate salt reduction.

Increase Flavor

Reducing the fat in recipes means that some flavor will be lost, since fat is a flavor carrier. There are easy ways to replace that flavor and maintain the integrity of the food.

Use fresh herbs and spices instead of the dried versions. Dried herbs and spices add flavor, but their fresh counterparts add more. The general rule is to use three times the amount of fresh herbs to dried. If a recipe calls for 1 teaspoon dried thyme, use 1 tablespoon fresh thyme instead. Citrus juices add flavor and can help food taste a bit more salty without adding sodium. They also add lots of vitamin C.

Eat Slowly

It can take up to twenty minutes for your stomach to signal to your brain that it is full. If you eat in ten or fifteen minutes, it's very easy to overeat because that signal hasn't come through. Put down your fork between bites, or try switching hands. It's more difficult to eat with your less dominant hand, so you will eat more slowly.

FACT

A recent study found that subjects who were blindfolded and told to eat until they felt full and satisfied ate 22 percent less than those who weren't blindfolded. You don't have to eat everything on your plate; pay attention to the cues your body gives you. The clean-plate-club mentality is responsible for some of the obesity crisis in this country.

Another study found that people who ate more slowly were also more satisfied and less hungry a few hours after eating. One of the best ways to encourage slower eating is to encourage conversation at the dinner table. Have some noncontroversial topics planned; talk about the person or event being celebrated at your party.

Use Small Plates

Visual cues are important in dining and weight regulation. Use smaller plates to set your table. Studies show that if we eat off large plates, in general we consume more food. Smaller plates look fuller and show off the food better, so our visual cue is satisfied.

Small plates also provide what nutritionists call an end signal. If you eat from a bag of potato chips, it's very easy to eat until the bag is empty. But putting chips into a small bowl will help your body realize there is an end to the food.

Since we tend to fill whatever plate or dish we are given, using smaller plates will automatically decrease the amount of food we eat. If it's too big of a change to go from a twelve-inch dinner plate to an eight-inch salad plate, try gradually reducing the plate size over time.

Food Safety and Parties

Food safety should be one of your top priorities. If the food you serve makes people sick, it doesn't matter how healthy the food is or how fun the party was. As the host, you are responsible for the health and safety of your guests; take this seriously. You have to keep an eye on the food, watch the time and temperature, and ensure that all the food is wholesome.

If some of your guests fall into a high-risk group—that is, pregnant, elderly, very young, or those with chronic diseases—you must be even more vigilant. Follow the basic rules of food safety:

- Promptly refrigerate food when you bring it home from the store
- Wash your hands after handling food
- Keep cooked and uncooked foods separate
- Do not store uncooked foods on top of cooked or ready-to-eat foods
- Keep hot foods hot and cold foods cold

- Do not let perishable food stand out at room temperature longer than two hours; one hour if the temperature is above 80°F
- Make sure your guests wash their hands too; offer hand wipes at picnics and other outdoor events
- Cook meat to a safe internal temperature before serving

Meat and eggs have special rules and regulations. Meat has to be cooked to a certain internal temperature to be safe. Keep raw meats away from food and be sure to wash your hands after handling it. Raw and undercooked eggs are not considered safe and shouldn't be served.

Meat Temperature Guidelines

Meat	Internal Temperature
Ground meat	165°F
Rare steak	135°F
Medium steak	145°F
Well-done steak	160°F
Turkey breast	165°F
Whole turkey	180°F
Chicken	165°F
Pork	155°F
Fish	140°F

If you're serving buffet style, it's important to rotate perishable foods so you always offer your guests safe, wholesome food. Set a small timer when you put out foods. If the timer goes off and there is still food on the platters, discard it and set out freshly prepared foods. Remember, you can refrigerate foods that have been sitting out, but returning those foods to a cooler if you're at a picnic isn't safe.

Party Planning

It's easy to plan a party; the amount of planning you have to do depends on how complicated the party is. A simple get-together for lunch just needs telephone invites, menu planning, and some table setting and decorating. But a wedding or baby shower means coordinating guests lists, setting a theme, and planning games, gifts, and food that will please the guests and especially the guest of honor.

The Theme

Is this a birthday party? A simple gathering of close friends? A celebration of a job promotion, a baby shower, or a holiday party? The theme is the beginning of party planning. This will automatically help you think about the guest list, the invitations, and the food.

A birthday party should be planned around the likes and dislikes of the special guest. A baby or wedding shower focuses on the bride or mother-to-be, while a job promotion can be planned around the hard-working star. Use the honored guest's favorite colors in your choices of flowers, balloons, and tableware, and include her favorite foods.

Supplies

You need to have the equipment and serving pieces to make and serve the food! When you choose your recipes, make a list of the supplies you'll need. If you're missing one or two, try to borrow them from family or friends. You can also rent everything from chairs to chafing dishes to outdoor tents. It's a good idea to start building a collection of sturdy classic serving pieces so you're prepared no matter the menu.

Guest List

When planning a guest list, you must consider the needs of your guests as well as the purpose of the party. A picnic in the park with a casual theme won't be appropriate for some groups, while a formal dinner can make others uncomfortable.

When making up your guest lists, think about people you think might enjoy each other's company. If your party is a payback for other invitations, include different people in the mix. A party is a great place to help others develop new friendships.

Be sure to only include the number of people that your house or party area can comfortably accommodate, and the number of people you feel confident feeding. Hosting too many people will simply make everyone uncomfortable. At the same time, a sparsely attended party can feel hollow and artificial. Plan the guest list carefully.

Invitations

The easiest way to invite people is just to call (or text message!). Be sure you allow enough time so people won't already have full calendars. Stationery stores, bookstores, and big-box retailers all have fabulous selections of invitations for any event. For a nice homemade touch, think about having your kids design the invitations, even for a formal event. They can be easily reproduced on a color copier.

The Food

When planning your menu, think about balancing the nutrition of the entire meal. If you want to serve something that isn't very nutrient dense, like baked chicken, balance it with a salad packed with fresh vegetables and dark greens and a healthy dessert that uses lots of fruit. Every single recipe doesn't have to be full of vitamins and minerals; it can have one or two good attributes and still fit into a healthy meal.

Planning a meal is a skill that just takes practice. You need to balance color, flavors, and temperature. Don't choose foods that are all brown, all hot, and all savory. A mix of sweet, sour, savory, bitter, along with hot and cold foods and gorgeous colors is best.

The first recipe to plan is the entrée. Remembering your guests' likes and dislikes, choose a recipe that is within your cooking skill range and that is appropriate to the season. You really wouldn't want to serve a big pot roast in the middle of summer, and grilled foods are always appropriate for warmer seasons.

Next choose side dishes and salads. If you are serving a pot roast, keep in mind that the roast's vegetables add flavor, color, and nutrition, allowing you to eliminate another dish. A fresh, crisp green salad is a good accompaniment, and breads are always a nice addition.

Balance last-minute recipes with make-ahead recipes. Using your slow cooker is always a good idea. In fact, if you can make two dishes in the slow cooker you'll be much calmer and more able to enjoy your own party.

Timetable and Shopping

It's a good idea to write down a timetable for your party. Start at the time you want to serve dinner and work backward from that point. Write everything down: the menu, the guest list, the shopping list, the serving pieces you'll need, plus the decorations, drinks, and supplies.

Don't expect to get everything done in one big shopping trip. Break the list down into several more easily manageable sections. Buy the most perishable goods, like fresh fruits and flowers, the day before the party. You might want to schedule one last shopping trip the night before the party just to make sure nothing has been forgotten.

Drinks

Always ask if your guests drink alcohol or if they have allergies or preferences. A big bowl of punch is the most cost-effective way to serve a large group of people, but a station for making individual drinks is a nice touch. Plan on about one bottle of wine for every three guests, one gallon of punch for ten people, and one or two cocktails per person. It's always best to have more than you need. Leftovers are one of the best things about a party.

Always offer a selection of nonalcoholic drinks along with wines or mixed drinks. Many people do not drink for health reasons, and others just don't like the taste. You'll also need a good selection of nonalcoholic drinks for the kids. Fill a big cooler or tub with ice and stock it with bottles and cans of fruit juice, sparkling water, and tea.

About the Recipes in this Cookbook

The nutritional information for the recipes in this book, as well as the information in the tables in this chapter, have been calculated by NutriBase Clinical Version 7.0 (*www.dietsoftware.com*). Total calories, fat, percentage of fat by calories, carbohydrates, fiber, sodium, calcium, vitamin A, and vitamin C content are included for each recipe.

You can substitute even lower-fat or fat-free ingredients in many of these recipes. Use your favorite fruits and vegetables, substitute chicken in a beef recipe, or change the flavor of a dip or soup. If you don't like onions or peas, leave them out. One of the most satisfying things about entertaining is tailoring the event to your taste. Have a wonderful party!

Chapter 2

Delicious Drinks and Appetizers

SERVES 10

Calories: 292.97
Fat: 7.00 grams
Fat as % of calories: 21.5%
Carbohydrates: 55.54 grams
Sodium: 142.33 mg
Vitamin A: 6% DV
Vitamin C: 4% DV
Calcium: 187.09 mg

INGREDIENTS

¼ cup granulated sugar
¼ cup brown sugar
⅓ cup cocoa
⅛ teaspoon salt
¾ cup water
1 cup dark chocolate chips
6 cups 1% chocolate milk
2 cups mini marshmallows
2 teaspoons vanilla
1 cup marshmallow creme

Angel Hot Chocolate

Melted marshmallows give this hot chocolate a fluffy consistency and creamy texture without adding any fat.

1. In large saucepan combine sugars, cocoa, salt, and water and mix well. Bring to a boil over high heat. Reduce heat to medium and boil for 2 minutes, stirring constantly to dissolve sugars. Remove from heat and stir in chocolate chips until melted.

2. Add milk and marshmallows. Cook and stir over medium heat until the marshmallows are melted and the mixture is steaming.

3. Stir in vanilla. Place a spoonful of marshmallow creme in the bottom of each mug and pour in the hot chocolate. Serve immediately.

SERVES 6

Calories: 120.54
Fat: 1.14 grams
Fat as % of calories: 8.5%
Carbohydrates: 34.82 grams
Fiber: 0.09 grams
Sodium: 54.46 mg
Vitamin A: 4% DV
Vitamin C: 0% DV
Calcium: 78.48 mg

INGREDIENTS

4 cups light root beer
2 cups light vanilla ice cream
½ cup crushed root beer candy

Light Root Beer Floats

Root beer floats are the essence of summer. Serve these with Banana–Orange Cupcakes (page 193) for a children's birthday party. You can use low-carb root beer and no-sugar ice cream if you'd like.

Chill six 1-cup mugs. Add ⅓ cup of root beer to each mug. Add ⅓ cup of the ice cream to each mug and stir gently. Slowly top with remaining root beer. Sprinkle with the crushed candy and serve immediately.

Low-Carb Beverages

Low-carb beverages, like low-carb root beer, use artificial sweeteners instead of sugar. If you use low-carb root beer and sugar-free ice cream in this recipe, the amount of carbohydrates per serving will drop to 4.23 grams. It's your choice whether you use artificial ingredients.

Healthy Fuzzy Navel

*A fuzzy navel is usually made with peach schnapps and vodka.
You can certainly add those to this drink, but this healthy
version is nonalcoholic.*

1. In large pitcher, combine peach nectar, orange juice, and gingerroot. Cover and chill for 2–3 hours to blend flavors.

2. When ready to serve, remove the gingerroot slices. Pour into a punch bowl and stir in ginger ale. Serve immediately.

SERVES 10

Calories: 114.20
Fat: 0.29 grams
Fat as % of calories: 2.3%
Carbohydrates: 28.16 grams
Fiber: 0.80 grams
Sodium: 11.38 mg
Vitamin A: 6% DV
Vitamin C: 100% DV
Calcium: 16.40 mg

INGREDIENTS
*4 cups peach nectar
4 cups orange juice
3 thin slices peeled gingerroot
1 16-ounce bottle ginger ale*

White Wine Sangria

*This sangria is a beautiful light pastel color. Encourage your guests to
eat the fruit after they're sipped the sangria!*

1. In large pitcher, combine lemon juice, orange juice, and lemonade concentrate; mix until concentrate dissolves. Add schnapps, rum, and wine; stir gently, cover, and chill overnight.

2. Place cherries, strawberries, and mango in bottom of punch bowl. Add wine mixture, then stir in ginger ale. Float lemon and lime slices in the bowl and top with raspberries. Serve immediately.

SERVES 16

Calories: 232.82
Fat: 0.24 grams
Fat as % of calories: 0.9%
Carbohydrates: 24.00 grams
Fiber: 1.69 grams
Sodium: 7.18 mg
Vitamin A: 2% DV
Vitamin C: 45% DV
Calcium: 12.23 mg

INGREDIENTS
*⅓ cup lemon juice
1 cup orange juice
1 6-ounce container frozen pink
   lemonade concentrate
½ cup peach schnapps
½ cup light rum
3 750-milliliter bottles white wine
1 cup each, chopped: cherries,
   strawberries, mango
2 16-ounce bottles ginger ale
1 lemon and 2 limes, thinly sliced
1½ cups raspberries*

SERVES 12

Calories: 85.71
Fat: 0.32 grams
Fat as % of calories: 4.2%
Carbohydrates: 21.74 grams
Fiber: 0.61 grams
Sodium: 30.92 mg
Vitamin A: 4% DV
Vitamin C: 0% DV
Calcium: 93.93 mg

INGREDIENTS
1 16-ounce bottle black tea
 concentrate
⅓ cup sugar
¼ cup honey
½ teaspoon ground cardamom
¼ cup cocoa powder
2 cups skim milk
1 32-ounce bottle ginger ale,
 chilled

Mocha Chai Punch

*A touch of honey and cardamom add nice flavor to a
milk-tea punch that's healthy and delicious.
Chai is a strong tea flavored with milk and spices.*

1. Pour the tea concentrate into large bowl or pitcher; set aside. In large saucepan, combine sugar, honey, cardamom, cocoa powder, and milk and mix well with wire whisk.

2. Cook sugar mixture over medium heat, stirring frequently, until it just comes to a simmer. Pour into the tea concentrate and stir well. Cover and chill for at least 24 hours.

3. When ready to serve, stir punch and pour into punch bowl. Add ginger ale and mix gently. Serve immediately.

Tea

Black tea contains a compound called theaflavin-3-monogallate, an antioxidant that inhibits the growth of cancer cells. It can also lower total cholesterol levels and may lower your risk of developing Parkinson's disease if consumed regularly. Green tea and white tea offer similar benefits, and they're all delicious.

Cantaloupe Punch

This is one healthy punch! If you prefer, you could add a bottle of white wine or sparkling wine instead of the club soda.

1. Purée cantaloupe in batches in blender or food processor. Place in large bowl and stir in lime juice.

2. In medium saucepan, combine sugar with water; bring to a boil. Reduce heat and simmer until sugar dissolves completely. Remove from heat and add orange juice. Cool completely.

3. Stir sugar mixture into cantaloupe along with apricot nectar and lemon juice. Cover and chill until ready to serve, at least 4 hours.

4. When ready to serve, stir cantaloupe mixture and pour into punch bowl. Add club soda and ice and serve.

SERVES 12

Calories: 123.89
Fat: 0.41 grams
Fat as % of calories: 2.9%
Carbohydrates: 30.91 grams
Fiber: 1.62 grams
Sodium: 31.88 mg
Vitamin A: 100% DV
Vitamin C: 150% DV
Calcium: 22.78 mg

INGREDIENTS

2 cantaloupes, peeled and cubed
¼ cup lime juice
½ cup sugar
1 cup water
2 cups orange juice
2 cups apricot nectar
½ cup lemon juice
1 16-ounce bottle club soda

Cranberry Punch

This is a delicious punch to serve during the holidays. You could add some sweetened dried cranberries to the punch for a little surprise.

1. Combine all ingredients except ginger ale in large bowl. Stir until blended, then cover and chill for 4–5 hours until very cold.

2. When ready to serve, pour into punch bowl and add ginger ale. Stir gently and serve immediately.

Frozen Rings

To keep punch cold without diluting it, make special rings of frozen juice along with fresh fruit. Just arrange fruit in a ring mold, then pour in some of the same ingredients used in the punch. Freeze until frozen solid. To use, dip mold into warm water for a few seconds, then invert, remove mold, and float the ring in the punch.

SERVES 16

Calories: 161.55
Fat: 0.21 grams
Fat as % of calories: 0.1%
Carbohydrates: 40.83 grams
Fiber: 0.26 grams
Sodium: 10.06 mg
Vitamin A: 10% DV
Vitamin C: 80% DV
Calcium: 14.17 mg

INGREDIENTS

1 12-ounce can frozen apple juice concentrate
1 12-ounce can pink lemonade concentrate
2 cups orange juice
2 12-ounce cans frozen cranberry juice concentrate
6 cups cold water
2 cups cranberry juice cocktail
1 16-ounce bottle ginger ale

SERVES 6

Calories: 50.11
Fat: 2.35 grams
Fat as % of calories: 42.4%
Carbohydrates: 6.76 mg
Fiber: 0.43 grams
Sodium: 100.36 mg
Vitamin A: 0% DV
Vitamin C: 10% DV
Calcium: 36.40 mg

INGREDIENTS

2 heads garlic
¼ teaspoon salt
⅛ teaspoon white pepper
½ teaspoon dried thyme leaves
1 tablespoon olive oil
2 teaspoons lemon juice

Roasted Garlic

When garlic is roasted it becomes nutty and sweet.
Spread it onto crackers or use it in recipes like the
Best Light Garlic Cheese Bread (page 138).

1. Preheat oven to 375°F. Remove some of the papery skins from the garlic heads. Cut each in half through the center, making four equal rounds. Place, cut side up, on a cookie sheet with sides.

2. Sprinkle with salt, pepper, and thyme and drizzle with olive oil. Sprinkle with lemon juice. Bake for 35–45 minutes or until garlic is golden and soft.

3. Let cool for 15 minutes, or until garlic is cool enough to handle. Squeeze cloves out of skins; discard skins. Serve as is, or mash and serve as an appetizer spread.

Fat in Low-Calorie Foods

When any fat at all is included in a very low-calorie food, like roasted garlic, the fat percentage of calories is going to be higher than your target of 30 percent. That doesn't mean the recipe is bad for you. Look at the kind of fat used; if it's monounsaturated olive oil, don't be concerned.

Tropical Salsa

This salsa packs a punch, both figuratively and nutritionally!
Its gorgeous colors will brighten up any platter.
Serve with bell pepper strips, crackers, and tortilla chips.

Drain pineapple, reserving juice. Combine all ingredients along with 3 tablespoons of the reserved juice in a large bowl; stir gently. Cover and chill for 2–3 hours to blend flavors before serving.

How to Peel a Mango

To peel mango, set it upright on work surface and cut down one side of the pit. Cut down the other side of the pit, then cut the two thinner sides from the pit. Hold the mango in your nondominant hand, and make criss-cross cuts through the flesh but not through the skin. Turn the mango halves inside-out, and cut the cubes from the skin.

SERVES 8

Calories: 98.05
Fat: 0.47 grams
Fat as % of calories: 4.3%
Carbohydrates: 24.61 grams
Fiber: 3.74 grams
Sodium: 152.73 mg
Vitamin A: 45% DV
Vitamin C: 210% DV
Calcium: 43.26 mg

INGREDIENTS

1 15-ounce can pineapple tidbits
2 oranges, peeled and chopped
1 mango, peeled and diced
2 red bell peppers, chopped
3 tomatoes, chopped
½ cup chopped green onion
½ cup chopped red onion
2 jalapeño peppers, minced
⅓ cup chopped cilantro
¼ cup lime juice
½ teaspoon salt
⅛ teaspoon pepper
¼ teaspoon cayenne pepper

Fresh Tomato Salsa

This salsa is delicious on everything from grilled chicken to grilled corn or potatoes. Serve it with baked sweet potato chips for a healthy treat.

1. In medium bowl, combine chopped tomatoes, drained tomatoes, grape tomatoes, and yellow tomatoes.

2. In small bowl, combine Roasted Garlic with remaining ingredients and mix well. Spoon over tomatoes and stir to coat. Cover and chill for 3–4 hours to blend flavors before serving.

Tomatoes

There are many types and varieties of tomatoes on the market. Grape tomatoes, which are about the size of grapes, are very sweet and tender. Yellow and orange tomatoes are easy to find, and heirloom tomatoes, grown from seeds saved from tomatoes that have been open-pollinated, are delicious and popular.

YIELDS 2 CUPS

Calories: 103.27
Fat: 3.43 grams
Fat as % of calories: 29.9%
Carbohydrates: 17.85 grams
Fiber: 4.28 grams
Sodium: 262.21 mg
Vitamin A: 35% DV
Vitamin C: 70% DV
Calcium: 48.42 mg

INGREDIENTS

4 tomatoes, chopped
1 14-ounce can fire-roasted
    diced tomatoes, drained
2 cups grape tomatoes
3 yellow tomatoes, chopped
2 tablespoons Roasted Garlic
    (page 24)
3 tablespoons lime juice
1 tablespoon olive oil
2 jalapeño peppers, minced
1 teaspoon seasoned salt
¼ teaspoon red pepper flakes
¼ teaspoon white pepper
1 teaspoon ground cumin

YIELDS 3 CUPS

Calories: 56.47
Fat: 0.22 grams
Fat as % of calories: 3.5%
Carbohydrates: 14.26 grams
Fiber: 1.97 grams
Sodium: 66.66 mg
Vitamin A: 10% DV
Vitamin C: 50% DV
Calcium: 15.43 mg

INGREDIENTS

1 8-ounce can pineapple tidbits
1 8-ounce can mandarin
    oranges
1 cup chopped strawberries
1 cup raspberries
3 tablespoons sugar
¼ cup lime juice
¼ teaspoon salt
Pinch cayenne pepper

SERVES 12

Calories: 125.91
Fat: 5.52 grams
Fat as % of calories: 39.4%
Carbohydrates: 16.17 grams
Fiber: 5.89 grams
Sodium: 130.17 mg
Vitamin A: 10% DV
Vitamin C: 35% DV
Calcium: 40.27 mg

INGREDIENTS

1 16-ounce can lima beans
1 14-ounce can low-salt sweet
    peas, drained
2 avocados, peeled and cubed
¼ cup lemon juice
½ cup nonfat sour cream
⅛ teaspoon salt
¼ teaspoon pepper
⅛ teaspoon cayenne pepper
1½ cups chopped tomatoes
1 jalapeño chili, minced
¼ cup minced cilantro

Fruit Salsa

Serve this versatile salsa with any grilled fish, as a topping for brownies, or as a dip with fruit. Chilling it will help to blend the flavors.

1. Drain pineapple and mandarin oranges, reserving 1 tablespoon juice from each. Combine pineapple and oranges with strawberries and raspberries in medium bowl and stir gently.

2. In bowl, combine reserved juice with sugar, lime juice, salt, and pepper; stir until sugar dissolves. Pour over fruit. Cover and chill for 3–4 hours.

Fruit Salsa

If you like it hot, you could add a minced jalapeño or habanero pepper to this salsa. It's also excellent served as an appetizer dip, especially with sweet potato chips and slices of fresh fruit. Fruit salsa is also delicious as a topping for grilled chicken or fish or as a topping for sorbets or ice cream.

Lighter Guacamole

Lima beans add a nutty taste and velvety texture, and peas add a bit of sweetness to this low-fat guacamole.

Drain the lima beans and rinse. Place in food processor along with the peas, 1½ avocados, lemon juice, sour cream, salt, and peppers. Process until smooth. Spoon into a bowl. Stir in the remaining cubed avocado, and stir and mash with a fork until mostly smooth. Stir in tomatoes, jalapeño, and cilantro. Serve immediately or store by pressing plastic wrap on the surface. Chill up to 24 hours.

Using Guacamole

You can serve guacamole as a dip, but there are other ways to use it. It makes a great sandwich spread with cooked chicken or turkey. You can use it to top hot tomato soup or as a topping for grilled fish or chicken. It's also delicious in layered dips, especially Layered Taco Dip Without the Guilt (page 30).

Layered Shrimp and Pesto Dip

This low-carb recipe is decadent and full of flavor yet high in vitamin A. Serve with crackers and breadsticks.

1. In small bowl, beat cream cheese until fluffy. Add sour cream and beat until smooth. Spread on a serving platter.

2. Spoon and spread Pesto over the cream cheese mixture. Top with shrimp, then sprinkle with green onions and chives. Cover and refrigerate for 2–3 hours before serving.

Fat or Carbs?

You have to make the choice! Food is composed of water, protein, fat, and carbohydrates. If you're on a low-carb diet, you will be consuming more fat just because the calories have to come from somewhere. Still, try to eat everything in moderation and don't shun any particular food unless you're allergic to it.

SERVES 8

Calories: 158.62
Fat: 13.21 grams
Fat as % of calories: 74.9%
Carbohydrates: 1.55 grams
Fiber: 0.11 grams
Sodium: 155.13 mg
Vitamin A: 15% DV
Vitamin C: 4% DV
Calcium: 52.58 mg

INGREDIENTS

1 8-ounce package cream cheese, softened
½ cup sour cream
1 cup Roasted Garlic Pesto (page 32)
1 cup small cooked shrimp
¼ cup chopped green onions
1 tablespoon minced chives

Berry Fruit Dip

Serve this beautiful dip with apple and pear slices, baked unsalted tortilla chips, and plain sugar cookies.

1. In food processor or blender, combine raspberries, strawberries, honey, orange juice, tofu, and salt; process or blend until smooth.

2. Place in small bowl; stir in dried cherries. Cover and chill until serving time, about 2–4 hours.

SERVES 8

Calories: 127.04
Fat: 1.36 grams
Fat as % of calories: 9.6%
Carbohydrates: 28.63 grams
Fiber: 2.50 grams
Sodium: 25.01 mg
Vitamin A: 25% DV
Vitamin C: 70% DV
Calcium: 39.50 mg

INGREDIENTS

1 cup raspberries
2 cups chopped strawberries
¼ cup honey
2 tablespoons orange juice
1 cup silken tofu
Pinch salt
½ cup chopped dried cherries

YIELDS 2 CUPS

Calories: 104.31
Fat: 3.96 grams
Fat as % of calories: 34.2%
Carbohydrates: 14.75 grams
Fiber: 0.12 grams
Sodium: 87.08 mg
Vitamin A: 10% DV
Vitamin C: 25% DV
Calcium: 74.25 mg

INGREDIENTS

1 3-ounce package nonfat
    cream cheese
1 cup low-fat sour cream
⅓ cup frozen orange juice
    concentrate, thawed
¼ cup honey
Pinch salt
2 teaspoons grated orange zest
1 tablespoon minced gingerroot
2 tablespoons chopped mint
1 tablespoon chopped thyme

Herbed Fresh Orange Dip

The combination of mint and thyme adds a fresh flavor and hint of lemon to this excellent dip. Serve it with baked potato chips, fresh fruit, and breadsticks.

In small bowl, beat cream cheese until fluffy. Gradually add sour cream and beat until smooth. Beat in remaining ingredients, then cover and refrigerate for 2–3 hours to blend flavors.

Low-Fat Dairy Products

Most recipes work better when you use a mixture of nonfat and low-fat products. The flavor and texture is better when there is some fat in the recipe. You can substitute full-fat products if you don't mind the extra fat, especially for special occasions.

SERVES 10–12

Calories: 156.61
Fat: 5.0 grams
Fat as % of calories: 28.7%
Carbohydrates: 21.97 grams
Fiber: 1.91 grams
Sodium: 544.12 mg
Vitamin A: 8% DV
Vitamin C: 6% DV
Calcium: 81.27 mg

INGREDIENTS

1 12-ounce tube low-fat
    refrigerated biscuits
¼ cup yellow cornmeal
1 tablespoon olive oil
½ cup chopped onion
½ cup frozen meatless soy
    crumbles
2 teaspoons chili powder
½ teaspoon dried oregano
    leaves
½ cup vegetarian refried beans
1 tomato, chopped
⅓ cup tomato sauce
1 cup shredded low-fat pepper
    jack cheese

Mini Mexican Pizzas

These little pizzas are delicious served with White Wine Sangria (page 21) before a cookout or a make-your-own enchiladas party. You can find the crumbles in the health food section of your supermarket's freezer division.

1. Preheat oven to 400°F. Separate dough into biscuits, then separate each biscuit into four thin pieces along the lines. Dip each side into cornmeal, then place on two ungreased cookie sheets.

2. In medium skillet, heat olive oil over medium heat. Add onion; cook and stir until tender, about 5 minutes. Stir in meatless crumbles, chili powder, and dried oregano; cook and stir until crumbles defrost. Add refried beans, tomatoes, and tomato sauce. Stir over low heat for 2 minutes, and remove from heat. Spoon mixture on top of dough rounds. Sprinkle with cheese. Bake for 8–10 minutes or until crusts are golden brown, topping is hot, and cheese is melted and beginning to brown.

Tomato–Egg Finger Sandwiches

You can roll the edges of these delicious little sandwiches
in some more chopped parsley for a pretty finish.

1. Melt butter in small saucepan over medium heat. Meanwhile, combine eggs, egg whites, milk, salt, and pepper in small bowl and beat well. Add to hot butter. Cook and stir over medium heat until eggs are set but still moist. Remove from heat.

2. Transfer eggs to a medium bowl and let cool. Using a knife, cut across the eggs to break them up. Stir in yogurt, mayonnaise, sour cream, and mustard and mix well.

3. Cut tomatoes in half and gently squeeze to seed. Chop coarsely. Add tomatoes and parsley to egg mixture and mix gently. Cover and chill for 3 hours. When ready to make sandwiches, cut the crusts off the sandwich bread and place on work surface.

4. Make sandwiches with the filling and the trimmed bread. Cut into 1" x 3" sandwiches using a very sharp knife. Cover and chill in refrigerator for 2–6 hours before serving.

SERVES 14

Calories: 159.72
Fat: 5.37 grams
Fat as % of calories: 30.2%
Carbohydrates: 23.25 grams
Fiber: 2.95 grams
Sodium: 246.61 mg
Vitamin A: 10% DV
Vitamin C: 10% DV
Calcium: 45.34 mg

INGREDIENTS

1 tablespoon butter
2 eggs
2 egg whites
3 tablespoons milk
⅛ teaspoon salt
⅛ teaspoon white pepper
½ cup plain low-fat yogurt
¼ cup nonfat mayonnaise
¼ cup nonfat sour cream
2 tablespoons Dijon mustard
3 large tomatoes
⅓ cup chopped flat-leaf parsley
12 slices firm whole wheat
   sandwich bread

SERVES 12

Calories: 225.04
Fat: 8.14 grams
Fat as % of calories: 32.4%
Carbohydrates: 30.36 grams
Fiber: 9.10 grams
Sodium: 353.93 mg
Vitamin A: 45% DV
Vitamin C: 140% DV
Calcium: 141.15 mg

INGREDIENTS

1 tablespoon olive oil
1 onion, chopped
4 cloves garlic, minced
1 15-ounce can pinto beans,
    drained
1 tablespoon chili powder
1 cup nonfat sour cream
1 4-ounce can chopped green
    chilies, drained
1 recipe Lighter Guacamole
    (page 26)
1 cup Fresh Tomato Salsa (page
    25)
2 tomatoes, chopped
2 red bell peppers, chopped
1 cup low-fat extra-sharp
    Cheddar cheese
3 green onions, chopped

Layered Taco Dip Without the Guilt

Make each layer in this gorgeous dip a little smaller so you can see them. Serve with vegetable strips as well as tortilla chips.

1. In large saucepan, heat olive oil over medium heat. Add onion and garlic; cook and stir until tender, about 6 minutes. Add pinto beans and chili powder; mash with potato masher until smooth. Cook and stir for 5 minutes until bubbly. Remove from heat and cool.

2. Spread the bean mixture on a serving platter. Combine sour cream and chilies in small bowl; spread on bean mixture. Top with Guacamole. Cover and refrigerate until ready to serve.

3. Top the dip with Salsa, tomatoes, peppers, cheese, and green onions. Serve with baked tortilla chips.

Refried Beans

If you're watching fat intake, you have several options. Vegetarian refried beans don't use lard, so they are a healthier alternative, but the best option is to make your own. You can use any kind of bean to make refried beans: black, kidney, pinto, or even chickpeas.

Oven-Baked Potato Skins

*These are great as an appetizer or as a side dish
with the Mushroom–Brie Meatloaf (page 79).*

SERVES 8–10

Calories: 150.49
Fat: 3.78 grams
Fat as % of calories: 22.6%
Carbohydrates: 22.96 grams
Fiber: 2.09 grams
Sodium: 289.23 mg
Vitamin A: 8% DV
Vitamin C: 30% DV
Calcium: 110.79 mg

INGREDIENTS
4 large russet potatoes
Butter-flavored cooking spray
¼ cup grated Romano cheese
½ teaspoon salt
¼ teaspoon pepper
1 tablespoon olive oil
1 onion, chopped
4 cloves garlic, minced
¾ cup nonfat sour cream
2 large tomatoes, chopped
⅓ cup chopped cilantro
*1 cup shredded extra-sharp low-
fat Cheddar cheese*

1. Wash and dry the potatoes. Prick the skins with a fork and place on a plate in microwave oven. Microwave on high for 7–9 minutes, turning once during cooking time, until potatoes are tender. Let cool for 10 minutes.

2. Cut the potatoes in half and scoop out the flesh, leaving about ¼" shell. Cover the flesh tightly and refrigerate for up to 2 days.

3. Preheat oven to 400°F. Cut the potato halves in half again lengthwise and spray both sides with a bit of the cooking spray. Sprinkle with Romano cheese, salt, and pepper and place upside down on a cookie sheet. Bake for 20 minutes, then turn the potatoes flesh side up and bake for 20–25 minutes longer until the shells are crisp.

4. Meanwhile, make the filling. Heat olive oil in medium saucepan over medium heat. Add onion and garlic; cook and stir for 10–12 minutes until onions start to turn brown. Remove from heat and place in medium bowl; let cool for 10 minutes.

5. Stir in the sour cream, tomatoes, and cilantro and refrigerate while potatoes finish baking. When potatoes are done, sprinkle with Cheddar cheese and return to oven. Bake for 5–10 minutes longer until cheese melts. Top potatoes with the sour cream mixture and serve immediately.

YIELDS 2 CUPS

Calories: 77.19
Fat: 5.45 grams
Fat as % of calories: 63.5%
Carbohydrates: 3.83 grams
Fiber: 1.43 grams
Sodium: 261.92 mg
Vitamin A: 70% DV
Vitamin C: 15% DV
Calcium: 99.99 mg

INGREDIENTS

2 cups packed basil leaves
3 tablespoons extra-virgin
    olive oil
2 heads Roasted Garlic (page 24)
1 10-ounce package frozen
    spinach, thawed
6 tablespoons grated
    Parmesan cheese
⅓ cup sour cream
½ teaspoon salt
⅛ teaspoon white pepper
1 teaspoon dried basil leaves
3 tablespoons lemon juice

SERVES 16

Calories: 56.20
Fat: 3.04 grams
Fat as % of calories: 54.4%
Carbohydrates: 3.74 grams
Fiber: 0.70 grams
Sodium: 79.26 mg
Vitamin A: 8% DV
Vitamin C: 35% DV
Calcium: 40.21 mg

INGREDIENTS

24 large mushrooms
2 tablespoons lemon juice
1 tablespoon olive oil
½ cup finely chopped onion
½ cup finely chopped red bell
    pepper
4 cloves garlic, minced
1 3-ounce package low-fat
    cream cheese, softened
¼ cup low-fat sour cream
1 6-ounce pouch salmon, drained
¼ cup grated Romano cheese
1 tablespoon chopped fresh
    dill weed

Roasted Garlic Pesto

This low-carb pesto can be used as a sandwich spread, folded into cooked pasta, or mixed with nonfat sour cream for an appetizer dip.

In food processor, combine basil, olive oil, and the Garlic cloves. Pulse until minced. Squeeze spinach to remove most of the water. Add to food processor; process until blended. Remove pesto to a medium bowl; stir in cheese, sour cream, salt, pepper, dried basil, and lemon juice. Cover by placing plastic wrap directly on the surface of the pesto; chill for 2–3 hours to blend flavors.

Freezing Pesto

Pestos freeze well. Divide the pesto into smaller portions by scooping it with either a tablespoon measure or ¼-cup measure. Place on a waxed paper-lined cookie sheet and freeze until firm. Then package the pesto in hard-sided freezer containers, label, and freeze. To thaw, let stand in fridge until soft.

Healthy Salmon-Stuffed Mushrooms

Salmon is full of omega-3 fatty acids, and mushrooms have vitamin D. Combine them in this appetizer for a healthy and low-carb snack.

1. Preheat oven to 375°F. Clean mushrooms by brushing with a soft brush. Remove the mushroom stems from the caps. Brush the caps with lemon juice and set aside. Trim the ends from the stems and finely chop the stems.

2. In saucepan, heat olive oil over medium heat. Add onion, red bell pepper, garlic, and mushroom stems; cook and stir until tender, about 6 minutes. Remove from heat and place in bowl. Add the cream cheese and sour cream to the vegetables and mix well. Add salmon, Romano cheese, and dill weed and mix gently. Stuff this mixture into the mushroom caps.

3. Bake for 20–25 minutes or until mushrooms are tender and filling is hot and beginning to brown on top. Let cool for 10 minutes, then serve.

Caramelized Onion Triangles

Make these little puffs ahead of time and freeze them.
When unexpected guests drop in, just bake them from frozen;
add another 5–6 minutes baking time.

1. In large skillet, melt butter over medium heat. Add onions; cook and stir until onions start to turn golden, about 12–15 minutes. Add garlic, marjoram, salt, and pepper; cook and stir for another 2–3 minutes.

2. Remove from heat and place in large bowl; cool for 30 minutes. Add cream cheese, sour cream, and Romano cheese to onion mixture; stir to combine.

3. Place a sheet of phyllo dough on work surface. Spray lightly with the cooking spray and top with another sheet. Cut into three 3" x 14" strips. Place 2 teaspoons of the onion mixture at base of each strip. Fold up strips as you would fold a flag. Spray with cooking spray and place on cookie sheet. Repeat with remaining phyllo and filling.

4. At this point the triangles can be frozen; freeze until solid, then pack into hard-sided freezer containers, label, and freeze. To bake them immediately, preheat oven to 375°F. Bake the triangles for 19–24 minutes until light golden brown.

YIELDS 48; SERVES 16

Calories: 102.21
Fat: 4.00 grams
Fat as % of calories: 35.2%
Carbohydrates: 13.66 grams
Fiber: 0.77 grams
Sodium: 179.32 mg
Vitamin A: 2% DV
Vitamin C: 4% DV
Calcium: 34.41 mg

INGREDIENTS

2 tablespoons butter
3 large onions, chopped
5 cloves garlic, minced
1 teaspoon dried marjoram leaves
¼ teaspoon salt
⅛ teaspoon white pepper
1 3-ounce package low-fat cream cheese, softened
½ cup nonfat sour cream
¼ cup grated Romano cheese
32 9" x 14" sheets frozen phyllo dough, thawed
Olive oil cooking spray

YIELDS 12

Calories: 65.52
Fat: 0.41 grams
Fat as % of calories: 5.6%
Carbohydrates: 11.01 grams
Fiber: 0.49 grams
Sodium: 119.92 mg
Vitamin A: 6% DV
Vitamin C: 2% DV
Calcium: 12.02 mg

INGREDIENTS

½ pound ground chicken breast
⅓ cup finely chopped onion
3 cloves garlic, minced
⅓ cup shredded carrot
⅓ cup finely shredded red
  cabbage
1 tablespoon minced jalapeño
  pepper
½ teaspoon five-spice powder
2 teaspoons hoisin sauce
1 teaspoon low-sodium soy
  sauce
⅛ teaspoon white pepper
2 tablespoons cornstarch
2 tablespoons chicken broth
12 7-inch spring roll wrappers
Nonstick cooking spray

Baked Egg Rolls

*Egg rolls are usually deep fried, which really increases the calorie and
fat counts. Be sure to use spring roll wrappers, which are thinner than
egg roll wrappers; they will be crisp even though baked.*

1. Preheat oven to 400°F. In medium saucepan, cook chicken with onion and
    garlic until chicken is cooked and vegetables are tender, about 5 minutes.

2. Add carrot, cabbage, and jalapeño pepper to chicken mixture; cook and
    stir for 4–5 minutes until carrots are crisp-tender. Drain well and place
    in medium bowl.

3. Add five-spice powder, hoisin sauce, soy sauce, and white pepper to
    chicken mixture and mix well. Let stand for 20 minutes.

4. Combine cornstarch and chicken broth in small bowl. Lay the spring
    roll wrappers on work surface. Place about 1 tablespoon of the chicken
    mixture in the center of each wrapper; brush edges with some of the
    cornstarch mixture. Roll up, enclosing filling.

5. Place rolls on large cookie sheet. Spray with cooking spray. Bake for 15
    minutes, then turn and bake another 10–15 minutes or until browned
    and crisp. Serve immediately.

Baked Spicy Tortilla Chips

Baking the tortilla chips reduces the fat content, and seasoning them yourself helps you control sodium.

1. Preheat oven to 400°F. Spray the tortillas on both sides with the olive oil cooking spray. Cut the tortillas into eight wedges each and place on two cookie sheets.

2. In small bowl combine remaining ingredients. Sprinkle over the tortilla wedges and toss to coat.

3. Bake for 9–11 minutes, stirring once during cooking time and rotating the cookie sheets once during cooking time, until the chips are crisp and golden brown. Remove and cool on paper towels. Store, covered, in airtight container at room temperature. You can refresh the chips, if necessary, by baking in a 400°F oven for 2–4 minutes until crisp.

Corn or Flour Tortillas?

You can use corn or flour tortillas to make these spicy chips. The corn tortillas provide a bit more nutrition and twice as much fiber than the flour tortillas. If you use flour tortillas, look for the flavored kinds. You can find red tortillas flavored with red pepper and blue ones made from blue corn.

SERVES 12

Calories: 74.87
Fat: 1.70 grams
Fat as % of calories: 20.4%
Carbohydrates: 13.75 grams
Fiber: 2.43 grams
Sodium: 154.07 mg
Vitamin A: 10% DV
Vitamin C: 2% DV
Calcium: 46.72 mg

INGREDIENTS
1 12-ounce package corn tortillas
Olive oil spray
3 tablespoons chili powder
½ teaspoon salt
1 teaspoon ground cumin
¼ teaspoon cayenne pepper
¼ cup finely grated Cotija cheese

SERVES 8–10

Calories: 184.28
Fat: 5.48 grams
Fat as % of calories: 26.8%
Carbohydrates: 30.85 grams
Fiber: 2.49 grams
Sodium: 336.58 mg
Vitamin A: 290% DV
Vitamin C: 45% DV
Calcium: 88.27 mg

INGREDIENTS
4 sweet potatoes, peeled
2 tablespoons butter, melted
3 tablespoons lime juice
1 teaspoon salt
3 tablespoons sugar
1½ teaspoons cinnamon
1 teaspoon ground ginger
¼ teaspoon ground nutmeg
*1 recipe Herbed Fresh Orange
    Dip (page 28)*

Sweet Potato Sticks with Herbed Fresh Orange Dip

*This unusual appetizer has the best flavor.
Sweet potatoes are very healthy for you, with lots of
vitamin A and fiber. The sticks are good even when cold!*

1. Preheat oven to 400°F. Cut the sweet potatoes into ¼-inch slices, then turn them and cut into ¼-inch strips. Cut each strip in half lengthwise so they are about 2–3" long, depending on the size of the sweet potatoes.

2. Place the sticks on two cookie sheets. In small bowl, combine butter, lime juice, and salt; mix well. Drizzle over the sticks and toss to coat. In another small bowl, combine sugar, cinnamon, ginger, and nutmeg. Sprinkle over the sticks and toss to coat.

3. Bake for 20–25 minutes, stirring twice during baking time, until the sticks are golden brown and crisp. When the sticks are done, remove to paper towels to cool for 5–10 minutes, then serve with the Dip.

Try It Savory

You can make these sweet potatoes savory and spicy if you'd like. Instead of the sugar, cinnamon, ginger, and nutmeg, use 2 tablespoons chili powder, 1 teaspoon cumin, ¼ teaspoon pepper, ⅛ teaspoon cayenne pepper, and ¼ cup of finely grated Cotija cheese. Bake as directed, but serve with a spicy tomato salsa.

Chapter 3

Good-for-You Breakfast

YIELDS 36 MUFFINS

Calories: 104.40
Fat: 1.36 grams
Fat as % of calories: 10%
Carbohydrates: 22.34 grams
Fiber: 1.46 grams
Sodium: 96.24 mg
Vitamin A: 6% DV
Vitamin C: 8% DV
Calcium: 20.19 mg

INGREDIENTS

1 cup apricot nectar
½ cup orange juice
1 cup raisins
½ cup dried cranberries
1 cup chopped dried apricots
1 teaspoon orange zest
2 cups all-purpose flour
¾ cup whole wheat flour
⅓ cup granulated sugar
½ cup brown sugar
1 teaspoon baking powder
1 teaspoon baking soda
½ teaspoon salt
3 tablespoons butter, melted
1 egg
½ cup nonfat light cream

Fruity Muffins

These cute little muffins are packed with vitamin A and fiber. They use just a tiny amount of real butter for great flavor with very little fat.

1. Preheat oven to 350°F. Spray 36 muffin cups with nonstick baking spray containing flour; set aside.

2. In medium saucepan, combine apricot nectar, orange juice, raisins, cranberries, apricots, and orange zest. Bring to a simmer over high heat. Lower heat to low and simmer for 3–4 minutes until fruits begin to plump. Remove from heat and let cool.

3. In large bowl, combine all-purpose flour, whole wheat flour, granulated sugar, brown sugar, baking powder, baking soda, and salt and mix well. Stir in fruit mixture along with butter, egg, and cream; mix just until blended.

4. Spoon mixture into prepared muffin cups. Bake for 17–24 minutes or until muffins are golden brown and toothpick inserted in center comes out clean. Let cool in pan for 5 minutes, then remove to wire rack to cool. Serve warm.

Low-Fat Banana–Almond Muffins

*Bananas and sour cream add flavor
and moistness to these gorgeous little muffins.*

1. Preheat oven to 375°F. Line 12 muffin cups with paper liners and set aside.

2. In large bowl, combine all-purpose flour, whole wheat flour, baking powder, baking soda, salt, 1 teaspoon cinnamon, ½ cup brown sugar, and 2 tablespoons granulated sugar and mix well.

3. In small bowl, combine bananas, sour cream, egg whites, canola oil, and vanilla and mix well. Add to dry ingredients and stir just until moistened. Stir in almonds. Spoon batter into prepared muffin cups.

4. In small bowl, combine ¼ cup brown sugar, 2 tablespoons sugar, wheat germ, and ½ teaspoon cinnamon and mix well. Add melted butter and mix until crumbly. Crumble over muffin batter.

5. Bake for 17–22 minutes, or until muffins are set and tops are golden brown. Remove to wire racks to cool.

YIELDS 12 MUFFINS

Calories: 232.54
Fat: 8.64 grams
Fat as % of calories: 33.4%
Carbohydrates: 36.15 grams
Fiber: 2.05 grams
Sodium: 114.65 mg
Vitamin A: 2% DV
Vitamin C: 4% DV
Calcium: 60.76 mg

INGREDIENTS

1 cup all-purpose flour
½ cup whole wheat pastry flour
1 teaspoon baking powder
½ teaspoon baking soda
¼ teaspoon salt
1½ teaspoons cinnamon, divided
¾ cup brown sugar, divided
¼ cup granulated sugar, divided
2 large ripe bananas, mashed
¼ cup low-fat sour cream
2 egg whites
⅓ cup canola oil
1 teaspoon vanilla
⅓ cup sliced toasted almonds
3 tablespoons wheat germ
2 tablespoons butter, melted

INGREDIENTS

1 cup orange juice
1¼ cups regular oatmeal
⅓ cup butter
⅓ cup low-fat sour cream
¾ cup brown sugar
½ cup granulated sugar, divided
1 egg
2 egg whites
2 teaspoons vanilla
½ cup all-purpose flour
½ cup whole wheat flour
1 teaspoon baking powder
½ teaspoon baking soda
¼ teaspoon salt
1½ teaspoons cinnamon, divided
¼ teaspoon cardamom
1½ cups dried cranberries
½ cup chopped walnuts

Cranberry–Oatmeal Muffins

*Serve these delicious muffins warm with some
whipped honey or raspberry jam.*

1. Preheat oven to 350°F. Spray 18 muffin cups with nonstick baking spray containing flour and set aside.

2. Pour orange juice into a microwave-safe measuring cup. Microwave on high for 2 minutes, then pour into large bowl. Add oatmeal and butter; stir until butter melts. Let stand for 20 minutes.

3. Add sour cream, brown sugar, ¼ cup granulated sugar, egg, egg whites, and vanilla and mix well. Add flours, baking powder, baking soda, salt, 1 teaspoon cinnamon, and cardamom and mix just until combined. Stir in dried cranberries and walnuts.

4. Spoon mixture into prepared muffin cups. In small bowl, combine ¼ cup sugar with ½ teaspoon cinnamon and sprinkle over muffins. Bake for 20–25 minutes or until muffins are golden brown. Remove to wire racks to cool.

Pasta and Bread

Because of low-carbohydrate diets, pasta and bread have been villainized in the American mind. But whole grain pastas and whole grain breads are important parts of a healthy diet, providing vitamins B and E and fiber too. Eliminating them from your diet is impractical and unhealthy in the long run.

Guilt-Free Cranberry Scones

*Hazelnuts have lots of good monounsaturated fat;
they help reduce LDL cholesterol levels. These scones are slightly
crumbly and slightly sweet, perfect for breakfast.*

1. Preheat oven to 375°F. Place 1 cup oatmeal in microwave-safe pie plate. Microwave for 3–4 minutes or until fragrant, stirring once during cooking time. Let oatmeal cool. Place the remaining ⅓ cup oatmeal in a food processor; process until ground.

2. In large bowl, combine buttermilk, orange juice, brown sugar, and egg and mix well. In medium bowl, combine whole wheat flour, all-purpose flour, baking powder, and baking soda and mix well. Cut in butter until particles are fine.

3. Stir in the toasted oatmeal and ground oatmeal, then add buttermilk mixture and stir just until combined. Add cranberries and hazelnuts and form into a ball.

4. Place dough on ungreased cookie sheet. Press into a ¾-inch thick circle about 9 inches across. With a sharp knife, cut into 10 wedges and separate slightly. In small bowl, combine sugar and cinnamon; mix well. Sprinkle over scones.

5. Bake for 13–18 minutes or until scones are light golden brown. Remove to wire rack to cool for 15 minutes, then serve warm.

SERVES 10

Calories: 336.22
Fat: 10.74 grams
Fat as % of calories: 27.8%
Carbohydrates: 53.92 grams
Fiber: 6.13 grams
Sodium: 167.74 mg
Vitamin A: 4% DV
Vitamin C: 4% DV
Calcium: 98.08 mg

INGREDIENTS

*1⅓ cups regular oatmeal
⅓ cup buttermilk
¼ cup orange juice
¼ cup brown sugar
1 egg
¾ cup whole wheat flour
¾ cup all-purpose flour
1½ teaspoons baking powder
½ teaspoon baking soda
4 tablespoons butter
1 cup chopped dried cranberries
½ cup chopped hazelnuts
1 tablespoon sugar
½ teaspoon cinnamon*

SERVES 16

Calories: 331.56
Fat: 11.85 grams
Fat as % of calories: 32.1%
Carbohydrates: 44.88 grams
Fiber: 4.01 grams
Sodium: 161.66 mg
Vitamin A: 2% DV
Vitamin C: 6% DV
Calcium: 81.96 mg

INGREDIENTS

1 16-ounce can pears
1 6-ounce can pear baby food
¼ cup canola oil
2 tablespoons lemon juice
3 tablespoons butter, softened
½ cup brown sugar
¾ cup granulated sugar
1 egg
3 egg whites
½ cup buttermilk
1 cup quick-cooking oatmeal
¼ cup flaxseed, ground
1½ cups all-purpose flour
1 cup whole wheat flour
2 teaspoons baking powder
½ teaspoon baking soda
¼ teaspoon salt
*1 cup chopped unsalted
   cashews*
¼ cup honey
*3 tablespoons reserved pear
   liquid*
3 tablespoons granulated sugar

High-Fiber Cashew–Pear Bread

*Wow—more than four grams of fiber in a half-inch slice of bread!
This delicious bread is fun to make, and your guests will love it too.*

1. Preheat oven to 350°F. Spray a 9" x 5" loaf pan with nonstick baking spray containing flour; set aside. Drain pears, reserving 3 tablespoons liquid. Purée pears in food processor or blender; set aside.

2. In large bowl, combine puréed pears, pear baby food, oil, lemon juice, butter, brown sugar, granulated sugar, egg, egg whites, and buttermilk and beat until blended. Stir in oatmeal and flaxseed. Add flours, baking powder, baking soda, and salt and mix until smooth. Stir in cashews.

3. Spoon batter into prepared pan. Bake for 45–55 minutes, or until bread is golden brown and begins to pull away from sides of pan. Let cool in pan for 5 minutes, then combine honey, reserved pear liquid, and 3 tablespoons granulated sugar in small bowl; spoon over the bread. Let stand for 5 minutes, then turn out onto wire rack to cool completely.

Brown Sugar Waffles

Place about ½ cup of oatmeal in a food processor and process until fine to equal ¼ cup ground oatmeal.

1. In small bowl, combine egg, buttermilk, orange juice, brown sugar, and butter; mix well and set aside.

2. In large bowl, combine flours, oatmeal, salt, baking powder, and baking soda and mix with a wire whisk. Stir in buttermilk mixture until just blended.

3. In small bowl, combine egg whites and lemon juice; beat until stiff peaks form. Fold into batter.

4. Spray a waffle iron with a nonstick baking spray containing flour. Using about ⅓ cup at a time, or according to waffle iron instructions, add batter to iron, close, and cook until steaming stops.

SERVES 8

Calories: 266.94
Fat: 10.14 grams
Fat as % of calories: 33.7%
Carbohydrates: 37.24 grams
Fiber: 2.77 grams
Sodium: 297.77 mg
Vitamin A: 6% DV
Vitamin C: 15% DV
Calcium: 145.46 mg

INGREDIENTS

1 egg
1¼ cups buttermilk
¾ cup orange juice
⅓ cup brown sugar
⅓ cup butter, melted
¾ cup all-purpose flour
¾ cup whole wheat pastry flour
⅓ cup ground oatmeal
⅛ teaspoon salt
1½ teaspoons baking powder
½ teaspoon baking soda
2 egg whites
1 teaspoon lemon juice

Sweet Apple Pancakes

Pancakes are easy as long as you don't overmix the batter and are careful to measure all the ingredients carefully.

1. In large bowl, combine applesauce, oil, egg, egg whites, shredded apple, milk, and orange juice and mix well.

2. In medium bowl, combine flours, brown sugar, baking powder, baking soda, apple pie spice, and salt and mix well. Add to applesauce mixture and stir just until combined. Do not overbeat.

3. Heat a large griddle or frying pan over medium heat. Spray griddle with nonstick cooking spray. Pour batter in ¼-cup portions onto griddle; sprinkle each with a spoonful of Granola. Cook until the sides look dry and bubbles begin to form and break on the surface, about 3–5 minutes. Turn and cook for 2–3 minutes on second side until done. Serve immediately.

SERVES 10

Calories: 273.84
Fat: 7.83 grams
Fat as % of calories: 25.7%
Carbohydrates: 45.48 grams
Fiber: 3.42 grams
Sodium: 190.87 mg
Vitamin A: 6% DV
Vitamin C: 25% DV
Calcium: 111.38 mg

INGREDIENTS

¼ cup applesauce
¼ cup canola oil
1 egg
2 egg whites
2 cups shredded Granny Smith apple
1 cup skim milk
1 cup orange juice
1½ cups all-purpose flour
1 cup whole wheat pastry flour
⅓ cup brown sugar
1 teaspoon baking powder
½ teaspoon baking soda
1 teaspoon apple pie spice
¼ teaspoon salt
1 cup Mixed Nut Granola (page 51)

SERVES 12

Calories: 335.76
Fat: 10.16 grams
Fat as % of calories: 27.2%
Carbohydrates: 53.64 grams
Fiber: 4.99 grams
Sodium: 235.62 mg
Vitamin A: 10% DV
Vitamin C: 15% DV
Calcium: 48.96 mg

INGREDIENTS

⅓ cup orange juice
⅓ cup buttermilk
⅓ cup peach nectar
1 egg
3 egg whites
⅓ cup honey
1 teaspoon cinnamon
½ teaspoon ginger
¼ teaspoon salt
2 teaspoons vanilla
1 loaf Cracked Wheat French
    Bread (page 139)
2 cups Mixed Nut Granola (page
    51), crushed
3 tablespoons butter

Honey Granola French Toast

Baking French toast in a big batch is not only easier on you,
but it cuts down on the fat content.

1. Start the day before you intend to eat the French toast. In large bowl, combine orange juice, buttermilk, peach nectar, egg, egg whites, honey, cinnamon, ginger, salt, and vanilla and beat until smooth.

2. Cut the Bread into ¾-inch slices on an angle to make slices larger. Place Bread slices in single layer in one or two baking dishes. Pour orange juice mixture over all. Cover and refrigerate overnight.

3. When ready to eat, place the crushed Granola on a plate. Melt butter and spread onto two cookie sheets with sides. Using a spatula, lift the Bread slices out of the baking dish one at a time and place in Granola. Turn to coat, then place in butter on cookie sheet.

4. Bake for 20–30 minutes or until bread is golden brown and crisp. Serve immediately.

Mixed Fruit Breakfast Pizza

These cute little pizzas taste like dessert, but they're loaded with fiber and vitamin C. Make the filling ahead of time, but assemble them just before serving.

1. In medium bowl, beat cream cheese until fluffy. Add honey, apricot preserves, and cinnamon and mix well.

2. Spread this mixture onto the toasted pita breads, and arrange the berries on top. In small microwave-safe bowl, heat apple jelly for 30 seconds at 50 percent power until melted, then spoon over the fruit. Serve immediately.

SERVES 6

Calories: 308.98
Fat: 7.71 grams
Fat as % of calories: 22.4%
Carbohydrates: 56.00
Fiber: 4.72 grams
Sodium: 274.46 mg
Vitamin A: 6%
Vitamin C: 25%
Calcium: 62.84 mg

INGREDIENTS

1 8-ounce package low-fat cream cheese, softened
¼ cup honey
⅓ cup apricot preserves
½ teaspoon cinnamon
6 whole wheat pita breads, toasted
1 cup sliced strawberries
1 cup raspberries
1 cup blueberries
3 tablespoons apple jelly

Fruity Breakfast Crepes

These sweet little crepes, full of fruit, are perfect for a breakfast buffet or brunch.

1. In medium bowl, beat cream cheese until light and fluffy. Gradually add sour cream and beat well. Add sugar and vanilla and beat until fluffy. Stir in preserves to marble.

2. In medium bowl, combine fruit and orange juice and mix. Let stand for 15 minutes, then drain.

3. Arrange Crepes on work surface. Gently divide the cream cheese mixture among them, then top with the drained fruit. Roll up Crepes and place on serving platter. Garnish with mint.

SERVES 8–10

Calories: 261.56
Fat: 8.85 grams
Fat as % of calories: 30.4%
Carbohydrates: 38.83 grams
Fiber: 3.02 grams
Sodium: 215.92 mg
Vitamin A: 10% DV
Vitamin C: 45% DV
Calcium: 115.02 mg

INGREDIENTS

1 8-ounce package low-fat cream cheese, softened
½ cup nonfat sour cream
¼ cup powdered sugar
1 teaspoon vanilla
½ cup apricot preserves
1 cup chopped oranges
1 cup raspberries
1 cup blueberries
3 tablespoons orange juice
10 Easy Sweet Crepes (page 198)
2 tablespoons chopped fresh mint

SERVES 8–10

Calories: 431.13
Fat: 30.77 grams
Fat as % of calories: 64.2%
Carbohydrates: 11.97 grams
Fiber: 1.05 grams
Sodium: 566.55 mg
Vitamin A: 25% DV
Vitamin C: 8% DV
Calcium: 310.29 mg

INGREDIENTS

14 eggs
⅓ cup heavy cream
½ teaspoon salt
⅛ teaspoon white pepper
½ cup butter, divided
3 tablespoons grated Parmesan cheese
2 shallots, minced
½ cup bottled Alfredo sauce
¼ cup heavy cream, whipped
10 Easy Sweet Crepes (page 198)
2 cups shredded Havarti cheese

SERVES 6–8

Calories: 191.23
Fat: 10.93 grams
Fat as % of calories: 47%
Carbohydrates: 2.18 grams
Fiber: 0.0 grams
Sodium: 386.45 mg
Vitamin A: 9% DV
Vitamin C: 0% DV
Calcium: 92.66 mg

INGREDIENTS

5 eggs
1½ cups liquid egg substitute
5 egg whites
½ cup nonfat light cream
½ teaspoon salt
¼ teaspoon white pepper
1 tablespoon olive oil
1 tablespoon butter
1 10-ounce container low-fat Alfredo sauce
¼ cup grated Parmesan cheese

Make-Ahead Creamy Breakfast Crepes

This is a delicious low-carb breakfast recipe that still lets you eat some grains.

1. In large bowl, beat eggs with ⅓ cup heavy cream, salt, and pepper until frothy. Grease a 2-quart casserole with 1 tablespoon of the butter and sprinkle with the Parmesan cheese; set aside.

2. In large saucepan, melt 3 tablespoons butter over medium heat. Add shallots; cook and stir until tender, about 5 minutes. Add egg mixture; cook and stir until eggs are set but still moist. Fold in the Alfredo sauce and whipped heavy cream, then place in casserole. Cover tightly and refrigerate up to 24 hours.

3. When ready to eat, preheat oven to 350°F. Divide egg mixture among the Crepes and sprinkle with Havarti cheese. Roll up Crepes. Place seamside down in a greased 13" x 9" glass baking dish and brush with 4 tablespoons melted butter. Bake for 20–25 minutes or until filling is hot. Serve immediately.

Low-Fat Make-Ahead Scrambled Eggs

Combining real eggs, egg whites, and liquid egg substitute makes scrambled eggs that taste like the real thing with just 11 grams of fat and 149 mg of cholesterol—compare that to 18 grams of fat and 445 mg of cholesterol for regular eggs.

1. In large bowl, combine eggs, egg substitute, egg whites, cream, salt, and pepper and mix well.

2. In large skillet, combine olive oil and butter over medium heat. Add egg mixture; cook and stir until eggs are almost set but still moist.

3. Remove from heat and stir in Alfredo sauce. Don't combine thoroughly. Place in prepared 2-quart casserole dish and sprinkle with Parmesan cheese.

4. Cover and refrigerate overnight or up to 12 hours. To reheat, preheat oven to 350°F. Bake the casserole for 25–35 minutes or until eggs are hot and set. Serve immediately.

Not-Your-Average Scrambled Eggs

By combining egg substitute with real eggs, you get the taste of real scrambled eggs with half the fat and cholesterol, and the vegetables add flavor and fiber.

1. Spray a large nonstick saucepan with nonstick cooking spray. Add onion and mushrooms; cook and stir until tender, about 6–7 minutes.

2. Meanwhile, in food processor or blender combine cream cheese, milk, and eggs; blend until smooth. Add liquid egg substitute, egg whites, pepper, and cheese; process or blend until smooth.

3. Pour egg mixture into saucepan and reduce heat to low. Cook, stirring frequently, until eggs are just set but still moist. Serve immediately.

SERVES 6

Calories: 148.95
Fat: 5.33 grams
Fat as % of calories: 32.2%
Carbohydrates: 5.94 grams
Fiber: 0.67 grams
Sodium: 319.80 mg
Vitamin A: 10% DV
Vitamin C: 2% DV
Calcium: 124.07 mg

INGREDIENTS

1 onion, chopped
1½ cups chopped mushrooms
1 3-ounce package nonfat cream cheese, softened
⅓ cup 1% milk
2 eggs
2 cups liquid egg substitute
4 egg whites
¼ teaspoon white pepper
2 tablespoons grated Romano cheese

Light Eggs Benedict

Making eggs Benedict with scrambled eggs lets you use egg substitute and egg whites to reduce the fat and cholesterol.

1. In large bowl, combine eggs, egg substitute, egg whites, milk, and pepper and mix well. In large skillet, melt butter over medium heat. Add egg mixture; cook and stir until eggs are just set and still moist. Remove from heat.

2. Stir in salmon, mozzarella cheese, Swiss cheese, ½ cup Alfredo sauce, and cooked and drained asparagus; set aside.

3. Split the English muffins and toast until golden brown. Place English muffins on broiler pan. Top each with some of the egg mixture and spoon remaining Alfredo sauce over each. Sprinkle with Romano cheese.

4. Preheat broiler. Broil the eggs Benedict 6 inches from the heat source for 4–7 minutes or until cheese sauce bubbles and begins to brown. Serve immediately.

SERVES 8

Calories: 312.32
Fat: 13.38 grams
Fat as % of calories: 38.5%
Carbohydrates: 15.64 grams
Fiber: 2.81 grams
Sodium: 480.22 mg
Vitamin A: 15% DV
Vitamin C: 15% DV
Calcium: 369.18 mg

INGREDIENTS

3 eggs
1 cup liquid egg substitute
4 egg whites
¼ cup 1% milk
¼ teaspoon white pepper
1 tablespoon butter
1 12-ounce pouch salmon, flaked
½ cup shredded part-skim mozzarella cheese
½ cup shredded Swiss cheese
1 10-ounce container low-fat Alfredo sauce
1 10-ounce package frozen chopped asparagus, cooked
4 whole wheat English muffins
¼ cup grated Romano cheese

SERVES 12

Calories: 325.34
Fat: 23.98 grams
Fat as % of calories: 66.3%
Carbohydrates: 6.56 grams
Fiber: 1.33 grams
Sodium: 573.11 mg
Vitamin A: 80% DV
Vitamin C: 60% DV
Calcium: 380.45 mg

INGREDIENTS

12 slices bacon
2 tablespoons butter
1 onion, chopped
1 leek, chopped
1 red bell pepper, chopped
3 cloves garlic, minced
*1 10-ounce package frozen
    chopped spinach, thawed*
*2 cups shredded Cheddar
    cheese*
2 cups shredded Havarti cheese
12 eggs
½ cup light cream
1 teaspoon dried thyme leaves
½ teaspoon salt
⅛ teaspoon white pepper
¼ cup grated Parmesan cheese

Crustless Bacon Quiche

*If you're eating low carb, this is the perfect breakfast entrée for you.
It's full of flavor and color, and the texture is perfect.
This recipe serves a crowd.*

1. Preheat oven to 350°F. Spray a 9" x 13" glass baking dish with nonstick cooking spray and set aside.

2. In large skillet, cook bacon until crisp; drain bacon on paper towels and crumble; set aside. Drain all but 1 tablespoon drippings from the skillet. Add butter to skillet and melt over medium heat.

3. Add onion and leek to skillet; cook and stir for 5 minutes. Add bell pepper and garlic and cook for another 2 minutes. Drain spinach well and add to skillet; cook and stir for 4 minutes longer. Remove from heat.

4. Place vegetable mixture into prepared baking dish and top with crumbled bacon. Layer Cheddar and Havarti cheese on top.

5. In large bowl, beat eggs with cream, thyme, salt, and pepper until smooth. Pour into baking dish. Sprinkle pie with Parmesan cheese. Bake for 35–45 minutes or until egg mixture is set and top is beginning to brown. Let stand for 5 minutes, then serve.

Fluffy Shrimp Quiche

A quiche is an excellent choice for a low-carb breakfast or brunch. The pie crust adds 14 carbs per serving, so if you omit it the recipe only has 5 grams per serving.

1. Preheat oven to 375°F. Make the Whole Wheat Pie Crust but omit the sugar. Prick the bottom of the Crust and bake for 7–8 minutes or until the Crust is just set.

2. Meanwhile, in medium saucepan, melt butter over medium heat. Add onion and garlic; cook and stir until crisp-tender, about 5 minutes. Add bell pepper; cook and stir for 3 more minutes. Drain shrimp and add to saucepan; stir gently and remove from heat.

3. In medium bowl, combine eggs, cream, milk, mustard, salt, pepper, and dill weed; beat until smooth.

4. Arrange vegetable mixture in the prebaked Pie Crust; top with feta, Cheddar and Havarti cheeses. Slowly pour egg mixture over all. Sprinkle with Parmesan cheese. Bake for 50–60 minutes or until quiche is puffed and golden brown. Let stand for 5 minutes, then serve.

SERVES 8–10

Calories: 394.00
Fat: 27.18 grams
Fat as % of calories: 63.5%
Carbohydrates: 19.00
Fiber: 2.58 grams
Sodium: 517.33 mg
Vitamin A: 25% DV
Vitamin C: 40% DV
Calcium: 322.71 mg

INGREDIENTS

1 Whole Wheat Pie Crust (page 188)
3 tablespoons butter
1 onion, chopped
3 cloves garlic, minced
1 red bell pepper, chopped
1 8-ounce package frozen cooked shrimp, thawed
5 eggs
½ cup heavy cream
½ cup whole milk
2 tablespoons Dijon mustard
¼ teaspoon salt
⅛ teaspoon pepper
½ teaspoon dried dill weed
1 4-ounce package feta cheese, crumbled
1 cup shredded Cheddar cheese
1 cup shredded Havarti cheese
¼ cup grated Parmesan cheese

SERVES 6

Calories: 213.47
Fat: 7.34 grams
Fat as % of calories: 30.9%
Carbohydrates: 32.99 grams
Fiber: 4.02 grams
Sodium: 125.69 mg
Vitamin A: 2% DV
Vitamin C: 60% DV
Calcium: 35.08 mg

INGREDIENTS

6 14" x 9" sheets phyllo dough,
    thawed
Butter-flavored cooking spray
6 tablespoons ground almonds
2 tablespoons butter, melted
⅓ cup seedless raspberry jam
2 tablespoons lemon juice
1 cup fresh raspberries
1 cup chopped strawberries
1 cup blueberries

Phyllo Berry Cups

You can make the phyllo cups and the berry filling ahead of time.
Fill the little cups just before serving.

1. Preheat oven to 375°F. Spray 12 muffin cups with nonstick baking spray containing flour; set aside.

2. Place a sheet phyllo dough on work surface and spray with cooking spray. Sprinkle with 1 tablespoon ground almonds and top with another sheet. Brush that sheet with half of the butter and sprinkle with 1 tablespoon almonds; top with a third sheet and spray that with cooking spray; top with another tablespoon of almonds.

3. Fold sheets in half to make a 9" x 7" rectangle. Cut into six 3" x 3½" squares. Place squares in muffin cups, pressing down to form a cup shape. Repeat with remaining dough, spray, butter, and almonds. Bake for 8–12 minutes or until pastry is golden brown and set. Remove from muffin cups and let cool on wire rack.

4. While pastry cools, combine jam and lemon juice in small saucepan. Heat over low heat, stirring frequently, until jam melts and mixture is smooth. Remove from heat and stir in berries. Fill the pastry cups with the berry mixture and serve.

Seasonal Fruit

With the global economy today, you can eat fruit any time of year, whether it's in season or not. The best fruit, of course, is grown in your own backyard or bought at a farmer's market. In the winter, you can use winter fruits like apples, kiwi, and pears in this easy recipe.

Mixed-Nut Granola

Granola is usually really high in fat. This one fits into the low-fat category—and all of the fat is healthy, from canola oil to nuts.

1. Preheat oven to 325°F. In large bowl, combine oatmeal, wheat germ, oat bran, and salt and mix well. Stir in all of the nuts, sesame seeds, and flax-seed.

2. In medium bowl, combine maple syrup, brown sugar, oil, orange juice, cinnamon, cardamom, and vanilla and mix well. Spoon over the oatmeal mixture and toss to coat.

3. Spoon mixture onto a large cookie sheet. Bake for 20–30 minutes, stirring once during baking time, until granola is toasted. Remove from oven and stir in apricots and blueberries. Let cool completely, then store in airtight container.

Granola

Granola may be the original health food from the 1960s. It's a combination of oats, seeds, nuts, and fat, baked and stirred until crisp and crunchy. You can substitute your favorite purchased granola for homemade in any recipe. Be sure to read labels so you know how much fat the cereal will add to the recipe.

**YIELDS 10 CUPS;
SERVING SIZE ½ CUP**

Calories: 372.11
Fat: 13.17 grams
Fat as % of calories: 31.8%
Carbohydrates: 57.77 grams
Fiber: 8.28 grams
Sodium: 64.89 mg
Vitamin A: 10% DV
Vitamin C: 5% DV
Calcium: 60.12 mg

INGREDIENTS
4 cups old-fashioned oatmeal
1 cup wheat germ
¾ cup oat bran
½ teaspoon salt
½ cup chopped hazelnuts
½ cup chopped almonds
⅓ cup chopped walnuts
⅓ cup sesame seeds
¼ cup flaxseed, ground
½ cup maple syrup
½ cup brown sugar
½ cup canola oil
⅓ cup orange juice
1 teaspoon cinnamon
¼ teaspoon cardamom
2 teaspoons vanilla
1 cup chopped dried apricots
1 cup dried blueberries

SERVES 6

Calories: 321.77
Fat: 1.90 grams
Fat as % of calories: 5.3%
Carbohydrates: 75.21 grams
Fiber: 4.40 grams
Sodium: 66.30 mg
Vitamin A: 45% DV
Vitamin C: 45% DV
Calcium: 180.74 mg

INGREDIENTS

4 ripe bananas, frozen
3 cups apricot nectar
1 16-ounce jar mango slices,
    drained
3 cups low-fat strawberry yogurt
1 8-ounce can crushed
    pineapple, undrained

Tropical Smoothies

Boy, is this smoothie good for you! It's high in fiber, very low in fat, and gives you almost half your daily requirements of vitamins A and C.

Combine all ingredients in food processor or blender; process or blend until mixed and smooth. Serve immediately.

Smoothies

You can make smoothies out of just about any fresh, frozen, or canned fruit. They are typically high in fat, but by making your own you can control the fat content. Just use low-fat or nonfat dairy products to combine with all of that healthy fruit. If you'd like, you can freeze a smoothie mixture in an ice cream maker for your own custom ice cream.

SERVES 8

Calories: 357.97
Fat: 9.21
Fat as % of calories: 23.1%
Carbohydrates: 66.65 grams
Fiber: 5.40 grams
Sodium: 81.28 mg
Vitamin A: 35%
Vitamin C: 80%
Calcium: 160.29 mg

INGREDIENTS

1 recipe Tropical Smoothies
    (page 52)
2 cups crisp rice flake cereal
½ cup sliced almonds
¼ cup wheat germ
¼ cup orange juice
3 tablespoons butter, melted
2 cups sliced strawberries

Smoothie Parfaits

You can use purchased low-fat granola to layer with the smoothie mixture and strawberries to make this elegant recipe even easier.

1. Place the Smoothies in a large bowl and cover; freeze until firm.

2. Meanwhile, preheat oven to 350°F. In medium bowl, combine cereal, almonds, and wheat germ and mix well. Add orange juice and butter and toss to coat. Spread in an even layer on cookie sheet.

3. Bake cereal mixture for 10–15 minutes, stirring once, until crisp and toasted. Let cool for 15 minutes, then remove to a bowl to cool completely, stirring once during cooling time.

4. When ready to serve, layer the frozen Smoothie mixture, cereal mixture, and strawberries in eight parfait glasses. Serve immediately.

Chapter 4

Festive, Guilt-Free Lunch

Calories: 315.92
Fat: 12.86 grams
Fat as % of calories: 36.6%
Carbohydrates: 34.85 grams
Fiber: 5.53 grams
Sodium: 369.33 mg
Vitamin A: 170% DV
Vitamin C: 30% DV
Calcium: 239.26 mg

INGREDIENTS

1 tablespoon olive oil
1 onion, chopped
3 cloves garlic, minced
2 cups diced carrot
1 potato, diced
½ teaspoon salt
⅛ teaspoon pepper
1 teaspoon dried oregano leaves
½ cup vegetable stock
1 cup frozen baby peas
*1 cup shredded low-fat Swiss
cheese*
*1 recipe Whole Wheat Pie Crust
(page 188)*
1 egg, beaten
¼ cup grated Parmesan cheese

Veggie Turnovers

*You can freeze these turnovers before baking.
Let stand in refrigerator overnight, then bake until hot and crisp,
adding a few minutes to the baking time.*

1. Preheat oven to 375°F. In large skillet, heat olive oil over medium heat. Add onion, garlic, and carrot; cook and stir for 5 minutes. Add potato; cook and stir for 3 minutes. Add salt, pepper, oregano, and vegetable stock, bring to a simmer, then cover and simmer for 6–8 minutes or until potatoes are tender.

2. Add peas; cook and stir until peas are hot. Remove from heat, drain, and pour mixture into medium bowl; let cool for 20 minutes. Then stir in Swiss cheese.

3. Divide Pie Crust into thirds and roll out ⅓ on floured surface to a 10" x 10" square. Cut into four 5" x 5" squares. Place a scant ⅓ cup filling in the center of each square. Brush the edges with beaten egg and fold over to form triangles; crimp edges with a fork. Repeat with remaining crust and filling.

4. Place turnovers on cookie sheet. Brush with any remaining egg and sprinkle with Parmesan cheese. Bake for 15–25 minutes or until crust is crisp and filling is hot. Let cool for 10 minutes, then serve.

Fluffy Vegetable Quiche

Just about any combination of vegetables can be used in this easy recipe; just make sure they are crisp-tender before adding to the crust.

1. Preheat oven to 375°F. Bake the Pie Crust for 5 minutes, remove from oven, and set aside on wire rack. In large saucepan, heat olive oil over medium heat. Add onion; cook and stir for 4 minutes. Add mushrooms; cook and stir for 4–5 minutes longer. Add peas; cook and stir until warm. Remove from heat, drain if necessary, and set aside.

2. In large bowl, combine ricotta, eggs, milk, flour, salt, and pepper and beat until smooth. Place Cheddar and feta cheeses in Pie Crust; top with vegetable mixture. Pour egg mixture over; sprinkle with Parmesan cheese. Bake for 35–45 minutes or until set and browned.

Feta Cheese

Feta cheese is very strongly flavored, so a little goes a long way. It's usually made from sheep's or goat's milk, but it can be made from cow's milk. You can find flavored feta cheeses in the supermarket to add more flavor with no effort. You can substitute crumbled firm goat cheese for feta if you'd like.

SERVES 8

Calories: 302.82
Fat: 12.78 grams
Fat as % of calories: 37.9%
Carbohydrates: 29.29 grams
Fiber: 4.72 grams
Sodium: 418.34 mg
Vitamin A: 15% DV
Vitamin C: 15% DV
Calcium: 210.97 mg

INGREDIENTS

1 Whole Wheat Pie Crust (page 188)
1 tablespoon olive oil
1 onion, chopped
1 8-ounce package sliced mushrooms
1½ cups baby frozen peas
½ cup part-skim ricotta cheese
2 eggs
1 cup skim milk
2 tablespoons flour
½ teaspoons salt
⅛ teaspoon pepper
½ cup shredded low-fat Cheddar cheese
¼ cup crumbled feta cheese
2 tablespoons grated Parmesan cheese

SERVES 8

Calories: 281.04
Fat: 10.78 grams
Fat as % of calories: 34.5%
Carbohydrates: 30.39 grams
Fiber: 3.95 grams
Sodium: 460.15 mg
Vitamin A: 60% DV
Vitamin C: 20% DV
Calcium: 231.39 mg

INGREDIENTS

1 tablespoon butter
1 onion, chopped
1 green bell pepper, chopped
1 cup grated carrot
1 cup cooked wild rice, drained
1 cup frozen cut-leaf spinach,
    thawed and drained
½ teaspoon salt
⅛ teaspoon pepper
½ teaspoon dried marjoram
    leaves
1 3-ounce package nonfat cream
    cheese, softened
2 eggs
3 egg whites
½ cup nonfat sour cream
1 Whole Wheat Pie Crust (page
    188)
1 cup shredded low-fat Swiss
    cheese

High-Fiber Wild Rice Quiche

Lots of vegetables add color, fiber, and nutrition to a light and fluffy quiche. This beautiful pie is perfect served with a fresh fruit salad.

1. Preheat oven to 375°F. In large skillet, melt butter over medium heat. Add onion, bell pepper, and carrot; cook and stir for 5–6 minutes until tender. Add wild rice, spinach, salt, pepper, and marjoram leaves; cook until liquid evaporates.

2. In food processor, combine cream cheese, eggs, egg whites, and sour cream; process until smooth.

3. Place wild rice mixture in Pie Crust and top with cheese. Pour the cream cheese mixture over all. Bake for 40–50 minutes or until pie is set and golden brown. Cool for 10 minutes, then slice to serve.

Quiches

Quiches are great for lunches. They can be filled with almost anything. Just make sure the vegetables and other ingredients aren't wet or soggy; that will make the quiche fail. You could add cooked shrimp, chicken, ham, or even meatballs to any quiche recipe. Add more chopped cooked vegetables for more nutrition.

Parmesan Orzo Salad

*This simple salad can be turned into a main dish by adding
cooked shrimp, chopped ham, or crabmeat.*

1. Bring a large pot of salted water to a boil. Meanwhile, in large bowl combine yogurt, sour cream, ½ cup cheese, buttermilk, mustard, and green onion and mix well.

2. Add vegetables to yogurt mixture and stir to coat. Cook pasta according to package directions, then drain and add to yogurt mixture. Stir to coat, then cover and refrigerate for 2–3 hours before serving. Stir salad before serving.

SERVES 8

Calories: 334.79
Fat: 7.78 grams
Fat as % of calories: 20.9%
Carbohydrates: 52.35 grams
Fiber: 3.71 grams
Sodium: 226.44
Vitamin A: 25% DV
Vitamin C: 120% DV
Calcium: 280.13 mg

INGREDIENTS

1 cup plain low-fat yogurt
¾ cup sour cream
½ cup grated Parmesan cheese
½ cup buttermilk
¼ cup Dijon mustard
⅓ cup chopped green onions
1 red bell pepper, chopped
1 green bell pepper, chopped
2 cups chopped red cabbage
1 yellow summer squash, chopped
1 16-ounce package orzo pasta

Pistachio Tea Sandwiches

*Use natural pistachios in these pretty little sandwiches,
not the ones that have been dyed red.*

1. In small bowl, combine cream cheeses and beat until fluffy. Add orange juice; beat until smooth. Stir in pistachios, apricots, and cranberries; set aside.

2. Arrange bread slices on work surface. Spread half of each type of bread with the cream cheese mixture. Top with remaining bread slices, matching types so sandwiches are made with the same variety of bread. Wrap sandwiches in plastic wrap and refrigerate up to 4 hours.

3. When ready to serve, unwrap sandwiches and cut each into 4 triangles. Arrange on platter and serve.

SERVES 6

Calories: 274.90
Fat: 8.88 grams
Fat as % of calories: 29.1%
Carbohydrates: 40.90 grams
Fiber: 5.44 grams
Sodium: 388.45 mg
Vitamin A: 15% DV
Vitamin C: 5% DV
Calcium: 91.69 mg

INGREDIENTS

1 3-ounce package low-fat cream cheese, softened
1 3-ounce package nonfat cream cheese, softened
2 tablespoons orange juice
⅓ cup chopped pistachios
½ cup chopped dried apricots
¼ cup chopped dried cranberries
6 slices thinly sliced pumpernickel bread
6 slices thinly sliced rye bread

SERVES 8

Calories: 389.96
Fat: 13.11 grams
Fat as % of calories: 30.2%
Carbohydrates: 46.31 grams
Fiber: 5.77 grams
Sodium: 322.24 mg
Vitamin A: 5% DV
Vitamin C: 7% DV
Calcium: 27.19 mg

INGREDIENTS

1 cup wild rice
2 cups chicken broth
*1 3-ounce package low-fat
    cream cheese, softened*
½ cup nonfat sour cream
¼ cup plain yogurt
¼ cup buttermilk
*2 teaspoons chopped fresh
    tarragon*
*½ teaspoon dried tarragon
    leaves*
½ teaspoon salt
⅛ teaspoon pepper
½ cup dried cranberries
½ cup chopped walnuts
*4 Slow Cooked Chicken Breasts
    (page 100), cubed*
1 avocado, peeled and diced

Avocado Wild Rice Chicken Salad

*Wild rice adds great taste and a lot of fiber to this elegant chicken salad,
    perfect for lunch on the porch under a lazily spinning ceiling fan.*

1. In medium saucepan, combine wild rice and chicken broth. Bring to a
   simmer over medium-high heat. Cover pan, reduce heat to low, and simmer for 40–45 minutes or until wild rice is tender and broth is absorbed.
   Fluff with fork.

2. In large bowl, beat cream cheese until fluffy. Gradually add sour cream,
   yogurt, and buttermilk, beating until smooth. Stir in both kinds of tarragon, salt, pepper, and wild rice.

3. Add cranberries, walnuts, and cubed chicken; stir to coat. Cover and chill
   for 3–4 hours. Fold in avocados just before serving. Serve immediately.

Grains and Legumes

Combining grains and legumes, like wild rice and edamame, provides complete protein, which is the key to a healthy vegetarian diet. By themselves,
these ingredients lack key amino acids that your body needs to repair cells.
When you combine these foods, your body can make a complete protein.

Beef and Berries Salad

*Start marinating the meat the day before you want
to serve this beautiful salad.*

1. Place beef in large resealable plastic bag. Add lemon juice, olive oil, garlic, and pepper; close bag and knead to mix. Place in casserole dish and refrigerate for 8–24 hours. Grill or broil steak for 4–5 minutes on each side until desired doneness. Let stand for 30 minutes, then slice thinly against the grain.

2. In food processor, combine frozen raspberries, yogurt, mayonnaise, orange juice, vinegar, salt, and pepper; blend well. Place spinach in serving bowl; top with fresh berries and steak. Drizzle with yogurt mixture and serve immediately.

Spinach

Spinach is a dark, leafy green vegetable that is very high in vitamin A and fiber. It also contains at least thirteen antioxidants, those magical little ingredients that can help protect against heart disease and cancer, especially prostate and ovarian cancers. It's also an excellent source of vitamin K, which can help prevent osteoporosis.

SERVES 6–8

Calories: 260.11
Fat: 10.90 grams
Fat as % of calories: 37.7%
Carbohydrates: 26.57 grams
Fiber: 5.53 grams
Sodium: 169.57 mg
Vitamin A: 50% DV
Vitamin C: 80% DV
Calcium: 78.76 mg

INGREDIENTS

1 pound beef sirloin steak
2 tablespoons lemon juice
1 tablespoon olive oil
1 clove garlic, minced
⅛ teaspoon pepper
1 cup frozen raspberries, thawed
½ cup raspberry yogurt
¼ cup low-fat mayonnaise
¼ cup orange juice
2 tablespoons raspberry vinegar
¼ teaspoon salt
⅛ teaspoon pepper
8 cups baby spinach leaves
2 cups fresh raspberries
2 cups sliced strawberries
1 cup blueberries

SERVES 6–8

Calories: 258.81
Fat: 7.36 grams
Fat as % of calories: 25.6%
Carbohydrates: 45.56 grams
Fiber: 5.03 grams
Sodium: 144.56 mg
Vitamin A: 10% DV
Vitamin C: 45% DV
Calcium: 87.39 mg

INGREDIENTS

1 cup wild rice
1 cup low-sodium vegetable broth
1 cup apple juice
1 cup lemon yogurt
⅓ cup low-fat sour cream
¼ teaspoon salt
⅛ teaspoon white pepper
⅓ cup orange juice
¼ cup chopped green onion
2 apples, chopped
2 pears, chopped
¼ cup lemon juice
1 cup red grapes
½ cup chopped toasted pecans

Fruity Wild Rice Salad

This delicious salad can be served as is, or add some cooked shrimp or ham. The apple juice and lemon yogurt add a sweetness that is delicious with the nutty wild rice.

1. In large saucepan, combine wild rice, broth, and apple juice. Bring to a simmer, cover, reduce heat to low, and cook for 35–40 minutes or until rice is tender. Drain well, if necessary.

2. Meanwhile, in large bowl, combine yogurt, sour cream, salt, pepper, and orange juice and mix well. When it is cooked, add wild rice and green onion.

3. Prepare apples and pears and toss with lemon juice in medium bowl. Add to wild rice mixture along with grapes and pecans. Cover and chill for 2–3 hours.

Wild Rice

Wild rice isn't a rice but a grass seed. It grows naturally in marshy areas and lakes in the northern part of the United States. It is high in fiber and B vitamins and has a good amount of protein and calcium. Rinse it before use, then cook just until it's tender. Wild rice can be expensive, so look for it on sale and freeze for longer storage.

Modern Chicken Salad Sandwiches

*Curry powder is a wonderful addition to a dressed-up chicken
fruit salad. Served open-face on toasted wheat bread,
these sandwiches are beautiful and delicious.*

1. In large bowl, combine mayonnaise, yogurt, apple juice, curry powder,
   salt, and blend well. Stir in green onions, cranberries, dried blueberries,
   almonds, and chicken. Cover and chill for 3–4 hours.

2. When ready to serve, toast the French Bread on both sides until golden.
   Gently fold fresh blueberries into chicken mixture and spoon onto toasted
   bread. Serve immediately.

SERVES 8

Calories: 416.21
Fat: 11.03 grams
Fat as % of calories: 23.9%
Carbohydrates: 57.91 grams
Fiber: 7.00 grams
Sodium: 378.58 mg
Vitamin A: 10% DV
Vitamin C: 12% DV
Calcium: 93.28 mg

INGREDIENTS
½ cup low-fat mayonnaise
⅓ cup plain yogurt
¼ cup apple juice
1 tablespoon curry powder
½ teaspoon salt
⅓ cup sliced green onions
½ cup dried cranberries
½ cup dried blueberries
½ cup sliced almonds
4 Slow Cooked Chicken Breasts
   (page 100), cubed
1 cup fresh blueberries
8 slices Cracked Wheat French
   Bread (page 139)

Curried Ham Sandwiches

*Curry powder and chutney are two Indian ingredients that add a lot
of flavor to recipes with little or no fat.*

1. In medium bowl, combine ham, green pepper, grapes, and green onion.
   In small bowl, combine chutney, curry powder, mayonnaise, orange
   yogurt, and orange juice; mix well. Add to ham mixture and stir to
   coat.

2. Spread butter on one side of each toasted slice of bread. Make sandwiches
   using ham filling and butter lettuce. Slice each sandwich in half diagonally and serve immediately.

SERVES 6

Calories: 351.42
Fat: 14.73 grams
Fat as % of calories: 37.7%
Carbohydrates: 44.63 grams
Fiber: 5.81 grams
Sodium: 912.60 mg
Vitamin A: 25% DV
Vitamin C: 60% DV
Calcium: 84.24 mg

INGREDIENTS
1½ cups diced ham
1 green pepper, chopped
2 cups red grapes, halved
⅓ cup chopped green onion
½ cup mango chutney
1 tablespoon curry powder
½ cup low-fat mayonnaise
¼ cup low-fat orange yogurt
¼ cup orange juice
2 tablespoons butter, softened
12 slices whole wheat bread,
   toasted
2 cups butter lettuce

SERVES 6

Calories: 256.85
Fat: 9.33 grams
Fat as % of calories: 32.7%
Carbohydrates: 34.07 grams
Fiber: 6.82 grams
Sodium: 456.38 mg
Vitamin A: 40% DV
Vitamin C: 70% DV
Calcium: 101.47 mg

INGREDIENTS

1 eggplant, chopped
1 red bell pepper, chopped
1 onion, chopped
5 cloves garlic, minced
*1 8-ounce package sliced
  mushrooms*
2 tablespoons olive oil
½ teaspoon salt
⅛ teaspoon pepper
1 8-ounce container hummus
½ cup nonfat sour cream
¼ cup crumbled feta cheese
6 whole wheat pita breads
2 cups butter lettuce leaves

SERVES 6

Calories: 240.98
Fat: 6.75 grams
Fat as % of calories: 25.2%
Carbohydrates: 32.54 grams
Fiber: 3.81 grams
Sodium: 138.30 mg
Vitamin A: 25% DV
Vitamin C: 20% DV
Calcium: 72.35 mg

INGREDIENTS

½ cup wild rice
1 cup water
1 cup cubed deli roast beef
1 cup sweet cherries, halved
⅓ cup sliced green onion
1 cup red grapes, halved
½ cup plain yogurt
⅓ cup low-fat sour cream
¼ cup orange juice
2 teaspoons curry powder
½ teaspoon salt
⅛ teaspoon pepper
*4 whole wheat pita breads,
  halved*
2 cups baby spinach leaves

Pita Hummus Sandwiches

*Roast the vegetables ahead of time,
and assemble the filling just before serving.*

1. Preheat oven to 350°F. Combine eggplant, bell pepper, onions, garlic, and mushrooms on cookie sheet with sides. Sprinkle with olive oil, salt, and pepper and toss to coat. Roast for 40–50 minutes or until vegetables are crisp-tender; remove with slotted spoon and place in large bowl.

2. In small bowl, combine hummus and sour cream; mix well. Stir into vegetables and add cheese. Cut pita breads in half. Line with lettuce, and spoon in vegetable mixture. Serve immediately.

Healthy Curried Beef Pitas

*You can get beef for sandwiches from any deli; just ask them to slice it
about ⅓-inch thick for this recipe, then cube it yourself.*

1. In small saucepan, combine wild rice and water. Bring to a boil over medium-high heat. Reduce heat to low, cover, and simmer for 35–45 minutes or until rice is tender. Drain if necessary and place in large bowl.

2. Add beef, cherries, green onions, and grapes and toss gently to mix. In small bowl, combine yogurt, sour cream, orange juice, curry powder, salt, and pepper and mix well. Pour over beef mixture and stir gently.

3. Line pita breads with the spinach leaves and spoon in beef mixture. Serve immediately.

Light Egg Salad Wraps

Egg salad, made with some tofu to reduce fat and cholesterol, is the perfect base for delicious sandwiches with a variety of chopped vegetables.

1. Drain the tofu by pressing between paper towels; crumble into large bowl. Add eggs, green onions, bell pepper, celery, and carrot and toss gently.

2. In small bowl combine yogurt, salad dressing, mustard, milk, salt, cayenne pepper, and tarragon and mix well. Add to egg mixture and stir gently to coat. At this point mixture can be refrigerated for up to 24 hours. When ready to eat, fold in grape tomatoes, then make wrap sandwiches with the lettuce and flour tortillas.

Hard-Boiled Eggs

To hard-boil eggs, place large eggs in a saucepan and cover with cold water. Bring to a boil over high heat. When water boils furiously, remove from heat, cover pan, and let stand for 15 minutes. Then drain eggs and run cold water into the pan until eggs are cold. Crack eggs under the water, then gently peel. Store in fridge up to 3 days.

SERVES 12

Calories: 315.08
Fat: 10.73 grams
Fat as % of calories: 30.6%
Carbohydrates: 42.91 grams
Fiber: 3.86 grams
Sodium: 738.60 mg
Vitamin A: 50% DV
Vitamin C: 30% DV
Calcium: 207.01 mg

INGREDIENTS

1 12-ounce package firm tofu, drained
4 hard-boiled eggs, chopped
⅓ cup chopped green onions
1 green bell pepper, chopped
4 stalks celery, chopped
1 cup grated carrot
½ cup low-fat yogurt
½ cup light whipped salad dressing
¼ cup Dijon mustard
⅓ cup skim milk
½ teaspoon salt
⅛ teaspoon cayenne pepper
1 teaspoon dried tarragon leaves
2 cups grape tomatoes, chopped
12 leaves butter lettuce
12 10-inch flour tortillas

SERVES 6

Calories: 340.25
Fat: 9.44 grams
Fat as % of calories: 24.9%
Carbohydrates: 50.56 grams
Fiber: 3.24 grams
Sodium: 909.85 mg
Vitamin A: 25% DV
Vitamin C: 25% DV
Calcium: 196.94 mg

INGREDIENTS

1 cup cubed cooked ham
⅓ cup chopped green onion
2 cups red grapes, halved
½ cup plain yogurt
2 tablespoons Dijon mustard
2 tablespoons lemon juice
½ cup low-fat mayonnaise
¼ cup crumbled feta cheese
6 10-inch flour tortillas
2 cups baby spinach leaves

Light Ham and Grape Wraps

Combining ham with some sweet fruit and tangy mustard and cheese adds great flavor to these simple wrap sandwiches.

1. In large bowl, combine ham, green onions, and grapes and mix well. In small bowl, combine yogurt, mustard, lemon juice, mayonnaise, and feta cheese. Stir into ham mixture until combined.

2. Place tortillas on work surface. Line with the spinach leaves, then divide ham mixture over the spinach. Roll up, folding in sides. Wrap in napkins and serve immediately.

SERVES 6

Calories: 285.11
Fat: 6.18 grams
Fat as % of calories: 19.5%
Carbohydrates: 34.27 grams
Fiber: 4.72 grams
Sodium: 414.70 mg
Vitamin A: 10% DV
Vitamin C: 40% DV
Calcium: 261.83 mg

INGREDIENTS

3-ounce package low-fat cream
    cheese, softened
½ cup low-fat mayonnaise
3 tablespoons lemon juice
1 cup chopped celery
¼ cup chopped green onion
1 Red Delicious apple, chopped
1 cup shredded low-fat Swiss
    cheese
¼ cup grated Parmesan cheese
1 12-ounce can white tuna,
    drained
12 6-inch corn tortillas
1 cup Fruit Salsa (page 26)

Grilled Tuna Salad Quesadillas

Quesadillas are a great choice for lunch, and the spicy fruit salsa adds more nutrition and flavor.

1. In medium bowl, beat cream cheese until fluffy. Add mayonnaise and lemon juice and beat until smooth. Add celery, green onion, apple, cheeses, and tuna and mix well.

2. Divide mixture among six of the tortillas and spread evenly. Top with rest of tortillas.

3. Heat a nonstick skillet or griddle over medium heat. Add quesadillas, three at a time, and cook until browned. Carefully flip and cook on second side until light brown. Cut into quarters, top with Fruit Salsa, and serve immediately.

Turkey Spring Rolls

*Rice wrappers are brittle rounds that you dip into
water to soften and fill with whatever you'd like.
You can find them in Asian markets and large supermarkets.*

1. In large bowl, combine rice, turkey, carrot, cucumber, peas, and red bell pepper and toss gently. In small bowl, combine fish sauce, lime juice, mint, basil, and chicken stock. Add to rice mixture and stir to coat.

2. Fill a large shallow bowl with warm water. One at a time, dip wrappers into the water to moisten. Place on work surface and top with ⅓ cup rice mixture. Roll up wrappers, folding in ends. Repeat with remaining wrappers and rice filling.

3. In small bowl, combine peanut butter, soy sauce, orange juice, sugar, and garlic and mix well. Serve as dippers for the spring rolls.

Peanut Butter

Peanut butter has no cholesterol and offers complete protein, along with B vitamins like folate and niacin—and it's inexpensive. Look for natural peanut butters, which do not contain any trans fat.

SERVES 8

Calories: 300.08
Fat: 11.36 grams
Fat as % of calories: 34.1%
Carbohydrates: 33.25 grams
Fiber: 3.26 grams
Sodium: 484.41 mg
Vitamin A: 80% DV
Vitamin C: 80% DV
Calcium: 45.90 mg

INGREDIENTS

1 cup cooked brown rice
1 cup diced cooked turkey
    breast
1 cup shredded carrot
½ cup peeled, shredded
    cucumber
½ cup frozen baby peas, thawed
1 red bell pepper, thinly sliced
2 teaspoons fish sauce
1 tablespoon lime juice
2 tablespoons chopped fresh
    mint
2 tablespoons chopped fresh
    basil
¼ cup chicken stock
16 8-inch rice wrappers
½ cup peanut butter
1 tablespoon low-sodium soy
    sauce
¼ cup orange juice
1 teaspoon sugar
2 cloves garlic, minced

Calories: 159.66
Fat: 5.93 grams
Fat as % of calories: 33.4%
Carbohydrates: 20.55 grams
Fiber: 1.63 grams
Sodium: 250.50 mg
Vitamin A: 2% DV
Vitamin C: 4% DV
Calcium: 177.14 mg

INGREDIENTS

3 cloves garlic, minced
3 tablespoons minced onion
1 tablespoon minced fresh
    rosemary
1 tablespoon minced thyme
    leaves
1 cup all-purpose flour
1 cup whole wheat pastry flour
¼ teaspoon salt
1½ teaspoons baking powder
1 teaspoon baking soda
¼ cup olive oil
2 tablespoons honey
1 egg
¾ cup buttermilk
¼ cup orange juice
1 cup diced low-fat Swiss
    cheese

Cheese–Herb Muffins

*These tender little muffins are delicious served with
a main dish salad for a light lunch.*

1. Preheat oven to 400°F. Spray 12 muffin cups with nonstick baking spray containing flour and set aside.

2. In small bowl, combine garlic, onion, rosemary, and thyme; set aside. In large bowl, combine all-purpose flour, whole wheat flour, salt, baking powder, and baking soda and mix well.

3. In another small bowl, combine olive oil, honey, egg, buttermilk, and orange juice and mix well. Add to flour mixture and blend just until dry ingredients are moistened. Fold in Swiss cheese.

4. Fill muffin cups with batter. Sprinkle muffins with onion mixture. Bake for 18–24 minutes or until muffins are golden brown. Let cool for 20 minutes; serve warm.

Pesto Tomato Soup

*Freshly made tomato soup tastes like nothing from a can,
even though you use canned ingredients to make it.
Enjoy this with some toasted cheese bread.*

1. In large stock pot, melt butter over medium heat. Add garlic and shallots; cook, stirring frequently until tender, about 5–6 minutes. Add tomatoes, sugar, vinegar, pepper, and basil leaves; cook and stir for 4 minutes.

2. Stir in tomato sauce, juice, and vegetable broth and bring to a simmer. Reduce heat to low and simmer for 15–20 minutes or until blended.

3. Cube cream cheeses and add to soup. Using an immersion blender or potato masher, blend the soup until smooth. Heat until soup is steaming. Serve with the Pesto.

SERVES 8

Calories: 159.99
Fat: 6.60 grams
Fat as % of calories: 37.1%
Carbohydrates: 18.93 grams
Fiber: 2.96 grams
Sodium: 674.05 mg
Vitamin A: 70% DV
Vitamin C: 60% DV
Calcium: 112.68 mg

INGREDIENTS

1 tablespoon butter
4 cloves garlic, minced
2 shallots, minced
5 tomatoes, chopped
1 tablespoon sugar
1 tablespoon balsamic vinegar
⅛ teaspoon white pepper
1 teaspoon dried basil leaves
1 8-ounce can tomato sauce
2 cups tomato juice
1 cup vegetable broth
1 3-ounce package low-fat
　　cream cheese
1 3-ounce package nonfat cream
　　cheese
½ cup Roasted Garlic Pesto
　　(page 32)

SERVES 6–8

Calories: 287.99
Fat: 7.71 grams
Fat as % of calories: 24.1%
Carbohydrates: 41.74 grams
Fiber: 3.98 grams
Sodium: 356.46 mg
Vitamin A: 60% DV
Vitamin C: 60% DV
Calcium: 65.29 mg

INGREDIENTS

3 tablespoons butter
1 onion, chopped
3 carrots, sliced
2 teaspoons curry powder
2 tablespoons flour
¼ teaspoon salt
1 48-ounce box low-sodium
  chicken broth
2 cups apple juice
3 Slow-Cooked Chicken Breasts
  (page 100), chopped
2 Granny Smith apples, chopped
2 Bosc pears, chopped
3 tablespoons lemon juice
3 tablespoons honey
1 cup nonfat light cream

Fruit and Chicken Soup

*This beautiful soup can be served warm or cold;
garnish with sliced fresh apples.*

1. In large soup pot, heat butter over medium heat. Add onion and carrot; cook and stir for 4 minutes. Add curry powder, flour, and salt; cook and stir for 4 minutes. Add chicken broth and apple juice; bring to a simmer.

2. Cover pot, reduce heat to low, and simmer for 6–7 minutes until carrots are very tender. Uncover and purée soup with immersion blender.

3. Add remaining ingredients except cream and bring to a simmer; simmer for 4–5 minutes until apples and pears are crisp-tender. Add cream and heat until steaming; serve immediately.

Curry Powder

Curry powder isn't a single spice but a blend of many spices. You can find it in grocery stores or you can make it yourself. Curry powder contains turmeric, which studies suggest to be a potent cancer-fighting ingredient. You can sprinkle it into sandwich spreads and use it to flavor everything from soups to salads.

High-Fiber Healthy Aloha Hash

Sweet potato, pineapple, coconut, and macadamia nuts are all reminiscent of the Hawaiian islands. Combined with ham, they make a delectable hash.

1. In large skillet, heat olive oil over medium heat. Add onion and garlic; cook and stir for 3 minutes. Add potatoes; cook and stir for 8–10 minutes or until potatoes are almost cooked.

2. Add ham; cook and stir for 3–4 minutes longer. Then add drained pineapple. In small bowl, combine reserved pineapple liquid, mustard, salt, and pepper; mix well. Add to skillet and bring to a simmer. Simmer for 5–6 minutes or until liquid is almost absorbed.

3. Sprinkle with coconut and nuts and serve immediately.

SERVES 6

Calories: 265.62
Fat: 9.09 grams
Fat as % of calories: 30.8%
Carbohydrates: 39.29 grams
Fiber: 5.03 grams
Sodium: 479.21 mg
Vitamin A: 230% DV
Vitamin C: 40% DV
Calcium: 61.37 mg

INGREDIENTS

1 tablespoon olive oil
1 onion, chopped
3 cloves garlic, minced
2 sweet potatoes, peeled and diced
2 russet potatoes, diced
1 cup diced ham
1 15-ounce can pineapple tidbits, drained, reserving juice
2 tablespoons Dijon mustard
¼ teaspoon salt
⅛ teaspoon white pepper
¼ cup toasted coconut
¼ cup chopped macadamia nuts

Chapter 5

Dinner Party: Meat Entrées

SERVES 8

Calories: 271.54
Fat: 9.07 grams
Fat as % of calories: 30.1%
Carbohydrates: 8.92 grams
Fiber: 1.45 grams
Sodium: 456.13 mg
Vitamin A: 30% DV
Vitamin C: 60% DV
Calcium: 65.64 mg

INGREDIENTS

2 1-pound pork tenderloins
½ teaspoon salt
⅛ teaspoon pepper
1 tablespoon butter
1 onion, chopped
1 red bell pepper, chopped
1 cup frozen baby peas, thawed
½ cup crumbled bleu cheese
2 tablespoons Dijon mustard
1 tablespoon honey

Vegetable-Stuffed Pork Tenderloin

Pork tenderloin is tender and mild,
beautifully flavored in this elegant and simple recipe.

1. Preheat oven to 400°F. Cut lengthwise through the tenderloins, cutting almost to the other side. Open the halves like a book, and place pork between sheets of waxed paper. Pound to ½-inch thickness, then sprinkle with salt and pepper.

2. In large skillet, melt butter over medium heat. Add onion and bell pepper; cook and stir for 5–7 minutes until crisp-tender. Remove from heat and add peas; cover and let stand for 5 minutes.

3. Spread onion mixture over the tenderloins and sprinkle with bleu cheese. Roll up tenderloins to enclose filling and tie every 2 inches with kitchen string to hold.

4. Place stuffed tenderloins on a cookie sheet. Roast for 15 minutes, then combine mustard and honey in a small bowl; brush over pork. Continue roasting for 15–25 minutes or until meat thermometer registers 155°F. Let stand for 10 minutes, then remove twine and slice to serve.

Pork Tenderloin

Pork tenderloin, the most tender cut of the meat, is just as lean as skinless chicken breast. The new ways of feeding farm animals have cut the amount of fat in many pork products by 16 percent. Tenderloin is easy to cook, tender, and mild, and it can be flavored in many different ways.

Pork with Grapefruit Salsa

*Slow cooked, tender, and juicy pork chops
are served with a cool, sweet, and tart salsa.*

1. Sprinkle pork chops with flour, salt, and pepper. Heat olive oil in large skillet; brown pork chops on each side, about 5 minutes total. Layer with onions in 4-quart slow cooker. Pour grapefruit juice over all. Cover and cook on low for 7–8 hours until pork is tender and registers 155°F.

2. Meanwhile, make salsa. In medium bowl, combine all remaining ingredients and mix well. Cover and chill until pork chops are ready.

Grapefruit

Grapefruit is one of the best sources of vitamin C. It also contains lycopene, a phytonutrient with antitumor properties. The fruit has a lot of pectin, a soluble fiber that helps fight heart disease.

SERVES 6

Calories: 285.36
Fat: 10.59 mg
Fat as % of calories: 34.6%
Carbohydrates: 25.21 grams
Fiber: 2.60 grams
Sodium: 350.60 mg
Vitamin A: 30% DV
Vitamin C: 190% DV
Calcium: 45.45 mg

INGREDIENTS

6 boneless pork loin chops
2 tablespoons flour
Salt and pepper to taste
2 tablespoons olive oil
2 onions, sliced
½ cup grapefruit juice
3 pink grapefruit, chopped
½ cup chopped green onions
1 red bell pepper, chopped
2 jalapeño peppers, minced
1 tablespoon sugar
⅛ teaspoon cayenne pepper
¼ cup chopped cilantro

Crisp Breaded Pork Chops

*Thin pork chops, pounded even thinner, cook in minutes. This is a
wonderful last-minute, low-carb recipe for entertaining.*

1. Place the chops between two pieces of waxed paper; pound until about ¼-inch thick. On plate, combine panko, cheese, and cornmeal; mix well. In shallow bowl, combine buttermilk, mustard, salt, and pepper and mix well.

2. Dip chops into buttermilk mixture, then into crumb mixture to coat. Place on wire rack and let stand for 15 minutes.

3. Melt butter in large skillet over medium-high heat. Add chops; cook for 3–4 minutes on each side until browned and crisp. Serve immediately.

SERVES 6

Calories: 298.81
Fat: 17.77 grams
Fat as % of calories: 53.5%
Carbohydrates: 7.49 grams
Fiber: 0.62 grams
Sodium: 881.42 mg
Vitamin A: 5% DV
Vitamin C: 5% DV
Calcium: 139.08 mg

INGREDIENTS

6 thin boneless pork chops
½ cup panko bread crumbs
½ cup grated Parmesan cheese
2 tablespoons cornmeal
¼ cup buttermilk
2 tablespoons Dijon mustard
½ teaspoon salt
⅛ teaspoon white pepper
2 tablespoons butter

Calories: 352.55
Fat: 13.88 grams
Fat as % of calories: 35.4%
Carbohydrates: 13.67 grams
Fiber: 0.43 grams
Sodium: 234.09 mg
Vitamin A: 0% DV
Vitamin C: 25% DV
Calcium: 49.35 mg

INGREDIENTS

1½ cups orange juice
½ cup chicken broth
*2 tablespoons low-sodium soy
    sauce*
*1 4-pound boneless pork loin
    roast*
2 tablespoons olive oil
6 cloves garlic, minced
1 onion, finely chopped
⅓ cup orange marmalade
⅛ teaspoon white pepper
1 teaspoon dried thyme leaves

Healthy Orange Pork Loin Roast

*Pork roast is glazed with a flavorful onion and orange mixture
that adds flavor and nutrition.*

1. Combine orange juice, chicken broth, and soy sauce in a large cooking bag. Add the roast; seal bag and turn to coat. Place bag in large casserole dish; refrigerate for 8–24 hours.

2. Preheat oven to 350°F. In large saucepan, heat olive oil over medium heat. Add garlic and onion; cook and stir until tender, about 5 minutes. Remove from pan with slotted spoon; place in 3-quart casserole dish.

3. Remove pork from marinade; reserve marinade. Brown pork on all sides in hot pan, about 5 minutes total. Add to casserole dish.

4. Add marinade, orange marmalade, pepper, and thyme leaves to pan; bring to a simmer, scraping up drippings. Pour over roast and cover tightly.

5. Roast pork for 1¾ to 2½ hours until internal temperature registers 155°F. Remove pork from pan and cover to keep warm. Pour juices into a saucepan and bring to a boil; boil hard for 3–4 minutes until thickened. Slice pork and serve with sauce.

Pork Loin with Maque Choux

*A tender orange- and wine-scented pork roast is served with
a chilled spicy corn mixture in this fabulous recipe.*

1. Preheat oven to 350°F. Sprinkle roast on all sides with half of the salt
   and pepper. Brown in olive oil in large skillet. Place in large roasting pan
   and pour wine and orange juice over. Cover and roast pork for 1¾ to
   2½ hours until internal temperature registers 155°F. Remove pork from
   pan and cover to keep warm.

2. Meanwhile, make the maque choux. Add onion and garlic to drippings
   in skillet and cook until crisp-tender, about 6 minutes. Add corn and red
   bell pepper; cook and stir for another 3 minutes. Add tomatoes, thyme,
   red pepper flakes, and remaining salt and pepper and bring to a simmer;
   simmer for 5 minutes. Add light cream and simmer for 5 minutes, then
   remove to a dish, stir in sour cream, cover, and refrigerate.

4. When pork registers 155°F on a meat thermometer, remove from oven.
   Cover and let stand for 10 minutes, then slice and serve with corn mixture.

SERVES 8

Calories: 418.65
Fat: 17.23 grams
Fat as % of calories: 37.0%
Carbohydrates: 22.48 grams
Fiber: 3.00 grams
Sodium: 352.80 mg
Vitamin A: 40% DV
Vitamin C: 170% DV
Calcium: 93.41 mg

INGREDIENTS

*1 3-pound boneless pork loin
   roast*
¾ teaspoon salt, divided
¼ teaspoon pepper, divided
1 tablespoon olive oil
½ cup dry white wine
½ cup orange juice
1 onion, chopped
3 cloves garlic, minced
3 cups frozen corn, thawed
2 red bell peppers, chopped
3 tomatoes, chopped
1 teaspoon dried thyme leaves
*⅛ teaspoon crushed red pepper
   flakes*
½ cup nonfat light cream
½ cup low-fat sour cream

INGREDIENTS

6 5-ounce boneless pork chops
3 tablespoons flour
Salt and pepper to taste
1 tablespoon olive oil
1 onion, chopped
1 green bell pepper, chopped
1 15-ounce can mandarin
    oranges, drained
¼ cup chili sauce
½ cup orange juice
2 tablespoons honey
1 teaspoon orange zest
2 tablespoons Dijon mustard

INGREDIENTS

2 tablespoons butter, divided
2 onions, chopped
3 cloves garlic, minced
2 Granny Smith apples, chopped
½ teaspoon salt
⅛ teaspoon pepper
¼ cup brown sugar
6 1-inch-thick boneless pork
    chops
¼ cup flour
½ cup chicken broth
½ cup apple juice
3 tablespoons Dijon mustard

Mustard–Orange Pork Chops

*Tender pork chops are simmered in a spicy orange and mustard sauce
for a delicious and healthy entrée.*

1. Sprinkle chops with flour, salt, and pepper. Heat olive oil in large skillet over medium heat. Add chops; brown on both sides, about 4 minutes total. Remove chops from skillet.

2. Add onion and bell pepper to skillet; cook and stir for 5 minutes. Return chops to skillet and add drained oranges; turn heat to low.

3. In small bowl, combine chili sauce, orange juice, honey, zest, and mustard; mix well. Add to skillet; bring to a simmer. Cover skillet and cook for 8–10 minutes or until pork is tender. Serve immediately.

Caramelized Onion–Apple Pork Chops

Caramelized onions are very sweet and tender.

1. Melt 1 tablespoon butter in large skillet over medium heat. Add onion and garlic; cook and stir until tender, about 6 minutes. Lower heat and stir frequently, until onions are deep golden brown, about 30 minutes.

2. Spoon onion mixture into medium bowl; stir in apples, salt, pepper, and sugar. Let cool for 15 minutes. Meanwhile, cut a pocket into the side of each chop.

3. Stuff some of the onion mixture into each chop, reserving the extra. Dredge chops in flour. Melt remaining 1 tablespoon butter in skillet; brown pork chops on both sides.

4. Place remaining onion mixture into 4-quart slow cooker; top with pork chops. Deglaze pan with chicken broth and apple juice; stir in mustard and pour over chops. Cover and cook on low for 8–9 hours until pork is tender.

Slow Cooker Braised Pork with Fruit

The slow cooker is a wonderful choice for entertaining because the food cooks happily all by itself while you do other things.

1. Sprinkle roast with salt, pepper, and flour. In large saucepan, heat olive oil over medium heat. Brown roast on all sides, about 6–8 minutes total. Remove to a 5- or 6-quart slow cooker.

2. Add onions and garlic to saucepan; cook and stir for 4–5 minutes to loosen pan drippings. Add to slow cooker along with all remaining ingredients.

3. Cover and cook on low for 7–8 hours, or until pork registers 160°F. Remove pork from slow cooker and cover to keep warm. Pour juices and fruit into a saucepan; bring to a boil and boil hard for 4–5 minutes to reduce sauce. Remove and discard bay leaf from sauce. Slice pork and serve with fruit and sauce.

SERVES 10–12

Calories: 433.99
Fat: 15.03 grams
Fat as % of calories: 31.1%
Carbohydrates: 35.12 grams
Fiber: 3.81 grams
Sodium: 306.88 mg
Vitamin A: 10% DV
Vitamin C: 8% DV
Calcium: 62.87 mg

INGREDIENTS

1 4-pound boneless pork shoulder roast
1 teaspoon salt
¼ teaspoon pepper
3 tablespoons flour
2 tablespoons olive oil
2 onions, chopped
6 cloves garlic, minced
1 cup chopped dried apricots
1 cup chopped dried figs
½ cup golden raisins
½ cup dark raisins
1 cup dry red wine
⅓ cup apple cider vinegar
½ cup chicken broth
1 teaspoon dried marjoram leaves
1 bay leaf

Calories: 294.81
Fat: 11.76 grams
Fat as % of calories: 35.9%
Carbohydrates: 22.08 grams
Fiber: 1.08 grams
Sodium: 429.57 mg
Vitamin A: 5% DV
Vitamin C: 15% DV
Calcium: 42.18 mg

INGREDIENTS

2 tablespoons butter
1 red onion, chopped
2 cups chopped red cabbage
1 red apple, chopped
½ teaspoon caraway seeds
6 6-ounce pork cutlets
½ teaspoon salt, divided
¼ teaspoon pepper, divided
4 tablespoons flour
2 tablespoons olive oil
1 cup chicken broth
1 cup pineapple juice
⅓ cup apple cider vinegar
¼ cup brown sugar

Cabbage-Stuffed Pork Rouladen

This meal is cooked on the stovetop, freeing up your oven for other uses. Serve this rich dish with a gelatin fruit salad, some homemade rolls, and a lemon pie for dessert.

1. In large saucepan, melt butter over medium heat. Add onion; cook and stir for 3 minutes. Add cabbage; cook and stir for 3 minutes longer. Then add apple and caraway seeds; cook and stir until food is tender, about 4–6 minutes longer.

2. Remove food from pan with slotted spoon; set aside.

3. If necessary, pound cutlets until they are ¼-inch thick. Place on work surface, sprinkle with ¼ teaspoon salt and ⅛ teaspoon pepper, and divide cabbage mixture among them. Roll up, enclosing cabbage mixture; secure with toothpicks. Dredge in flour, shaking off excess.

4. Drain saucepan and return to heat; add olive oil. Brown rouladen on all sides, about 3–4 minutes, then remove from pan. Add chicken broth, pineapple juice, vinegar, brown sugar, ¼ teaspoon salt, and ⅛ pepper to pan, and bring to a simmer, scraping to remove drippings. Simmer for 4 minutes.

5. Return rouladen to pan and bring back to a simmer. Cover pan, reduce heat to low, and simmer for 20–25 minutes or until pork is cooked and sauce is thickened. Serve immediately.

Cabbage

Cabbage is a cruciferous vegetable, that family of foods that are nutritional powerhouses. These foods help prevent cancer, are nutrient dense, and provide lots of vitamin C. Cabbage also keeps well, for up to a week, in the refrigerator. You can chop it with a chef's knife or use the slicing blade of your food processor.

Mushroom–Brie Meatloaf

To make the soft Brie easier to slice, place it in the freezer for 20 minutes. This low-carb meatloaf is also relatively low in fat.

1. Preheat oven to 350°F. In large skillet, heat olive oil over medium heat. Add onion and garlic; cook and stir for 3 minutes. Add mushrooms, salt, and pepper; cook and stir until liquid evaporates, about 8–9 minutes.

2. Remove from heat and place in large bowl. Add ½ cup chili sauce and crumbled bread; mix well. Gently work in beef, pork, Brie, and parsley with your hands.

3. Form into a large loaf shape and place in roasting pan. Brush with remaining chili sauce and bake for 60–70 minutes or until internal temperature registers 165°F. Let stand for 10 minutes, then slice to serve.

SERVES 8

Calories: 301.84
Fat: 14.57 grams
Fat as % of calories: 43.4%
Carbohydrates: 11.12 grams
Fiber: 1.27 grams
Sodium: 326.93 mg
Vitamin A: 10% DV
Vitamin C: 15% DV
Calcium: 54.28 mg

INGREDIENTS
½ tablespoon olive oil
½ onion, chopped
3 cloves garlic, minced
1 cup chopped cremini mushrooms
1 cup chopped button mushrooms
Salt and pepper to taste
¾ cup chili sauce, divided
1 slice whole wheat bread,
    crumbled
1½ pounds 85% lean ground beef
½ pound ground pork
½ cup minced Brie cheese
¼ cup minced fresh parsley

Honey-Glazed Filet Mignon

Filet mignon is the most expensive cut of meat, but there's absolutely no waste and the taste and texture can't be beat.

1. Season steaks with salt and pepper. Heat a large nonstick skillet over medium heat and add olive oil. Add steaks to pan; cook for 4 minutes until easy to turn. Carefully turn steaks and cook for 3–5 minutes until desired doneness. Remove from pan and cover with foil to keep warm.

2. Add garlic and shallots to pan; turn to medium-high. Cook and stir to loosen pan drippings. Add honey and wine and bring to a boil. Boil for a few minutes to reduce sauce. Return steaks to pan and cook for 1 minute to heat through, spooning sauce over steaks. Serve immediately.

SERVES 6

Calories: 307.25
Fat: 13.42 grams
Fat as % of calories: 29.1%
Carbohydrates: 11.36 grams
Fiber: 0.05 grams
Sodium: 254.48 mg
Vitamin A: 2% DV
Vitamin C: 2% DV
Calcium: 29.37 mg

INGREDIENTS
6 4-ounce filet mignon steaks
½ teaspoon salt
⅛ teaspoon pepper
1 tablespoon olive oil
3 cloves garlic, minced
2 shallots, minced
3 tablespoons honey
¼ cup dry red wine

Calories: 321.46
Fat: 13.26 grams
Fat as % of calories: 37.1%
Carbohydrates: 27.78 grams
Fiber: 5.21 grams
Sodium: 472.36 mg
Vitamin A: 110% DV
Vitamin C: 25% DV
Calcium: 361.26 mg

INGREDIENTS

½ pound sweet Italian sausage
½ pound 85% lean ground beef
2 onions, chopped
4 cloves garlic, minced
1 cup grated carrot
1 cup diced portabello
  mushrooms
2 14.5-ounce cans diced
  tomatoes, undrained
1 6-ounce can tomato paste
¼ cup minced fresh basil
½ teaspoon dried Italian
  seasoning
⅛ teaspoon pepper
12 whole wheat lasagna noodles
1 15-ounce container part-skim
  ricotta cheese
1 3-ounce package nonfat cream
  cheese, softened
1 egg
1 10-ounce package frozen
  chopped spinach, drained
¼ teaspoon ground nutmeg
2 cups shredded part-skim
  mozzarella cheese
⅓ cup grated Parmesan cheese

Healthy and Rich Lasagna

Using leaner meats and low-fat dairy products helps reduce the fat in this flavorful and still rich-tasting lasagna.

1. In large saucepan, combine sausage and ground beef; brown over medium heat, stirring to break up meat. Drain well, remove meat from pan, and drain on paper towels; set aside.

2. Bring a large pot of water to a boil. Meanwhile, add onions, garlic, carrot, and mushrooms to saucepan; cook and stir over medium heat until vegetables are tender and liquid evaporates. Add tomatoes, tomato paste, basil, Italian seasoning, pepper, and meat to saucepan and bring to a simmer. Reduce heat to low and simmer for 20 minutes.

3. Cook lasagna noodles as directed on package until al dente. While noodles are cooking, in medium bowl combine ricotta, cream cheese, and egg and mix well. Stir in spinach, nutmeg, and mozzarella cheese.

4. Preheat oven to 350°F. Spray a 9" x 13" baking pan with nonstick cooking spray. Place a spoonful of tomato mixture in bottom of pan; top with ⅓ of the noodles and ⅓ of the ricotta cheese mixture. Top with ⅓ of the meat mixture, then repeat layers, ending with meat mixture. Sprinkle with Parmesan cheese. Bake for 45–55 minutes or until lasagna bubbles and cheese melts and browns.

Part-Skim Mozzarella

Part-skim mozzarella is one of the best low-fat cheeses for melting. Even though it's lower in fat, it still melts well and stays nice and creamy. It's also easy to shred and keeps well in the fridge for several weeks. Don't substitute fresh mozzarella for the processed kind; it has a lot more water and a much softer texture.

Low-Carb Beef with Peppers

*Even though bell peppers contain sugar, a carbohydrate, they are so high
in vitamins A and C that they are considered very nutrient dense.*

1. Trim flank steak and cut across the grain into ½-inch slices. In large skillet, heat olive oil over medium heat. Add steak strips; brown on all sides, about 5 minutes, then remove with slotted spoon and set aside.

2. Add onion to skillet; cook and stir for 2 minutes. Then add all the bell peppers. Sprinkle with salt and pepper; cook and stir for 4–5 minutes or until crisp-tender.

3. Return beef to skillet and add broth. Bring to a simmer, then cover and cook for 4–5 minutes. Uncover and add Pesto; heat through and serve immediately.

SERVES 6–8

Calories: 335.90
Fat: 15.53 grams
Fat as % of calories: 41.6%
Carbohydrates: 12.55 grams
Fiber: 3.89 grams
Sodium: 564.18 mg
Vitamin A: 80% DV
Vitamin C: 160% DV
Calcium: 142.22 mg

INGREDIENTS

1½ pounds flank steak
2 tablespoons olive oil
1 onion, chopped
1 red bell pepper, sliced
1 green bell pepper, sliced
1 yellow bell pepper, sliced
1 orange bell pepper, sliced
½ teaspoon salt
⅛ teaspoon pepper
½ cup beef broth
¾ cup Roasted Garlic Pesto
(page 32)

Cranberry Beef Pot Roast

*Fresh cranberries, cranberry juice, and orange juice add flavor and
nutrition to this elegant pot roast.*

1. Combine onion, garlic, mushrooms, cranberries, and sugar in a 4-quart slow cooker. Trim excess fat from beef and brown on all sides in a large pan over medium heat. Place beef on top of onion mixture in slow cooker.

2. Drain any fat from pan, then deglaze with cranberry and orange juices; bring to a simmer. Add salt, pepper, and cloves and stir well, then pour over roast in slow cooker. Spread roast with cranberry sauce.

3. Cover and cook on low for 8–9 hours or until beef is tender. Remove beef and cover with foil. Combine cornstarch and water in small bowl. Add cornstarch mixture to slow cooker; cook on high for 15 minutes until thickened. Serve with roast.

SERVES 8

Calories: 317.81
Fat: 6.77 grams
Fat as % of calories: 19.2%
Carbohydrates: 17.55 grams
Fiber: 1.06 grams
Sodium: 353.43 mg
Vitamin A: 5% DV
Vitamin C: 25% DV
Calcium: 17.14 mg

INGREDIENTS

1 onion, chopped
4 cloves garlic, minced
½ cup diced mushrooms
1 cup cranberries, cut in half
2 tablespoons sugar
2½ pounds boneless top round
beef
1 cup cranberry juice
½ cup orange juice
1 teaspoon salt
⅛ teaspoon pepper
¼ teaspoon ground cloves
½ cup cranberry sauce
2 tablespoons cornstarch
¼ cup water

SERVES 6

Calories: 347.36
Fat: 11.85 grams
Fat as % of calories: 30.7%
Carbohydrates: 19.42 grams
Fiber: 4.08 grams
Sodium: 585.89 mg
Vitamin A: 110% DV
Vitamin C: 100% DV
Calcium: 47.54 mg

INGREDIENTS

2 tablespoons butter, divided
1 onion, chopped
3 cloves garlic, minced
3 carrots, diced
1½ pounds bottom round steak
1 red bell pepper, thinly sliced
¼ cup flour
½ teaspoon salt
⅛ teaspoon pepper
2 4-ounce cans sliced
 mushrooms, drained
½ cup beef broth
1 14.5-ounce can diced
 tomatoes, undrained
2 tablespoons mustard
1 tablespoon Worcestershire
 sauce

Slow Cooker Beef Rouladen

Beef, thinly pounded and stuffed with vegetables,
makes an excellent main dish for entertaining.

1. In large skillet, melt 1 tablespoon butter over medium heat. Add onion, garlic, and carrots; cook and stir until tender, about 7 minutes. Remove from heat and place in medium bowl; let cool for 15 minutes.

2. Meanwhile, cut round steak into 6 equal portions. Trim excess fat, then place between sheets of waxed paper and pound until ¼-inch thick. Divide bell pepper strips among beef, then top with onion mixture. Roll up, enclosing filling; secure with toothpicks.

3. On plate, combine flour, salt, and pepper and mix. Dredge beef rolls in flour mixture. In same skillet, melt remaining 1 tablespoon butter. Brown beef rolls on all sides. Place mushrooms in 4-quart slow cooker; top with beef rolls.

4. Deglaze skillet with beef broth; add tomatoes, mustard, and Worcester-shire sauce and bring to a simmer. Pour into slow cooker. Cover and cook on low for 7–8 hours or until beef is tender. Serve rouladen with sauce.

Beef Roasts

If you have a choice, choose select or prime beef rather than choice. This beef has less surface fat but more marbling. Marbling, or fat inside the muscle, adds moisture and flavor to the beef. Top and bottom round roast are two of the cuts of beef that meet the standard of lean or extra lean.

Today's Beef Stroganoff

Less beef helps lower the fat content, and more mushrooms add to the meaty flavor in this excellent company dish.

1. Toss sirloin with 1 tablespoon flour, salt, and pepper. Heat olive oil in medium skillet over medium heat. Brown sirloin for about 4 minutes. Place in 4- to 5-quart slow cooker. Add onions and garlic to skillet; cook for 4 minutes, stirring to scrape up drippings. Add to slow cooker.

2. Add mushrooms, carrots, beef stock, and apple juice to slow cooker. Cover and cook on low for 7–8 hours or until beef and mushrooms are tender.

3. In food processor, combine sour cream with cream cheese and blend until smooth. Add remaining 2 tablespoons flour and ½ cup of the hot liquid from the slow cooker and blend. Add to slow cooker, cover, and cook on high for 30 minutes. Serve over hot cooked noodles.

Beef

There are dozens of cuts of beef that are classified as low fat—defined as anything that contains 10 grams or less of fat per serving. These include sirloin tip, round roast (both top and bottom), brisket, 95% lean ground beef, shoulder pot roast, and chuck shoulder steak, among others. For more information, visit *www.mibeef.org/conleancuts.htm*.

SERVES 6–8

Calories: 333.91
Fat: 9.36 grams
Fat as % of calories: 25.5%
Carbohydrates: 38.45 grams
Fiber: 5.57 grams
Sodium: 438.10 mg
Vitamin A: 140% DV
Vitamin C: 40% DV
Calcium: 107.46 mg

INGREDIENTS

1 pound sirloin tip, cubed
3 tablespoons flour, divided
½ teaspoon salt
⅛ teaspoon pepper
1 tablespoon olive oil
2 onions, chopped
5 cloves garlic, minced
1 8-ounce package sliced mushrooms
2 cups sliced cremini mushrooms
2 cups sliced carrots
3 cups low-sodium beef stock
1½ cups apple juice
1 cup low-fat sour cream
1 3-ounce package nonfat cream cheese
4 cups hot, cooked whole wheat noodles

INGREDIENTS

2 tablespoons butter
1 onion, chopped
1 red bell pepper, chopped
1 cup sliced cremini mushrooms
1 pound sliced deli roast beef
1 cup part-skim ricotta cheese
1 tablespoon flour
Salt and pepper to taste
1 teaspoon dried marjoram leaves
1 cup shredded low-fat Swiss cheese
1 recipe Whole Wheat Pie Crust (page 188), unbaked
3 tablespoons grated Romano cheese

INGREDIENTS

1 egg white
2 cloves garlic, minced
1 slice Cracked Wheat French Bread (page 139)
½ cup finely shredded carrot
¼ cup tomato juice
½ teaspoon salt
⅛ teaspoon white pepper
½ teaspoon dried marjoram
¼ cup chopped flat-leaf parsley
1½ pounds ground turkey breast

Beef Galette

A galette is a rustic pie, made by filling a pie crust with a meat mixture, then just folding over the edges.

1. Preheat oven to 375°F. In large saucepan, melt butter over medium heat. Add onion, red bell pepper, and mushrooms; cook and stir until vegetables are tender and liquid evaporates, about 10–11 minutes. Remove from heat and place in large bowl.

2. Add beef, ricotta, flour, salt, pepper, marjoram, and Swiss cheese and mix gently. Roll out Pie Crust to a 12-inch circle and place on cookie sheet. Place beef mixture in center of pie dough, leaving a 2-inch border. Gently fold pie dough edges over the beef mixture, leaving a 4-inch open space in the center.

3. Sprinkle with Romano cheese. Bake for 25–35 minutes or until crust is golden brown and filling is bubbling. Let stand for 10 minutes, then slice to serve.

Healthy Meatballs

Turkey breast, carrots, and tomato juice all add nutrition to these flavorful meatballs. When you bake them, they're even lower in fat!

1. Preheat oven to 400°F. In large bowl, combine all ingredients except turkey breast; mix well. Add turkey; mix gently until combined.

2. Shape into 36 meatballs, about 1-inch wide. Spray a cookie sheet with sides with nonstick cooking spray and arrange meatballs 1-inch apart. Bake for 15–20 minutes or until meatballs register 165°F. Remove to wire rack to cool. Use in recipes or serve immediately.

Best Meatballs

To make the best meatballs, there are some rules to follow. Most meatball recipes call for vegetables and bread to lighten the texture and add nutrition. Be sure you combine all the ingredients except the meat and mix well, then add the meat. Don't overmix or the meatballs will be tough.

Light Sweet and Sour Meatballs

Sweet and sour is a flavor combination everyone loves.
Serve with a spinach salad.

1. In large saucepan, heat olive oil over medium heat. Add onion and garlic; cook and stir for 4 minutes. Add bell peppers; cook and stir for 3 minutes. Sprinkle with flour, salt, and pepper; cook until bubbly, about 3 minutes.

2. Add pineapple tidbits with liquid, orange juice, soy sauce, cider vinegar, and sugar. Bring to a boil, stirring frequently, until sugar dissolves. Simmer for 5 minutes.

3. Add Meatballs to sauce and stir gently. Bring back to a simmer; simmer for 5–7 minutes or until meatballs are hot. Serve immediately over rice.

Bell Peppers

Bell peppers are mild and sweet and can be found in many colors. Whether you choose red, orange, yellow, green, or purple, these vegetables are full of vitamins A and C. To prepare, cut in half and pull out the section that holds the seeds. Place the peppers skin side down and cut into strips, then cut crosswise to chop.

SERVES 6

Calories: 349.83
Fat: 7.21 grams
Fat as % of calories: 18.5%
Carbohydrates: 50.34 grams
Fiber: 3.62 grams
Sodium: 470.02 mg
Vitamin A: 40% DV
Vitamin C: 100% DV
Calcium: 50.39 mg

INGREDIENTS

1 tablespoon olive oil
1 onion, chopped
3 cloves garlic, minced
1 green bell pepper, chopped
1 red bell pepper, chopped
2 tablespoons flour
½ teaspoon salt
⅛ teaspoon white pepper
1 20-ounce can pineapple tidbits
½ cup orange juice
2 tablespoons low-sodium soy sauce
⅓ cup apple cider vinegar
¼ cup sugar
¾ recipe Healthy Meatballs (page 84), baked
4 cups hot, cooked brown rice

INGREDIENTS

1 15-ounce can pineapple tidbits
2 tablespoons butter
1 onion, chopped
3 cloves garlic, minced
3 carrots, sliced
¼ teaspoon salt
⅛ teaspoon pepper
1 teaspoon dry mustard powder
4 cups whole wheat bread cubes
½ cup dried currants
2 ½-inch thick low-salt boneless
    ham steaks
½ cup orange juice

Stuffed Ham

This unusual way of serving ham steaks is a meal all by itself. The sweet and tart filling contrasts beautifully with the suave and salty ham.

1. Preheat oven to 350°F. Drain pineapple, reserving juice; set both aside. In large saucepan, melt butter over medium heat. Add onion, garlic, and carrots; cook until tender, about 7 minutes. Sprinkle with salt and pepper; remove from heat.

2. Stir in mustard powder and ⅓ cup reserved pineapple juice; mix well. Add bread cubes, reserved pineapple tidbits, and currants; toss to mix.

3. Place one ham steak on a flat rack in a roasting pan. Top with pineapple mixture, then with second ham steak. Pour orange juice and remaining pineapple juice over all.

4. Bake for 45–55 minutes or until ham and stuffing is hot, basting with pan juices several times during baking. Slice thinly to serve.

Ham Steaks

You can sometimes find packaged ham steaks in the meat department of grocery stores, but you may have to ask the butcher. Be sure to specify low-salt ham steaks, and ask her to slice them ½-inch thick or thinner to cut down on sodium levels. Ham steaks are an economical way to serve a large number of people with less cost.

Chapter 6

Dinner Party: Poultry Entrées

INGREDIENTS

1 tablespoon olive oil
1 onion, chopped
3 carrots, sliced
4 boneless, skinless chicken
    breasts, cubed
⅓ cup flour
¼ teaspoon salt
⅛ teaspoon white pepper
⅓ cup Dijon mustard
1 13-ounce can low-fat
    evaporated milk
¼ cup chicken broth
3 tablespoons lemon juice
1 teaspoon dried thyme leaves,
    divided
30 9" x 14" sheets phyllo dough,
    thawed
⅓ cup dry bread crumbs
¼ cup finely chopped walnuts
4 tablespoons butter, melted
Olive oil spray

Chicken in Phyllo

A combination of cooking spray and butter makes flaky layers with less fat than puff pastry in this special party recipe.

1. In large saucepan, heat olive oil over medium heat. Add onion and carrot; cook and stir until tender, about 6 minutes. Toss chicken breasts with flour, salt, and pepper. Add to skillet; cook and stir until browned, about 5 minutes.

2. Add mustard, evaporated milk, chicken broth, lemon juice, and ½ teaspoon thyme leaves to saucepan. Bring to a simmer, then reduce heat to low and simmer for 10 minutes or until chicken is thoroughly cooked and sauce has thickened. Set aside.

3. Unroll phyllo dough. In small bowl, combine bread crumbs, walnuts, and remaining ½ teaspoon thyme leaves. Preheat oven to 400°F. Lay a sheet of phyllo on the work surface, keeping the rest covered with plastic wrap. Brush sparingly with 1 teaspoon melted butter and sprinkle with a bit of the bread crumb mixture. Top with another sheet; spray with olive oil spray. Repeat layers, using five sheets in all, alternating butter and bread crumb mixture and olive oil spray in between sheets. Do not butter or spray on top sheet.

4. Repeat with remaining sheets, making six stacks. Divide chicken mixture over bottom part of each stack on the short side. Fold over once, starting at short side, then fold in ends. Roll up like a jelly roll, enclosing filling. Place on cookie sheet.

5. Repeat with remaining stacks and filling. Brush the filled rolls with any remaining butter and sprinkle with any remaining bread mixture. Bake for 15–20 minutes or until rolls are golden brown. Serve immediately.

Baked Crisp Parmesan Chicken

You can double or triple this easy recipe to feed more people. Just make sure there's a bit of space between each chicken breast on the rack.

1. Place chicken in a glass baking dish and sprinkle on both sides with salt, pepper, paprika, and marjoram. In small bowl, combine buttermilk and mustard; pour over chicken. Cover and refrigerate for 8–24 hours.

2. Preheat oven to 350°F. Place a rack in a large, shallow roasting pan. Combine cheese, bread crumbs, and melted butter on a plate. Remove chicken from marinade and shake off excess. Dip into cheese mixture to coat.

3. Place chicken on rack. Bake for 30–35 minutes or until meat thermometer registers 160°F. Remove chicken from oven and let stand for 5 minutes, then serve immediately.

SERVES 6

Calories: 234.28
Fat: 8.43 grams
Fat as % of calories: 31.2%
Carbohydrates: 5.77 grams
Fiber: 0.43 grams
Sodium: 536.80 mg
Vitamin A: 4% DV
Vitamin C: 2% DV
Calcium: 141.10 mg

INGREDIENTS

6 boneless, skinless chicken breasts
1 teaspoon salt
⅛ teaspoon pepper
1 teaspoon paprika
1 teaspoon dried marjoram leaves
1 cup buttermilk
¼ cup mustard
½ cup grated Parmesan cheese
⅓ cup dry bread crumbs
2 tablespoons butter, melted

Chicken Tortellini with Squash

This rich-tasting dish is very nutrient dense, with more than enough vitamin A and calcium to keep your body happy.

1. Preheat oven to 350°F. In a large skillet, heat olive oil over medium heat. Add onion, garlic, and chicken; cook until onion is tender and chicken is cooked.

2. Remove chicken and vegetables from skillet; place in 2-quart casserole. Add squash and chicken broth to skillet. Bring to a simmer over high heat. Cover pan, reduce heat to low, simmer until squash is almost tender.

3. Add frozen tortellini to skillet; cover and simmer for 2–3 minutes longer or until tortellini is thawed and squash is tender.

4. Add tortellini and squash mixture to casserole along with Alfredo sauce, thyme, and pepper; mix gently. In small bowl, combine bread crumbs and melted butter; toss to coat. Sprinkle over casserole.

5. Bake, uncovered, for 30–40 minutes or until casserole is hot and bubbling and bread crumbs are browned. Serve immediately.

SERVES 8

Calories: 438.55
Fat: 14.46 grams
Fat as % of calories: 29.7%
Carbohydrates: 44.42 grams
Fiber: 1.78 grams
Sodium: 761.49 mg
Vitamin A: 122% DV
Vitamin C: 15% DV
Calcium: 221.03 mg

INGREDIENTS

1 tablespoon olive oil
1 onion, chopped
3 cloves garlic, minced
1 pound boneless, skinless chicken breasts, cubed
2 cups peeled, cubed butternut squash
1 cup chicken broth
2 9-ounce packages frozen chicken tortellini
1 16-ounce jar low-fat Alfredo sauce
1 teaspoon dried thyme leaves
⅛ teaspoon pepper
½ cup whole wheat bread crumbs
2 tablespoons butter, melted

SERVES 8

Calories: 295.42
Fat: 9.98 grams
Fat as % of calories: 30.5%
Carbohydrates: 13.58 grams
Fiber: 1.65 grams
Sodium: 366.98 mg
Vitamin A: 51% DV
Vitamin C: 6% DV
Calcium: 185.16 mg

INGREDIENTS

8 boneless, skinless chicken breasts
1 tablespoon olive oil
1 onion, chopped
1 cup grated carrots
3 cloves garlic, minced
½ cup diced cooked low-salt ham
¾ cup low-fat four-cheese Alfredo sauce
1 cup shredded Swiss cheese
¼ cup skim milk
1 egg, beaten
2 cups soft whole wheat bread crumbs
1 teaspoon paprika
¼ teaspoon white pepper

Low-Fat Chicken Cordon Bleu

Chicken cordon bleu is typically fried in butter, then baked until golden brown. This easy recipe omits the frying step to save on calories.

1. Preheat oven to 325°F. Using a very sharp knife, carefully cut the chicken breasts in half so they open up like a book. Do not cut all the way through the chicken; you're butterflying the breast. Set aside.

2. In medium skillet, heat olive oil over medium heat. Add onion, carrot, and garlic; cook and stir until vegetables are tender, about 7–9 minutes. Remove from heat and add ham; turn into medium bowl.

3. Add sauce and cheese to bowl and stir to mix. Divide mixture among the butterflied chicken breasts. Gently roll up the chicken to enclose the filling; secure with a toothpick.

4. In shallow bowl, combine milk and egg and mix well. On plate, combine bread crumbs with paprika and pepper; mix well. Dip chicken into milk mixture, then into bread crumbs to coat. Place in two 13" x 9" glass baking dishes.

5. Bake chicken for 15 minutes, then carefully turn with a large spatula and bake for 15–20 minutes longer or until chicken is thoroughly cooked. Remove toothpicks and serve.

Chicken en Papillote

Baking chicken in an enclosed container yields tender and moist meat, flavored with the other ingredients. It's a beautiful presentation too.

1. Preheat oven to 400°F. In large skillet, melt butter over medium heat. Add leek, garlic, and carrot; cook and stir until tender, about 6–7 minutes.

2. Cut six 12" x 16" sheets of parchment paper, fold in half into 12" x 8" rectangles, and cut half a heart shape. Unfold into heart shapes. Place a chicken breast near the fold on one side of each heart. Sprinkle with salt, pepper, and thyme.

3. Lay lemon slices on top of each chicken breast. Spoon vegetable mixture on top of chicken and drizzle each with olive oil and wine. Fold one half of each heart over the food, and seal by crimping the edges together. Place bundles on cookie sheets.

4. Bake for 25–30 minutes or until paper bundles expand and turn brown; chicken should be at 165°F on a meat thermometer. Serve the bundles to your guests, warning them to be careful with steam when they cut them open.

En Papillote

To cook en papillote, you can use parchment paper or heavy-duty foil. Parchment paper generally makes a prettier presentation. If you're grilling food in a package, foil will stand up to the heat of the grill. If baking, the paper is just fine; it will turn brown but will not burn. Crimp the edges tightly to hold in the steam and flavor.

SERVES 6

Calories: 222.50
Fat: 7.98 grams
Fat as % of calories: 32.2%
Carbohydrates: 6.39 grams
Fiber: 1.11 grams
Sodium: 307.22 mg
Vitamin A: 100% DV
Vitamin C: 15% DV
Calcium: 36.87 mg

INGREDIENTS

1 tablespoon butter
1 leek, rinsed and chopped
4 cloves garlic, minced
1½ cups shredded carrots
6 boneless, skinless chicken breasts
½ teaspoon salt
⅛ teaspoon white pepper
1 teaspoon dried thyme
1 lemon, thinly sliced
2 tablespoons olive oil
⅓ cup dry white wine

SERVES 6

Calories: 329.87
Fat: 12.85 grams
Fat as % of calories: 35.1%
Carbohydrates: 19.30 grams
Fiber: 3.81 grams
Sodium: 454.29 mg
Vitamin A: 100% DV
Vitamin C: 10% DV
Calcium: 97.99 mg

INGREDIENTS

1 tablespoon olive oil
1 onion, chopped
4 cloves garlic, minced
¾ cup solid-pack pumpkin purée
½ cup chopped toasted pecans
½ teaspoon salt
⅛ teaspoon pepper
¼ cup grated Parmesan cheese
1 teaspoon dried thyme leaves
*6 boneless, skinless chicken
    breasts*
¼ cup whole wheat flour
1 teaspoon paprika
¼ cup dried bread crumbs
⅓ cup buttermilk
2 tablespoons butter

Pumpkin-Stuffed Chicken Breasts

*This unusual recipe is really fun to serve.
It's delicious, especially for the holidays, and so good for you!*

1. Preheat oven to 350°F. In large saucepan, heat olive oil over medium heat. Add onion and garlic; cook and stir until the onion begins to brown and caramelize, about 7–9 minutes.

2. Add pumpkin, pecans, salt, pepper, Parmesan, and thyme and remove from heat. Let cool for 30 minutes.

3. Pound chicken breasts until they are about ⅓-inch thick. Divide the pumpkin mixture among the chicken breasts and roll up to enclose filling; secure with toothpicks.

4. On plate, combine flour, paprika, and bread crumbs. Dip chicken into buttermilk, then into flour mixture.

5. In large skillet, melt butter over medium heat. Add chicken; brown on both sides. Place chicken on wire rack in large roasting pan. Roast, uncovered, for 30–40 minutes or until chicken is thoroughly cooked. Remove toothpicks and serve immediately.

Making Stuffed Chicken

The most important step in making any stuffed chicken is pounding the breasts. They have to be pounded thinly enough to roll easily, but there can't be any rips or tears in the flesh. Work slowly and check your progress often. If you make holes in the chicken, freeze it to save for another use and start over.

Grilled Citrus Chicken

*You could also grill chicken thighs in this marinade for a dish with
130 calories and 7.23 grams of fat per serving.*

1. Cut slits in chicken breast and insert garlic slivers. Place chicken in a shallow casserole dish.

2. In small bowl, combine remaining ingredients and mix well. Pour over chicken, cover, and marinate in refrigerator for 18–24 hours.

3. When ready to eat, prepare and preheat grill. Remove chicken from marinade; reserve marinade. Grill chicken for 4–6 minutes on each side, brushing occasionally with reserved marinade, turning once, until meat thermometer registers 160°F. Discard remaining marinade.

SERVES 6

Calories: 177.60
Fat: 5.99 grams
Fat as % of calories: 30.3%
Carbohydrates: 1.95
Fiber: 0.10 grams
Sodium: 464.98 mg
Vitamin A: 0% DV
Vitamin C: 10% DV
Calcium: 19.57 mg

INGREDIENTS

6 boneless, skinless chicken
   breasts
6 cloves garlic, slivered
¼ cup olive oil
¼ cup lemon juice
¼ cup orange juice
1 teaspoon grated lime zest
1 tablespoon minced rosemary
2 teaspoons paprika
1 teaspoon salt
⅛ teaspoon crushed red pepper

Apple and Raisin–Stuffed Chicken Breasts

*Apples and raisins are the perfect complement to tender and juicy
chicken breasts. This is a good alternative dish to a Thanksgiving turkey.*

1. Preheat oven to 350°F. In medium saucepan, melt butter over medium heat. Add onion, apple, and garlic; cook and stir until tender, about 6–7 minutes. Add raisins, salt, and pepper and remove from heat. Stir in sour cream. Let cool.

2. Cut a 4-inch slit in the thick side of each chicken breast. Stuff with the apple mixture and close with toothpicks. Place chicken in shallow baking dish and pour broth and apple juice over.

3. Bake for 35–45 minutes or until chicken registers 160°F. on a meat thermometer. Remove toothpicks and serve immediately.

SERVES 6

Calories: 254.21
Fat: 5.28 grams
Fat as % of calories: 20.5%
Carbohydrates: 22.05 grams
Fiber: 2.29 grams
Sodium: 352.87 mg
Vitamin A: 5% DV
Vitamin C: 25% DV
Calcium: 47.57 mg

INGREDIENTS

1 tablespoon butter
1 onion, chopped
1 apple, chopped
4 cloves garlic, minced
½ cup raisins
½ teaspoon salt
⅛ teaspoon pepper
¼ cup low-fat sour cream
6 boneless, skinless chicken
   breasts
1 cup chicken broth
½ cup apple juice

Roast Chicken

If you're serving more than four people, roast more chickens! This versatile low-carb recipe can be seasoned any way you'd like.

1. Preheat oven to 375°F. Rinse chicken and pat dry. Rub with butter, inside and out. Sprinkle with salt, inside and out. Sprinkle outside with pepper and paprika.

2. Place chicken on rack in shallow roasting pan. Squeeze one quarter of the lemon over the chicken, then place remaining three quarters inside the chicken along with the parsley.

3. Roast for 55–65 minutes, basting with pan juices halfway through cooking time, until a meat thermometer inserted into the thigh registers 180°F. Remove chicken from oven, let stand for 10 minutes, then slice to serve.

Light Garlic Chicken Dijon Pilaf

This skillet dish is easy for entertaining. Choose a nice-looking skillet and put it directly on the table for ease in serving.

1. Cut chicken into 1-inch pieces and sprinkle with salt, pepper, and basil. In large skillet, melt butter over medium heat. Add chicken, onion, and garlic; cook and stir until chicken is almost cooked, about 5–6 minutes.

2. Add carrot and rice to skillet; cook and stir for 2–3 minutes. Add chicken broth and mustard. Bring to a simmer.

3. Reduce heat to low, cover, and cook for 35–40 minutes or until rice is tender and liquid is absorbed. Sprinkle with cheese and stir. Then sprinkle with parsley and serve.

Chicken Pasta with Cherries

*There are so many wonderful different shapes of pasta
on the market. Farfalle look like little bow ties,
but you could also use penne, mostaccioli, or shell pasta.*

1. Bring a large pot of salted water to a boil. Meanwhile, combine olive oil and butter in large skillet over medium heat. Add onion, celery, and garlic; cook and stir until crisp-tender, about 5 minutes. Sprinkle with flour, celery salt, pepper, and thyme leaves; cook and stir until bubbly.

2. Add milk, cherry juice, and sour cream to onion mixture; cook and stir until mixture thickens and begins to bubble. Add cherries and chicken and cook for 5 minutes; remove from heat.

3. When water comes to a boil, add pasta. Cook until al dente according to package directions. When pasta is done, drain, reserving ¼ cup cooking water.

4. Return skillet to medium heat and add drained pasta and cooking water. Cook and stir until mixture starts to bubble, about 4–5 minutes. Add cheese; cook and stir until cheese melts. Sprinkle with almonds and serve immediately.

SERVES 8

Calories: 529.12
Fat: 11.40 grams
Fat as % of calories: 19.4%
Carbohydrates: 63.91 grams
Fiber: 2.86 grams
Sodium: 242.80 mg
Vitamin A: 35% DV
Vitamin C: 10% DV
Calcium: 339.91 mg

INGREDIENTS

1 tablespoon olive oil
2 tablespoons butter
1 onion, chopped
4 stalks celery, chopped
4 cloves garlic, minced
¼ cup flour
½ teaspoon celery salt
⅛ teaspoon white pepper
1 teaspoon dried thyme leaves
2 cups skim milk
½ cup cherry juice
½ cup low-fat sour cream
1 cup chopped dried cherries
1 cup halved fresh cherries
4 cups cooked, cubed chicken
*1 16-ounce package farfalle
    pasta*
*1 cup shredded low-fat Swiss
    cheese*
½ cup sliced toasted almonds

SERVES 6–8

Calories: 363.60
Fat: 12.62 grams
Fat as % of calories: 31.2%
Carbohydrates: 7.71 grams
Fiber: 0.60 grams
Sodium: 397.83 mg
Vitamin A: 2% DV
Vitamin C: 6% DV
Calcium: 33.74 mg

INGREDIENTS

¾ cup dried potato flakes
¾ cup crushed crisp rice cereal
1 teaspoon seasoned salt
¼ teaspoon pepper
1 teaspoon paprika
2 egg whites
¼ cup mustard
4 pounds bone-in, skinless
    chicken parts

Light Oven-Fried Chicken

This delicious recipe is just like fried chicken only better.

1. Preheat oven to 400°F. Place potato flakes, crushed cereal, salt, pepper, and paprika on a plate. In a shallow bowl, combine egg whites and mustard; beat well.

2. Coat chicken in egg mixture, then roll in cereal mixture to coat. Place on a rack in a large shallow roasting pan. Roast for 55–65 minutes or until chicken is thoroughly cooked. Serve immediately.

Seasoned Salt

Seasoned salt is a great item to have in your spice cupboard. If you can't find it in the supermarket, make your own by combining ¼ cup salt with 2 tablespoons dried parsley flakes, 1 teaspoon onion powder, 1 teaspoon garlic powder, 2 teaspoons pepper, 1 tablespoon mustard powder, and 2 tablespoons dried chives. Store in an airtight container.

SERVES 6

Calories: 476.35
Fat: 18.90 grams
Fat as % of calories: 35.6%
Carbohydrates: 39.89 grams
Fiber: 5.02 grams
Sodium: 638.17 mg
Vitamin A: 30% DV
Vitamin C: 90% DV
Calcium: 337.75 mg

INGREDIENTS

2 tablespoons butter
1 tablespoon olive oil
1 onion, chopped
5 cloves garlic, minced
2 green bell peppers, chopped
2 jalapeños, minced
2 tablespoons chili powder
¼ cup flour
Salt and pepper to taste
1½ cups chicken broth
1 cup skim milk
3 cups cubed, cooked chicken
1 cup shredded low-fat pepper
    jack cheese
6 Triple Onion Scones (page 137)
3 tablespoons chopped cilantro

Tex-Mex Chicken à la King

Chicken à la king is a classic comfort food recipe. This version is updated with the zesty flavors of Tex-Mex cooking.

1. In large skillet, combine butter and olive oil over medium heat. Add onion and garlic; cook and stir for 5 minutes. Add bell peppers and jalapeños; cook and stir for 3–4 minutes longer.

2. Add chili powder, flour, salt, and pepper; cook and stir until bubbly. Add chicken broth and milk; cook and stir until mixture bubbles and thickens. Stir in chicken. Bring back to a simmer, then cook, stirring frequently, for 8–9 minutes until chicken is hot. Stir in cheese until melted.

3. Place the hot baked Scones on plates (you can split them if you'd like) and top with the chicken mixture. Sprinkle with cilantro and serve immediately.

Pecan-Crusted Chicken Breasts

Pecans, mustard, and garlic make a delicious and crunchy coating on simple chicken breasts.

1. On a plate, combine pecans, flour, salt, pepper, and marjoram. In shallow bowl, combine eggs, garlic, and mustard and beat well.

2. Dip chicken into egg mixture, then into pecan mixture to coat, pressing coating into chicken. Let stand on wire rack for 20 minutes.

3. Melt butter in a large skillet over medium heat. Add chicken; cook for 5–7 minutes on each side, turning once, until chicken is thoroughly cooked. Serve immediately.

SERVES 8

Calories: 411.06 grams
Fat: 29.33 grams
Fat as % of calories: 64.2%
Carbohydrates: 7.91 grams
Fiber: 3.41 grams
Sodium: 469.81 mg
Vitamin A: 5% DV
Vitamin C: 0% DV
Calcium: 43.56 mg

INGREDIENTS

2 cups chopped pecans
⅓ cup whole wheat flour
1 teaspoon salt
¼ teaspoon pepper
1 teaspoon dried marjoram leaves
2 eggs, beaten
3 cloves garlic, minced
¼ cup Dijon mustard
8 boneless, skinless chicken breasts
¼ cup butter

High-Fiber Blueberry Hazelnut–Stuffed Chicken Breasts

Blueberries and hazelnuts are two of the so-called super foods that can help reduce your cholesterol levels.

1. Preheat oven to 350°F. In medium skillet, melt butter over medium heat. Add chopped hazelnuts; cook and stir until fragrant. Remove from heat and stir in blueberries.

2. Place chicken breasts on work surface; cover with waxed paper and pound until ⅓-inch thick. Place blueberry mixture on chicken; fold in sides and roll up; secure with toothpicks. Beat egg whites until foamy. Combine flour, wheat germ, ground hazelnuts, salt, and pepper on plate.

3. Dip chicken into egg whites, then into flour mixture to coat. Place on wire rack in baking dish. Bake for 25–35 minutes until chicken is thoroughly cooked.

SERVES 6

Calories: 442.03
Fat: 18.50 grams
Fat as % of calories: 37.6%
Carbohydrates: 36.90 grams
Fiber: 6.28 grams
Sodium: 285.26
Vitamin A: 2% DV
Vitamin C: 2% DV
Calcium: 47.42 mg

INGREDIENTS

2 tablespoons butter
¾ cup chopped hazelnuts
¾ cup dried blueberries
6 boneless, skinless chicken breasts
2 egg whites
⅓ cup whole wheat flour
⅓ cup wheat germ
¼ cup ground hazelnuts
½ teaspoon salt
⅛ teaspoon pepper

Calories: 240.78
Fat: 7.13 grams
Fat as % of calories: 26.7%
Carbohydrates: 11.56 grams
Fiber: 1.68 grams
Sodium: 501.55 mg
Vitamin A: 2% DV
Vitamin C: 9% DV
Calcium: 117.97 mg

INGREDIENTS

1 cup plain yogurt
⅓ cup lemon juice
1 tablespoon curry powder
1 teaspoon ground turmeric
1 teaspoon ground ginger
⅛ teaspoon ground cardamom
½ teaspoon crushed red pepper
1 teaspoon grated lemon zest
6 boneless, skinless chicken
   breasts
2 cups soft whole wheat bread
   crumbs
1 teaspoon dried oregano
½ teaspoon salt
⅛ teaspoon pepper
½ cup crumbled feta cheese

Velvet Indian Chicken

*Yogurt and lemon juice make this chicken very tender and moist. The
bread crumb topping, broiled in the oven, makes a crisp crust.*

1. In a 13" x 9" baking dish, combine yogurt with lemon juice, curry pow-
    der, turmeric, ginger, cardamom, red pepper flakes, and lemon zest; mix
    well. Add chicken breasts and turn to coat. Cover and refrigerate for 24
    hours.

2. Set oven to broil. Combine bread crumbs, oregano, salt, and pepper on
    plate. Remove chicken from marinade and roll in bread crumb mixture
    to coat. Place chicken on broiler pan.

3. Broil chicken 6 inches from heat source for 10–12 minutes on each side,
    turning once, until chicken is thoroughly cooked. Sprinkle with feta
    cheese and serve.

Yogurt

The difference in fat grams between 1 cup of plain regular yogurt and low-fat
yogurt is 7.9 grams versus 3.8 grams. That's not that much of a difference,
especially when used in a recipe that serves a lot of people. The full-fat yogurt
has almost twice the vitamin A of low-fat yogurt, so don't feel bad about using
the full-fat version of this product.

The All-New Chicken Kiev

A butter sauce, rather than plain butter, fills these chicken rolls. Regular chicken Kiev has 700 calories and 50 grams of fat per serving!

1. In medium skillet, melt butter over medium heat. Add onion and garlic; cook and stir until tender, about 7 minutes. Stir in flour, salt, and pepper; cook and stir until bubbly.

2. Add lemon juice and milk; cook and stir until very thick and bubbly. Cool sauce, then chill until very cold. Divide mixture into 8 portions, shape portions into a rectangle about 2" x 1", then freeze until firm.

3. Preheat oven to 400°F. Place chicken breasts in between sheets of waxed paper; pound until thin and even, about ⅓-inch thick. Place frozen sauce mixture on each breast; fold in sides and roll up to enclose filling; secure with toothpicks.

4. Beat egg whites until foamy; place on plate. Combine bread crumbs, cheese, parsley, and olive oil on another plate. Dip chicken bundles in egg whites, then in bread crumb mixture to coat. Place on wire rack in roasting pan.

5. Bake for 25–30 minutes or until chicken is thoroughly cooked. Serve immediately.

SERVES 8

Calories: 278.67
Fat: 10.09 grams
Fat as % of calories: 32.5%
Carbohydrates: 14.07 grams
Fiber: 0.88 grams
Sodium: 381.51 mg
Vitamin A: 6% DV
Vitamin C: 15% DV
Calcium: 83.70 mg

INGREDIENTS

¼ cup butter (no substitutes)
1 onion, finely chopped
5 cloves garlic, minced
3 tablespoons flour
½ teaspoon salt
⅛ teaspoon white pepper
¼ cup lemon juice
¾ cup 1% milk
8 boneless, skinless chicken breasts
2 egg whites
½ cup dried bread crumbs
2 tablespoons grated Romano cheese
1 tablespoon dried parsley flakes
2 tablespoons olive oil

Low-Fat Pesto Chicken Pasta

It doesn't take a lot of pesto, a traditionally high-fat food, to add flavor to a dish. Less than a cup makes this elegant dish delicious, and it serves eight.

1. Bring a large pot of salted water to a boil. Meanwhile, heat olive oil in large saucepan over medium heat. Add shallots; cook and stir until tender, about 4 minutes.

2. Toss chicken with flour, salt, and pepper and add to saucepan. Cook and stir until chicken is almost cooked. Add broth and cream; bring to a simmer. Cook and stir until sauce begins to thicken. Add tomatoes to chicken mixture.

3. Cook pasta until al dente according to package directions. Drain pasta and add to chicken mixture along with Pesto and cheese. Cook and stir over medium heat until heated through, then serve immediately.

SERVES 8

Calories: 450.44
Fat: 12.48 grams
Fat as % of calories: 24.9%
Carbohydrates: 51.60 grams
Fiber: 2.08 grams
Sodium: 516.72 mg
Vitamin A: 70% DV
Vitamin C: 25% DV
Calcium: 160.26 mg

INGREDIENTS

2 tablespoons olive oil
3 shallots, chopped
4 boneless, skinless chicken breasts, cubed
¼ cup flour
Salt and pepper to taste
1½ cups chicken broth
½ cup light cream
3 tomatoes, chopped
1 16-ounce package penne pasta
¾ cup Roasted Garlic Pesto (page 32)
¼ cup grated Parmesan cheese

Slow-Cooked Chicken Breasts

When you need cooked chicken for a sandwich or a salad, this is a simple, time-saving method for cooking it so it stays moist and tender.

1. Sprinkle chicken with poultry seasoning and pepper. Place in a 4- or 5-quart slow cooker; sprinkling each layer with garlic. Pour stock and lemon juice over all.

2. Cover and cook on low for 6–7 hours or until chicken registers 165°F. Place chicken in shallow casserole dish and pour liquid from slow cooker over. Cover and refrigerate until chilled.

3. Use as directed in recipes. You can also chop the chicken and freeze it in 1-cup amounts for storage up to 3 months.

SERVES 6

Calories: 145.54
Fat: 3.10 grams
Fat as % of calories: 19.2%
Carbohydrates: 0.88 grams
Fiber: 0.07 grams
Sodium: 63.99 mg
Vitamin A: 0% DV
Vitamin C: 2% DV
Calcium: 18.28 mg

INGREDIENTS

6 boneless, skinless chicken breasts
1 teaspoon poultry seasoning
⅛ teaspoon pepper
3 garlic cloves, minced
1 cup chicken stock
1 tablespoon lemon juice

Honey Mustard Turkey Tenderloins

Turkey tenderloins are a very tender cut with a low fat content. They cook quite quickly and are delicious and easy to serve and eat.

1. Cut turkey tenderloins in half crosswise and place in shallow baking dish. In small bowl, combine olive oil, mustard, honey, salt, pepper, and yogurt and pour over turkey. Cover and marinate in refrigerator for 18–24 hours.

2. When ready to eat, preheat oven to 325°F. Combine bread crumbs, cheese, and thyme on a plate. Remove turkey from marinade and shake off excess. Roll turkey in bread crumb mixture to coat. Place on cookie sheet.

3. Bake for 20 minutes, then carefully turn turkey over and bake for 20–30 minutes longer, until juices run clear. Serve immediately.

Mustard

Mustard seeds are part of the *brassica* family, which includes cauliflower and broccoli. They are high in phytonutrients, which can help prevent the development of some forms of cancer. The seeds also have good amounts of selenium and magnesium, which are anti-inflammatory and can also help reduce high blood pressure.

SERVES 6

Calories: 455.75
Fat: 14.08 grams
Fat as % of calories: 27.8%
Carbohydrates: 13.38 grams
Fiber: 1.23 grams
Sodium: 439.67 mg
Vitamin A: 0% DV
Vitamin C: 0% DV
Calcium: 102.84 mg

INGREDIENTS

3¾-pound turkey tenderloins
2 tablespoons olive oil
⅓ cup Dijon mustard
¼ cup honey
½ teaspoon salt
¼ teaspoon pepper
¼ cup yogurt
2 cups soft whole wheat bread crumbs
¼ cup grated Parmesan cheese
1 teaspoon dried thyme leaves

SERVES 6–8

Calories: 455.00
Fat: 9.70 grams
Fat as % of calories: 19.2%
Carbohydrates: 60.81 grams
Fiber: 4.32 grams
Sodium: 382.01 mg
Vitamin A: 5% DV
Vitamin C: 10% DV
Calcium: 223.94 mg

INGREDIENTS

2 tablespoons butter
1 tablespoon olive oil
1 onion, chopped
4 cloves garlic, minced
2 stalks celery, chopped
¼ cup flour
½ teaspoon salt
⅛ teaspoon pepper
½ teaspoon dried mint leaves
1 teaspoon dried thyme leaves
1 cup dried cranberries
2 cups chicken stock
1 cup 1% milk
3 cups cooked cubed turkey
1 12-ounce package spaghetti
   pasta
1 cup shredded low-fat Swiss
   cheese
3 tablespoons grated Parmesan
   cheese

Low-Fat Turkey and Cranberry Tetrazzini

You can easily make this dish ahead of time and refrigerate it until you're ready to eat. Just add 15 minutes or so to the baking time.

1. Preheat oven to 350°F. Bring a large pot of salted water to a boil. Spray a 2½-quart casserole with nonstick cooking spray; set aside. In large saucepan, melt butter and olive oil over medium heat. Add onion and garlic; cook and stir until tender, about 6 minutes. Add celery; cook and stir for 2 minutes longer.

2. Add flour, salt, pepper, mint, and thyme to saucepan; cook and stir until bubbly. Add cranberries, chicken stock, and milk; cook and stir until mixture bubbles and starts to thicken. Add turkey and stir.

3. Cook pasta according to package directions until al dente. Drain and add to saucepan with turkey. Add Swiss cheese and cook until melted. Pour into prepared casserole dish.

4. Sprinkle with Parmesan cheese. Bake for 45–50 minutes or until casserole bubbles and its top starts to brown.

Pasta

Pasta has gotten a bad reputation because of the low-carb diet trend, but it has nourished populations for generations. You can now find whole-grain pastas in the market, which have a lower glycemic index. The taste is stronger, so use it in highly flavored dishes. You can mix it with plain pasta until you're used to the taste.

Chapter 7

Dinner Party: Seafood Entrées

SERVES 8–10

Calories: 518.47
Fat: 14.43 grams
Fat as % of calories: 23.7%
Carbohydrates: 74.32 grams
Fiber: 4.87 grams
Sodium: 363.29 mg
Vitamin A: 130% DV
Vitamin C: 70% DV
Calcium: 65.26 mg

INGREDIENTS

2 tablespoons butter
1 onion, chopped
4 cloves garlic, minced
2 cups long-grain brown rice
1 cup orange juice
4 carrots, sliced
1 teaspoon salt
⅛ teaspoon white pepper
1 tablespoon curry powder
2 cups apricot nectar
1 cup chicken broth
1½ cups finely chopped dried apricots
2 pounds salmon fillets
⅔ cup apricot preserves

Crockpot Salmon with Curried Apricot Pilaf

The rich flavor of salmon is accented with the tart and sweet flavor of apricots in this elegant dish.

1. In large skillet, melt butter over medium heat. Add onion and garlic; cook and stir for 5 minutes until crisp-tender. Add brown rice; cook and stir for 2–3 minutes longer until rice is coated with the butter.

2. Pour orange juice into skillet; stir until mixture boils. Pour into 4-quart slow cooker. Add carrots, salt, pepper, curry powder, apricot nectar, chicken broth, and chopped apricots. Cover and cook on low for 6–7 hours or until rice is tender; stir.

3. Spread salmon fillets with the apricot preserves; place into slow cooker. Cover and cook on low for 1–1½ hours or until salmon flakes when tested with fork.

Salmon and the Slow Cooker

Most fish doesn't cook very well in the slow cooker because the extended cooking time can easily overcook the flesh. You can adapt recipes by choosing a long-cooking food, like rice or potatoes, then adding the fish at the very end of the cooking time. Make sure that you keep checking the fish; it's done when it flakes easily with a fork.

Indian Salmon and Vegetable Stir-Fry

*This colorful and quick dish is a nice change of pace
from traditional stir-fry recipes.*

1. In small bowl, combine chicken broth, chutney, cornstarch, and cayenne pepper; mix well and set aside.

2. In large skillet, heat olive oil over medium-high heat. Add onion, curry powder, and cauliflower; stir-fry for 4 minutes. Add water, cover skillet, and simmer for 3 minutes until cauliflower is crisp-tender.

3. Add red bell pepper; stir-fry for 2 minutes longer. Add salmon fillets; cover skillet and cook for 3 minutes. Add peas and chutney mixture; stir-fry for 3–5 minutes longer or until salmon is cooked and sauce bubbles. Serve immediately over hot cooked rice.

SERVES 6

Calories: 361.33
Fat: 12.29 grams
Fat as % of calories: 30.6%
Carbohydrates: 37.99 grams
Fiber: 6.89 grams
Sodium: 256.76 mg
Vitamin A: 30% DV
Vitamin C: 230% DV
Calcium: 67.79 mg

INGREDIENTS
1 cup chicken broth
½ cup mango chutney
1 tablespoon cornstarch
⅛ teaspoon cayenne pepper
2 tablespoons olive oil
1 onion, chopped
1 tablespoon curry powder
3 cups cauliflower florets
¼ cup water
1 red bell pepper, chopped
1 pound thin salmon fillets
2 cups frozen baby peas, thawed
3 cups cooked brown rice

Grilled Salmon with Peach Salsa

*Salmon steaks are rich and smoky tasting when cooked on the grill.
Pair them with a fruity and spicy salsa and you have a healthy dish
that's a winner.*

1. Place salmon steaks in a large baking dish. In small bowl, combine lemon juice, oil, salt, and pepper and pour over steaks. Cover and marinate for 2–4 hours in refrigerator.

2. In medium bowl, combine Salsa with peaches; cover and refrigerate.

3. When ready to eat, prepare and preheat grill. Remove salmon from marinade; discard marinade. Cook salmon 6 inches from medium coals for 10–15 minutes, turning once, until salmon flakes when tested with fork. Serve salmon with Salsa.

SERVES 6

Calories: 474.50
Fat: 17.76 grams
Fat as % of calories: 33.7%
Carbohydrates: 38.46 grams
Fiber: 5.81 grams
Sodium: 475.33 mg
Vitamin A: 70% DV
Vitamin C: 300% DV
Calcium: 80.62 mg

INGREDIENTS
6 5-ounce salmon steaks
3 tablespoons lemon juice
1 tablespoon olive oil
½ teaspoon salt
⅛ teaspoon white pepper
2 cups Tropical Salsa (page 25)
2 peaches, peeled and cubed

Calories: 289.94
Fat: 7.33 grams
Fat as % of calories: 22.7%
Carbohydrates: 15.52 mg
Fiber: 2.17 grams
Sodium: 291.43 mg
Vitamin A: 10% DV
Vitamin C: 60% DV
Calcium: 49.09 mg

INGREDIENTS

¼ cup lemon juice
2 tablespoons olive oil
2 tablespoons Dijon mustard
¼ teaspoon white pepper
1 teaspoon dried thyme leaves
6 6-ounce red snapper fillets
2 cups Fruit Salsa (page 26)

Lemon Grilled Red Snapper with Fruit Salsa

The mustard and lemon add a nice tang to the soft, mild fish, and the Fruit Salsa looks gorgeous and it tastes wonderful.

1. Prepare and preheat grill. In small bowl, combine lemon juice, olive oil, mustard, pepper, and thyme leaves; mix well. Place the fish fillets in a glass baking dish; spread the mustard mixture over both sides. Let stand for 30 minutes.

2. Place fish on grill. Grill, uncovered, 6 inches from medium coals for 8–10 minutes, turning once during grilling time, until fish flakes with a fork. Place on serving platter and top with the Fruit Salsa. Serve immediately.

SERVES 6

Calories: 308.33
Fat: 9.50 grams
Fat as % of calories: 27.7%
Carbohydrates: 31.44 grams
Fiber: 3.19 grams
Sodium: 475.01 mg
Vitamin A: 90% DV
Vitamin C: 15% DV
Calcium: 110.35 mg

INGREDIENTS

1 tablespoon olive oil
1 onion, chopped
3 cloves garlic, minced
1 cup chopped mushrooms
1 cup sliced carrots
1 cup skim milk
1½ cups long-grain brown rice
3 cups fish stock
2 cups chicken broth
1 pound thin red snapper fillets
1 tablespoon lemon juice
1 tablespoon butter
⅓ cup grated Parmesan cheese
3 tablespoons chopped flat-leaf
 parsley

Light Snapper Risotto

*Risotto is a special dish for a party.
It's not difficult to make; it just takes patience.*

1. In large saucepan, heat olive oil over medium heat. Add onion and garlic; cook and stir for 3 minutes. Add mushrooms and carrot; cook and stir for 3–4 minutes longer. Add milk and bring to a boil. Add rice and return to a boil.

2. Add the fish stock and chicken broth 1 cup at a time, stirring the mixture constantly. Wait to add the next cup until the liquid is almost absorbed. Continue cooking until the rice is tender, about 20–25 minutes total.

3. Place fish on top of rice mixture; cover and cook for 5–6 minutes until fish flakes when tested with a fork. Add lemon juice, butter, and cheese then stir; remove from heat and cover. Let stand for 5 minutes, then uncover, gently stir in parsley, and serve.

Baked Stuffed Tex-Mex Trout

*A whole fish stuffed with a spicy rice mixture
is the centerpiece for a celebration.*

1. In medium saucepan, combine rice, 1½ cups chicken broth, and chili powder and bring to a boil. Reduce heat, cover, and cook for 30–40 minutes or until rice is tender. Drain if necessary.

2. In large skillet, heat olive oil over medium heat. Add onion and all of the peppers; cook and stir for 5–6 minutes or until crisp-tender. Remove from heat and stir in cooked rice and cilantro.

3. Preheat oven to 350°F. Spray a roasting pan with nonstick cooking spray. Sprinkle cavity of fish with salt and peppers. Stuff with rice filling and tie with kitchen string. Place in prepared pan.

4. Pour remaining ½ cup chicken broth, butter, and lime juice over fish. Bake fish, basting occasionally with pan juices, for 50–60 minutes or until fish flakes easily when tested with fork. Serve immediately.

Cooking Fish

Generally, the rule is to cook fish for 10 minutes per inch of thickness. Fish fillets are usually about ½-inch thick, while fish steaks are 1-inch thick. When broiling thin fillets, there's no need to turn them. By not turning, the delicate fillets will hold their shape. This rule applies whether you're grilling, baking, or broiling fish.

SERVES 6–8

Calories: 378.84
Fat: 13.61 grams
Fat as % of calories: 32.9%
Carbohydrates: 21.29 grams
Fiber: 2.12 grams
Sodium: 477.62 mg
Vitamin A: 30% DV
Vitamin C: 170% DV
Calcium: 150.63 mg

INGREDIENTS
¾ cup long-grain brown rice
2 cups chicken broth, divided
2 teaspoons chili powder
1 tablespoon olive oil
1 onion, chopped
1 jalapeño pepper, minced
2 red bell peppers, chopped
1 poblano pepper, chopped
⅓ cup chopped cilantro
1 3-pound whole trout, cleaned
1 teaspoon salt
¼ teaspoon cayenne pepper
¼ teaspoon white pepper
1 tablespoon butter, melted
2 tablespoons lime juice

INGREDIENTS

1 tablespoon olive oil
1 tablespoon butter
1 onion, chopped
1 fennel bulb, thinly sliced
3 carrots, sliced
4 cloves garlic, minced
1 8-ounce package sliced
*   mushrooms*
6 5-ounce fish fillets
½ teaspoon salt
⅛ teaspoon white pepper
1 teaspoon dried tarragon leaves
1 lemon, thinly sliced
1 tablespoon olive oil
2 tablespoons dry white wine

Fish en Papillote

*Fennel, with its licorice flavor, is the perfect complement
to tender and mild fish.*

1. Preheat oven to 400°F. In large skillet, heat olive oil and butter over medium heat. Add onion, fennel, carrots, and garlic; cook and stir for 5 minutes. Add mushrooms; cook and stir for 5–6 minutes longer until vegetables are tender.

2. Cut six 12" x 16" sheets of parchment paper, fold in half into 12" x 8" rectangles, and cut half a heart shape. Unfold into heart shapes. Place a fish fillet near the fold on one side of each heart. Sprinkle with salt, pepper, and tarragon.

3. Lay lemon slices on top of each fillet. Spoon vegetable mixture on top of fish and drizzle each with olive oil and wine. Fold one half of each heart over the food and seal by crimping the edges together. Place bundles on cookie sheets.

4. Bake for 15–18 minutes or until paper bundles expand and turn brown; fish should flake easily when tested with a fork. Serve the bundles to your guests, warning them to be careful with steam when they cut them open.

Fish Fillets with Veggie Salsa

*A warm and spicy salsa is served over glazed
fish fillets in this simple recipe.*

SERVES 6

Calories: 246.01
Fat: 4.55 grams
Fat as % of calories: 16.6%
Carbohydrates: 20.17 grams
Fiber: 2.26 grams
Sodium: 461.72 mg
Vitamin A: 130% DV
Vitamin C: 20% DV
Calcium: 54.96 mg

INGREDIENTS

1 tablespoon olive oil
1 red onion, chopped
2 cloves garlic, minced
2 cups shredded carrots
*1 cup chopped portobello
    mushrooms*
2 jalapeño peppers, minced
¼ cup lime juice
½ teaspoon salt
⅛ teaspoon cayenne pepper
½ cup chopped cilantro
6 6-ounce fish fillets
¼ teaspoon salt
⅛ teaspoon pepper
¼ cup honey
1 tablespoon chili powder

1. In large saucepan, heat olive oil over medium heat. Add onion, garlic, carrots, and mushrooms; cook and stir for 5 minutes. Add jalapeño peppers; cook and stir for 2 minutes longer. Remove from heat and place in medium bowl. Add lime juice, ½ teaspoon salt, cayenne pepper, and cilantro to vegetables in bowl. Stir and set aside.

2. Set oven to broil. Spray a broiler pan with nonstick cooking spray and place fish fillets on pan. Broil for 3 minutes, then remove from oven and carefully turn.

3. In small bowl, combine ¼ teaspoon salt, pepper, honey, and chili powder and mix well. Spoon over fish. Return to broiler and broil for 3–5 minutes longer or until fish flakes when tested with fork. Serve fish with warm salsa.

Salsa

When making your own salsas, pick fruits and vegetables that are very high in nutrients. Zucchini, for instance, has a nice mild flavor and texture, but it doesn't have a lot of vitamins. Pick carrots, tomatoes, peppers, apricots, and strawberries. Choosing brightly colored fruit and vegetables is the key.

Calories: 364.73
Fat: 11.56 grams
Fat as % of calories: 28.5%
Carbohydrates: 30.09 grams
Fiber: 5.37 grams
Sodium: 351.68 mg
Vitamin A: 350% DV
Vitamin C: 35% DV
Calcium: 81.10 mg

INGREDIENTS
4 sweet potatoes, peeled
1 onion, chopped
4 cloves garlic, minced
2 tablespoons olive oil
½ teaspoon salt
¼ teaspoon pepper
½ cup ground pecans
⅓ cup wheat germ
¼ cup whole wheat flour
⅛ teaspoon cayenne pepper
8 6-ounce cod fillets
⅓ cup honey mustard

SERVES 6

Calories: 276.71
Fat: 8.45 grams
Fat as % of calories: 27.5%
Carbohydrates: 1.50 grams
Fiber: 0.02 grams
Sodium: 407.77 mg
Vitamin A: 5% DV
Vitamin C: 5% DV
Calcium: 170.03 mg

INGREDIENTS
1 tablespoon butter
2 cloves garlic, minced
1 tablespoon chopped fresh
    rosemary
¼ cup dry white wine
2 tablespoons lemon juice
6 6-ounce fish fillets
1 cup sliced shaved ham
1 cup shredded low-fat
    mozzarella cheese

Pecan Fish with Sweet Potatoes

This one-dish dinner is pretty and easy, and it's full of vitamin A and omega-3 fatty acids to protect your heart.

1. Preheat oven to 400°F. Slice the sweet potatoes to ¼-inch thickness. Combine with onion and garlic in large roasting pan. Drizzle with olive oil and sprinkle with salt and ¼ teaspoon pepper. Roast for 40–45 minutes, turning once with a spatula during roasting time.

2. Meanwhile, combine pecans, wheat germ, flour, and cayenne pepper on plate. Coat fish fillets with honey mustard on one side only and press that side into the pecan mixture.

3. When sweet potatoes are tender, place fish, pecan side up, on top of them. Roast for another 10–15 minutes or until fish flakes when tested with a fork. Serve immediately.

Easy Fish Cordon Bleu

This simple recipe is a good one to keep in your back pocket when unexpected company drops by.

1. Preheat oven to broil. In small saucepan, melt butter over medium heat. Add garlic and rosemary; cook and stir until fragrant. Add wine and lemon juice; cook and stir until liquid is reduced to 3 tablespoons; remove from heat.

2. Spray broiler pan with nonstick cooking spray; arrange fish on pan. Spoon butter mixture over fish. Broil for 5–6 minutes or until fish is just cooked through.

3. Arrange ham on fish, then top with the cheese. Broil for 2–3 minutes longer or until cheese melts and begins to brown. Serve immediately.

Healthy Fish Enchiladas

Fish adds a mild flavor and great texture to these simple enchiladas.
Use your favorite vegetables and add more spice if you'd like.

1. Preheat oven to 400°F. In large skillet heat olive oil over medium heat and sauté onion, garlic, and jalapeño pepper until crisp-tender, about 5 minutes. Add red and green bell pepper; cook and stir for 4 minutes longer.

2. Place fish on top of vegetables; season with salt and pepper. Cover and cook for 6–8 minutes or until fish flakes when tested with fork. Add Salsa and ½ cup of the cheese and stir gently to combine.

3. Divide fish mixture among the tortillas and roll up. Place seam-side down in 13" x 9" glass baking pan, cover with enchilada sauce and sprinkle with 1 cup cheese. Bake for 15–25 minutes or until thoroughly heated.

Canned Sauces

You can certainly make your own enchilada or tomato sauce, but there are some good-quality canned products available. Get in the habit of reading labels, and choose the products with the lowest sodium content and fewest artificial ingredients. Keep a good supply of these products on hand for quick and easy meals.

SERVES 6–8

Calories: 328.56
Fat: 11.17 grams
Fat as % of calories: 30.6%
Carbohydrates: 18.82 grams
Fiber: 3.10 grams
Sodium: 503.37 mg
Vitamin A: 30% DV
Vitamin C: 100% DV
Calcium: 207.68 mg

INGREDIENTS

2 tablespoons olive oil
1 onion, chopped
3 cloves garlic, minced
1 jalapeño pepper, minced
1 red bell pepper, chopped
1 green bell pepper, chopped
6 6-ounce fish fillets
½ teaspoon salt
⅛ teaspoon pepper
1 cup Fresh Tomato Salsa (page 25)
1½ cups shredded low-fat pepper jack cheese
12 6-inch corn tortillas
1 8-ounce can enchilada sauce

Calories: 193.78
Fat: 5.94 grams
Fat as % of calories: 27.6%
Carbohydrates: 8.05 grams
Fiber: 0.97 grams
Sodium: 548.91 mg
Vitamin A: 25% DV
Vitamin C: 90% DV
Calcium: 271.17 mg

INGREDIENTS

1 tablespoon butter
1 leek, chopped
3 cloves garlic, minced
1 red bell pepper, chopped
1 cup sliced mushrooms
2 tablespoons flour
½ teaspoon salt
⅛ teaspoon pepper
1 teaspoon dried basil leaves
½ cup skim milk
¾ cup low-fat sour cream
2 eggs
3 egg whites
1 6-ounce can tuna, drained
1 cup low-fat Swiss cheese
3 tablespoons grated Romano
  cheese

Crustless Veggie Tuna Quiche

A quiche is a great recipe for entertaining at a brunch.
This healthy version is filled with vegetables.

1. Preheat oven to 375°F. Spray a 9-inch pie pan with nonstick baking spray containing flour and set aside. In large skillet, melt butter over medium heat. Add leek and garlic; cook and stir for 3 minutes. Add red bell pepper and mushrooms; cook and stir for 3–4 minutes longer.

2. Stir in flour, salt, pepper, and basil and cook and stir until bubbly. Add milk and sour cream; cook and stir until mixture starts to thicken. Remove from heat and stir in eggs and egg whites.

3. Stir in tuna and Swiss cheese. Pour into prepared pie pan and sprinkle with Romano cheese. Bake for 40–50 minutes or until quiche is puffed and golden brown. Serve immediately.

Mushrooms

Surprisingly, mushrooms have a good amount of vitamin D, the sunshine vitamin, even though they are grown in the dark. The latest research, shows that exposure of mushrooms to just 5 minutes of ultraviolet (UV) light greatly increases their vitamin D content. They also have selenium, a mineral that acts as an antioxidant, which helps reduce cancer risk.

Updated Seafood Lasagna

Make this elegant dish ahead of time and refrigerate it. Then when you're ready to entertain, just pop it in the oven.

1. Preheat oven to 350°F. Bring a large pot of water to a boil over high heat. Spray a 13" x 9" glass baking dish with nonstick cooking spray and set aside.

2. In large skillet, heat olive oil and butter over medium heat. Add onion and garlic; cook and stir until tender, about 6–7 minutes. Add flour; cook and stir until bubbly.

3. Add milk; cook and stir with wire whisk until mixture thickens and bubbles. Stir in cream cheese, Havarti, and mozzarella cheese and cook until melted and smooth. Remove from heat and add nutmeg, salt, and pepper.

4. In large bowl, combine spinach, shrimp, crabmeat, peas, and lemon juice; mix gently. Cook noodles in boiling water until almost al dente; drain well.

5. Spoon a thin layer of the cheese sauce in bottom of prepared baking dish. Top with three noodles, some of the seafood mixture, and more cheese sauce. Repeat layers, ending with cheese sauce. Sprinkle with Parmesan cheese.

6. Bake for 50–60 minutes or until casserole is bubbling and cheese on top begins to brown. If you refrigerated the casserole, bake an additional 15–20 minutes until bubbly. Let stand for 10 minutes, then cut into squares to serve.

SERVES 12

Calories: 401.30
Fat: 13.70
Fat as % of calories: 30.7%
Carbohydrates: 36.75 grams
Fiber: 2.50 grams
Sodium: 388.44 mg
Vitamin A: 70% DV
Vitamin C: 20% DV
Calcium: 324.77 mg

INGREDIENTS

2 tablespoons olive oil
1 tablespoon butter
1 onion, chopped
3 cloves garlic, minced
⅓ cup flour
2 cups 1% milk
1 8-ounce package low-fat cream cheese, cubed
1 cup shredded Havarti cheese
1 cup shredded part-skim mozzarella cheese
¼ teaspoon nutmeg
½ teaspoon salt
¼ teaspoon white pepper
1 10-ounce package frozen cut-leaf spinach, thawed
1 pound medium cooked shrimp, thawed
1 8-ounce package imitation crabmeat, thawed
2 cups frozen baby peas, thawed
2 tablespoons lemon juice
9 whole wheat lasagna noodles
⅓ cup grated Parmesan cheese

INGREDIENTS

⅓ cup apricot preserves
3 cloves garlic, minced
⅓ cup chili sauce
¼ cup orange juice
1 tablespoon grated fresh
    gingerroot
½ teaspoon salt
⅛ teaspoon pepper
2 red bell peppers
2 yellow summer squash
2 red sweet onions
36 large raw shrimp, deveined

INGREDIENTS

1 cup low-fat strawberry yogurt
¼ cup low-fat mayonnaise
⅓ cup orange juice
½ teaspoon ground ginger
½ teaspoon salt
⅛ teaspoon cayenne pepper
2 mangoes, peeled and cubed
2 cups red grapes
2 cups cubed cantaloupe
¼ cup chopped green onion
2 cups cooked medium shrimp
1 12-ounce package small shell
    pasta
¼ cup toasted coconut

Vegetable Shrimp Kebabs

The sauce for these skewers is delicious and full of flavor!

1. Prepare and preheat grill. In small bowl, combine preserves, garlic, chili sauce, orange juice, gingerroot, salt, and pepper and mix well.

2. Seed bell peppers and cut into 1-inch strips. Cut the summer squash into ½-inch slices. Cut each red onion into 8 wedges.

3. Thread vegetables and shrimp onto six 12-inch metal skewers. Place skewers in a large glass baking dish and pour preserves mixture over. Let stand for 30 minutes.

4. Prepare and preheat grill. Remove skewers from marinade, reserving marinade. Grill skewers 6 inches from medium coals for 7–9 minutes, turning once and brushing with reserved marinade, until shrimp curl and turn pink and vegetables are crisp-tender. Serve immediately.

Caribbean Shrimp Salad

For summer entertaining, there's nothing better than this gorgeous salad, full of fresh flavors and nutrition.

1. Bring a large pot of water to a boil. Meanwhile, in large bowl combine yogurt, mayonnaise, orange juice, ginger, salt, and pepper and mix well. Stir in mangoes, grapes, cantaloupe, green onion, and shrimp; cover and refrigerate.

2. Cook pasta according to package directions until al dente. Drain well and stir into salad. Cover and chill for 4–5 hours to blend flavors. Sprinkle with toasted coconut just before serving.

Baked Stuffed Shrimp

*This gorgeous dish is low-carb and still gives you a
good amount of vitamin A.*

1. Preheat oven to 375°F. Spray a 13" x 9" baking dish with cooking spray
   and set aside.

2. In medium skillet, combine olive oil and 2 tablespoons butter; melt over
   medium heat. Add shallots, garlic, and carrots; cook and stir until tender, about 6 minutes. Add wine, salt, and cayenne pepper and cook for
   2 minutes longer. Remove from heat.

3. Add crab, bread crumbs, marjoram, and Swiss cheese and mix gently; set
   aside.

4. Pat the shrimp dry and slit down the back without cutting all the way
   through. Stuff the shrimp with the crab mixture and place, stuffing side
   up, in prepared dish. Drizzle with melted butter.

5. Bake for 20–23 minutes or until shrimp are cooked and stuffing is hot
   and begins to brown. Serve immediately.

SERVES 6

Calories: 227.13
Fat: 12.00 grams
Fat as % of calories: 47.5%
Carbohydrates: 9.34 grams
Fiber: 1.28 grams
Sodium: 472.27 mg
Vitamin A: 80% DV
Vitamin C: 6% DV
Calcium: 146.87 mg

INGREDIENTS

1 tablespoon olive oil
2 tablespoons butter
2 shallots, minced
4 cloves garlic, minced
1 cup diced carrot
¼ cup dry white wine
½ teaspoon salt
⅛ teaspoon cayenne pepper
1 cup diced crabmeat
1 cup soft whole wheat bread
   crumbs
1 teaspoon dried marjoram
   leaves
½ cup shredded low-fat Swiss
   cheese
24 jumbo shrimp, peeled and
   deveined
2 tablespoons butter, melted

SERVES 6

Calories: 433.55
Fat: 10.05 grams
Fat as % of calories: 20.9%
Carbohydrates: 59.62 grams
Fiber: 8.14 grams
Sodium: 580.78 mg
Vitamin A: 90% DV
Vitamin C: 110% DV
Calcium: 108.61 mg

INGREDIENTS

1 tablespoon olive oil
4 cloves garlic, minced
1½ cups long-grain brown rice
2 cups low-sodium chicken
    broth
1 cup tomato juice
1 tablespoon butter
1 cup shredded carrots
1 onion, chopped
1 red bell pepper, chopped
1 pound medium raw shrimp,
    shelled
¼ cup chopped fresh cilantro
1 15-ounce can black beans,
    drained
½ cup low-fat sour cream

Cilantro Shrimp with Beans and Rice

Beans and rice are an excellent high-fiber combination. This could be a vegetarian main dish if you use vegetable broth and omit the shrimp.

1. In large saucepan, heat olive oil over medium heat. Add garlic; cook and stir for 2 minutes. Add brown rice; cook and stir for 2 minutes longer. Add chicken broth and tomato juice; bring to a simmer. Reduce heat to low, cover pan, and simmer for 35–45 minutes or until rice is tender.

2. Meanwhile, in large skillet melt butter over medium heat. Add carrots, onion, and red bell pepper; cook and stir until tender, about 5–6 minutes. Add shrimp; cook and stir until shrimp curl and turn pink, about 3–4 minutes. Stir in cilantro and remove from heat.

3. When rice is done, add shrimp mixture, black beans, and sour cream. Cook and stir over medium heat for 4–5 minutes or until thoroughly heated. Serve immediately.

Black Beans

Black beans, also known as turtle beans because they look like turtle shells, are rich in antioxidants and fiber. They have a rich, nutty flavor and a smooth, velvety texture. The latest studies show that adding black beans to your diet may actually help prevent cancer cells from forming.

Crab and Fruit au Gratin

Rich crabmeat and tart and sweet fruits combine to make an excellent casserole perfect for company.

1. Preheat oven to 375°F. Spray a 2-quart casserole with nonstick cooking spray; set aside. Drain apricot halves, reserving juice; chop apricots and set aside. Drain mandarin oranges, discard juice; set aside.

2. In large skillet, heat olive oil and 1 tablespoon butter over medium heat. Add onion; cook and stir until tender, about 6 minutes. Add flour, salt, pepper, and tarragon; cook and stir until bubbly.

3. Add chicken broth, ¾ cup reserved apricot juice, and sour cream. Cook and stir until bubbly and thickened. Stir in reserved fruits, dried cherries, crabmeat, and Swiss cheese; remove from heat.

4. Spoon crab mixture into prepared casserole dish. In small bowl, combine bread crumbs, Parmesan cheese, and 1 tablespoon melted butter; mix well. Sprinkle over casserole. Bake for 30–40 minutes or until casserole is bubbling and top is brown.

Choosing Crab

Dungeness crab is called for in these recipes because it has a lot less sodium than Alaskan king crab. If the crab in the market isn't labeled, ask the fishmonger or butcher where it's from. You can substitute imitation crab or surimi in some of these recipes, especially the highly flavored ones; it's made of pollock and flavorings.

SERVES 6

Calories: 388.61
Fat: 12.29 grams
Fat as % of calories: 28.5%
Carbohydrates: 42.71 grams
Fiber: 3.24 grams
Sodium: 714.30 mg
Vitamin A: 80% DV
Vitamin C: 50% DV
Calcium: 320.81 mg

INGREDIENTS

1 15-ounce can apricot halves
1 15-ounce can mandarin oranges
1 tablespoon olive oil
1 tablespoon butter
1 onion, chopped
3 tablespoons flour
½ teaspoon salt
⅛ teaspoon pepper
1 teaspoon dried tarragon leaves
1 cup chicken broth
½ cup nonfat sour cream
½ cup dried cherries
1 pound Dungeness crabmeat
1 cup shredded low-fat Swiss cheese
1 cup soft whole wheat bread crumbs
¼ cup grated Parmesan cheese

INGREDIENTS

2 tablespoons butter
1 onion, chopped
3 cloves garlic, minced
¾ cup chopped hazelnuts
½ cup silken tofu
3 tablespoons Dijon mustard
1 cup soft whole wheat bread
    crumbs
1 teaspoon Old Bay seasoning
1½ pounds Dungeness crabmeat
½ cup chopped dried blueberries
½ cup wheat germ

INGREDIENTS

2 tablespoons olive oil
1 onion, chopped
1½ pounds sea scallops
¼ teaspoon salt
⅛ teaspoon pepper
1 teaspoon dried basil
3 cups chopped tomatoes
½ cup Roasted Garlic Pesto
    (page 32)
½ cup nonfat light cream

High-Fiber Hazelnut Crab Cakes

Crab cakes are really an indulgent treat. Using whole wheat crumbs instead of buttery crackers and silken tofu instead of mayonnaise reduces the fat and ups the fiber.

1. In medium saucepan, melt butter over medium heat. Add onion and garlic; cook and stir until tender, about 6 minutes. Add hazelnuts; cook and stir until nuts are fragrant. Remove from heat and place in large bowl.

2. Add tofu, mustard, bread crumbs, and Old Bay seasoning; stir well. Gently fold in crab, then fold in blueberries. Cover and chill mixture for 6–8 hours.

3. When ready to eat, preheat broiler. Shape crab into 6 cakes and roll in wheat germ. Place on broiler pan. Broil crab cakes for 8–9 minutes on each side, until golden brown and crisp. Serve immediately.

Pesto Scallops

This super-quick dish is delicious and gorgeous. You could serve it over pasta or rice to soak up the wonderful sauce.

1. In large skillet, heat olive oil over medium heat. Add onion; cook and stir until tender, about 6 minutes. Remove onion from skillet; do not wipe out skillet. Return skillet to medium-high heat.

2. Sprinkle scallops with salt, pepper, and basil and add to skillet. Cook without stirring until scallops move easily and are deep golden brown on one side.

3. Turn scallops and immediately add onion, tomatoes, Pesto, and cream to skillet. Cook for 3–4 minutes or until scallops are just cooked through and cream is hot. Stir gently and serve immediately.

Chapter 8

Dinner Party: Vegetarian Entrées

INGREDIENTS

1¼ cups wild rice
1 onion, chopped
3 cloves garlic, minced
2 cups vegetable broth
½ cup orange juice
2 cups frozen edamame, thawed
⅓ cup grated Parmesan cheese
1 tablespoon butter

Wild Risi Bisi

Risi bisi is an Italian side dish made with plain rice and peas. Using wild rice and soybeans instead ups the nutritional value; adding cheese makes this a delicious light vegetarian main dish.

1. In 3-quart slow cooker, combine wild rice, onion, garlic, vegetable broth, and orange juice. Cover and cook on low for 7–8 hours or until wild rice is tender.

2. Stir in the edamame, cover, and cook on high for 30 minutes. Uncover and add cheese and butter. Turn off heat, cover, and let stand for 10 minutes. Fluff with a fork and serve.

INGREDIENTS

4 cups Mixed Rice Pilaf (page 150)
⅓ cup grated Parmesan cheese
1 egg
2 egg whites
1 tablespoon Dijon mustard
1 cup cubed Cheddar cheese
½ cup dried bread crumbs
¼ cup ground hazelnuts
1 cup Fruit Salsa (page 26)

Mixed Rice Pilaf Balls

Melted cheese in the center of crisp rice balls adds the perfect touch, and the salsa adds some sweetness and spice.

1. Place Pilaf in microwave-safe bowl. Microwave on 50 percent power for 2–3 minutes or until hot. Remove from microwave and immediately add Parmesan cheese; beat well. Add egg, egg whites, and Dijon mustard and mix until combined. Cool completely, about 30 minutes.

2. Preheat oven to 425°F. Form rice mixture into 1-inch balls. Insert a cube of Cheddar cheese into each ball. On shallow plate, combine bread crumbs and hazelnuts. Roll rice balls in this mixture and place on cookie sheet.

3. Bake for 15–20 minutes or until balls are golden brown and crisp on the outside. Serve with Salsa.

Parmesan Wild Rice and Chickpeas

Don't rinse the chickpeas; just drain them. You want some of the liquid they are packed in to help thicken the recipe.

1. In medium saucepan, combine wild rice and 2 cups vegetable stock. Bring to a simmer, then cover and cook for 30–40 minutes or until rice is tender. Drain if necessary and set aside.

2. In large skillet, heat olive oil over medium heat. Add onion and carrots; sprinkle with salt, pepper, and marjoram. Cook and stir until crisp-tender, about 7–8 minutes.

3. Add chickpeas, wild rice, and ½ cup vegetable stock; bring to a simmer. Then add cream cheese, sour cream, and Parmesan cheese; cook and stir until mixture is blended.

SERVES 6

Calories: 316.59
Fat: 8.98 grams
Fat as % of calories: 25.5%
Carbohydrates: 45.56 grams
Fiber: 5.58 grams
Sodium: 607.45 mg
Vitamin A: 80% DV
Vitamin C: 1% DV
Calcium: 147.44 mg

INGREDIENTS

1 cup wild rice
2½ cups vegetable stock
1 tablespoon olive oil
1 onion, chopped
3 carrots, sliced
½ teaspoon salt
⅛ teaspoon pepper
½ teaspoon marjoram leaves
1 15-ounce can chickpeas, drained
1 3-ounce package low-fat cream cheese, softened
½ cup nonfat sour cream
⅓ cup grated Parmesan cheese

Lighter Indian Stir-Fry

A delicious stir-fry with spices and fresh vegetables is a great entertaining recipe.

1. In small bowl, combine 1 cup vegetable stock, cornstarch, cayenne pepper, and chutney; mix well and set aside.

2. In large skillet or wok, heat oil over medium-high heat. Add onion, garlic, and gingerroot; stir-fry for 3 minutes. Add cauliflower and carrots; stir-fry for 3 minutes. Add ½ cup vegetable stock and curry powder and cook for 5–6 minutes until vegetables are tender.

3. Stir in green bell pepper and peas; stir-fry for 2 minutes. Stir cornstarch mixture and add to skillet. Stir-fry for 4–5 minutes until sauce thickens and bubbles. Serve over brown rice.

SERVES 6

Calories: 234.49
Fat: 4.41 grams
Fat as % of calories: 16.9%
Carbohydrates: 42.83 grams
Fiber: 5.55 grams
Sodium: 211.78 mg
Vitamin A: 90% DV
Vitamin C: 70% DV
Calcium: 47.94 mg

INGREDIENTS

1½ cups vegetable stock, divided
1 tablespoon cornstarch
⅛ teaspoon cayenne pepper
¼ cup mango chutney
1 tablespoon canola oil
1 onion, chopped
3 cloves garlic, minced
1 tablespoon minced gingerroot
2 cups cauliflower florets
3 carrots, sliced
1 tablespoon curry powder
1 green bell pepper, chopped
1 cup frozen baby peas, thawed
3 cups hot cooked brown rice

INGREDIENTS

2 tablespoons olive oil
1 onion, chopped
2 cups sliced button
*   mushrooms*
1 cup chopped portabello
*   mushrooms*
2 cloves garlic, minced
2 carrots, sliced
½ teaspoon salt
⅛ teaspoon white pepper
1 teaspoon dried tarragon leaves
1½ cups long-grain brown rice
4 cups vegetable broth
½ cup dry white wine, if desired
⅓ cup grated Parmesan cheese

Onion and Mushroom Risotto

Brown rice provides a healthy alternative to traditional arborio rice. The vegetables are sautéed beforehand to give added texture and taste to the finished meal.

1. In large saucepan, heat olive oil over medium heat. Add onion, mushrooms, garlic, and carrot; cook and stir until crisp-tender, about 5–7 minutes. Add salt, pepper, tarragon, and rice; cook and stir for 4 minutes longer.

2. Meanwhile, place stock in a medium saucepan and warm over low heat. Add wine to rice mixture; cook and stir until absorbed. Then start adding the broth, about ½ cup at a time, stirring the mixture constantly.

3. Keep adding broth, stirring constantly, until rice is tender, about 30–35 minutes. Add cheese, cover pan, and remove from heat. Let stand for 5 minutes, then stir and serve.

Risotto

Risotto is traditionally made with arborio rice, a short-grain rice with a high starch content. But you can make it with ordinary rice, and using brown rice adds more fiber and B vitamins. Almost constant stirring is the secret to good risotto. The stirring action helps the rice release more starch, which makes the risotto creamy.

Spanish Lima Beans and Rice

Spanish rice is taken to the next level with the additions of adobo sauce, a spicy red sauce, and lima beans, which help complete the protein in the rice.

1. In large saucepan, heat olive oil over medium heat. Add onion and garlic; cook and stir for 5 minutes. Sprinkle with salt and pepper, then add rice. Cook and stir for 3–4 minutes until rice is coated.

2. Add vegetable broth and bring to a simmer. Reduce heat, cover, and simmer for 25–30 minutes or until rice is almost tender. Add green bell pepper, tomatoes, adobo sauce, chili powder, and lima beans.

3. Bring back to a simmer; simmer for 5–6 minutes or until rice is tender and lima beans are hot. Serve immediately.

Lima Beans

Lima beans are delicious; they are soft and nutty with a creamy texture. They are sometimes called butter beans. These little nuggets have a significant amount of fiber and are also high in folate, a B vitamin that can help lower the levels of homocysteine. Elevated homocysteine levels can indicate a risk for heart disease.

SERVES 6

Calories: 364.45
Fat: 8.47 grams
Fat as % of calories: 20.9%
Carbohydrates: 61.72 grams
Fiber: 7.74 grams
Sodium: 741.44 mg
Vitamin A: 15% DV
Vitamin C: 25% DV
Calcium: 65.49 mg

INGREDIENTS

2 tablespoons olive oil
2 onions, chopped
3 cloves garlic, minced
½ teaspoon salt
⅛ teaspoon cayenne pepper
1½ cups long-grain brown rice
3 cups vegetable broth
1 green bell pepper, chopped
1 14.5-ounce can diced tomatoes, undrained
1 tablespoon adobo sauce
2 teaspoons chili powder
1 10-ounce package frozen lima beans, thawed

Calories: 258.87
Fat: 8.49 grams
Fat as % of calories: 29.5%
Carbohydrates: 39.01 grams
Fiber: 5.91 grams
Sodium: 408.52 mg
Vitamin A: 120% DV
Vitamin C: 550% DV
Calcium: 124.01 mg

INGREDIENTS

½ cup brown rice
1 cup vegetable stock
2 tablespoons olive oil
1 onion, chopped
4 cloves garlic, minced
½ cup golden raisins
½ teaspoon salt
½ teaspoon dried oregano
   leaves
¼ cup minced parsley
¼ cup minced fresh mint leaves
3 tablespoons lemon juice
2 tomatoes, chopped
⅓ cup crumbled feta cheese
6 red bell peppers
1 cup dry white wine
¼ cup grated Parmesan cheese

Greek Stuffed Peppers

These beautiful stuffed peppers are delicious served hot or cold.
The combination of oregano, parsley, mint, and feta cheese
evokes the cuisine of Greece.

1. In small saucepan, combine rice and stock; bring to a simmer over medium-high heat. Cover, reduce heat to low, and simmer for 35–40 minutes until rice is tender. Set aside.

2. In large skillet, heat olive oil over medium heat. Add onion and garlic; cook and stir for 5 minutes. Add raisins, salt, oregano, parsley, mint, lemon juice, and tomatoes and bring to a simmer. Cook for 5–6 minutes to blend flavors.

3. Preheat oven to 375°F. Stir rice and feta cheese into tomato mixture and remove from heat. Cut the bell peppers in half lengthwise; remove seeds and membranes.

4. Arrange the peppers in a large roasting pan. Fill with the rice mixture. Pour the wine around the peppers. Cover with foil and bake for 30–35 minutes or until peppers are tender. Uncover, sprinkle with Parmesan cheese, and bake for 10 minutes longer until cheese melts. Serve immediately.

Vegetable Lasagna Rolls

*These pretty little rolls are full of creamy cheese and spinach,
topped with a rich artichoke–tomato sauce.*

1. Preheat oven to 350°F. Bring a large pot of water to a boil. In large skillet, heat olive oil over medium heat. Add onion and garlic; cook and stir for 5 minutes. Add carrot and stir.

2. Finely chop the artichoke hearts and add to onion mixture along with rosemary and pepper; cook and stir for 3 minutes. Add pasta sauce and bring to a simmer.

3. Cook lasagna noodles according to package directions until al dente. Meanwhile, in medium bowl combine ricotta and cream cheese and mix well. Add mozzarella cheese. Drain spinach by squeezing in a kitchen towel and stir into cheese mixture.

4. Drain noodles and rinse with cold water; drain again. Spread on work surface. Spread about ⅓ cup of the ricotta mixture on each noodle and roll up.

5. Place half of artichoke sauce in 13" x 9" baking pan. Top with filled noodles and rest of the artichoke sauce. Sprinkle with Parmesan cheese. Bake for 35–45 minutes until casserole bubbles and cheese browns.

Rosemary: Fresh Versus Dried

Dried rosemary may be more readily available, but fresh rosemary has a more intense taste and tender leaf. Dried rosemary leaves can become very hard and brittle and can be difficult to eat. More and more grocery stores are stocking fresh rosemary; ask your grocer if you can't find it.

SERVES 9

Calories: 381.10
Fat: 10.09 grams
Fat as % of calories: 23.8%
Carbohydrates: 56.80 grams
Fiber: 3.70 grams
Sodium: 539.34 mg
Vitamin A: 130% DV
Vitamin C: 25% DV
Calcium: 315.27 mg

INGREDIENTS

1 tablespoon olive oil
1 onion, chopped
4 cloves garlic, minced
1 cup grated carrots
1 14-ounce can artichoke hearts, drained
2 teaspoons minced fresh rosemary
⅛ teaspoon pepper
1 26-ounce jar chunky pasta sauce
9 whole wheat lasagna noodles
1 cup part-skim ricotta cheese
1 3-ounce package nonfat cream cheese, softened
1 cup shredded part-skim mozzarella cheese
1 10-ounce package frozen chopped spinach, thawed
¼ cup grated Parmesan cheese

INGREDIENTS

2 tablespoons butter
1 onion, chopped
4 cloves garlic, minced
2 jalapeño peppers, minced
3 carrots, sliced
1 red bell pepper, chopped
3 tablespoons flour
½ teaspoon salt
⅛ teaspoon cayenne pepper
1 13-ounce can nonfat evaporated milk
1½ cups vegetable broth
1 3-ounce package nonfat cream cheese
1 cup salsa
2 tablespoons Dijon mustard
1 16-ounce package whole wheat rotini pasta
1½ cups shredded low-fat Cheddar cheese
1½ cups shredded low-fat pepper jack cheese
2 tablespoons grated Cotija cheese

Tex-Mex Mac and Cheese

This sophisticated macaroni and cheese uses rotini pasta and lots of spice to wake up your taste buds. Full-fat cheeses are used because melting is important.

1. Bring a large pot of water to a boil. In large saucepan, melt butter over medium heat. Add onion, garlic, jalapeño peppers, and carrot; cook and stir for 6–7 minutes until crisp-tender. Add bell pepper; cook and stir for 4 minutes longer.

2. Add flour, salt, and pepper to saucepan; cook and stir until bubbly. Add milk, broth, cream cheese, salsa, and mustard; bring to a simmer, then reduce heat and stir until thickened.

3. Cook pasta until al dente according to package directions. Add cheeses to saucepan; cook and stir until cheese melts. Drain pasta and add to saucepan; cook and stir over low heat until pasta is coated and sauce thickens. Serve immediately.

Cheese: Full Fat or Low Fat?

Low-fat cheeses don't have as much flavor as their full-fat counterparts, but if you choose an extra sharp variety, you won't taste the difference. Choosing a strongly flavored cheese like feta or goat's milk also helps. Low-fat cheeses don't melt as well as their full fat counterparts, so use full fat if melted cheese is important to the recipe.

Pasta with Garlic Bread Crumbs

Bread crumbs are a classic substitute for cheese in older Italian recipes. This simple dish is quick and delicious.

1. Bring a large pot of salted water to a boil over high heat. Meanwhile, heat butter in large skillet over medium heat. Add garlic and shallots; cook and stir until tender and fragrant.

2. Add bread crumbs to skillet; cook and stir until golden and crisp, about 5–6 minutes. At the same time, add the pasta to the boiling water. Cook until al dente according to package directions.

3. Scoop the pasta out of the cooking water using a large sieve and add to the bread crumb mixture. Add a ladle of the pasta cooking water to the skillet along with the cheese and parsley; toss over low heat until combined. Serve immediately.

SERVES 6

Calories: 408.05
Fat: 9.31 grams
Fat as % of calories: 20.5%
Carbohydrates: 68.33 grams
Fiber: 2.48 grams
Sodium: 327.07 mg
Vitamin A: 15% DV
Vitamin C: 15% DV
Calcium: 196.76 mg

INGREDIENTS

2 tablespoons butter
3 cloves garlic, minced
2 shallots, minced
4 slices whole wheat bread, crumbled
1 16-ounce package whole wheat fettuccine pasta
¾ cup grated Parmesan cheese
½ cup minced fresh parsley

Roasted Vegetable Tart

This recipe is an excellent way to use leftover roasted vegetables. The cheesy filling has lots of flavor and a smooth, velvety texture.

1. Preheat oven to 400°F. Roll out the crust and line a 10-inch tart pan with removable bottom. Press the crust onto the bottom and sides, then roll a rolling pin over the edges to cut off excess dough. Prick bottom well and bake for 8 minutes; remove to wire rack.

2. Arrange the Vegetables in the Crust; sprinkle with Havarti and set aside. In medium bowl, combine eggs, egg whites, ricotta, buttermilk, flour, pepper, basil, and thyme and beat until combined. Slowly pour into tart pan.

3. Sprinkle top with the Cotija cheese. Bake for 10 minutes, then reduce heat to 350°F and bake for 15–25 minutes longer or until tart is set and top is browned. Let cool for 10 minutes, then slice to serve.

SERVES 6–8

Calories: 338.72
Fat: 13.74 grams
Fat as % of calories: 36.5%
Carbohydrates: 42.56 grams
Fiber: 6.28 grams
Sodium: 350.53 mg
Vitamin A: 70% DV
Vitamin C: 35% DV
Calcium: 235.00 mg

INGREDIENTS

1 recipe Whole Wheat Pie Crust (page 188)
4 cups Roasted Root Vegetables (page 145)
½ cup shredded Havarti cheese
2 eggs
2 egg whites
½ cup part-skim ricotta cheese
½ cup buttermilk
2 tablespoons flour
⅛ teaspoon pepper
½ teaspoon dried basil leaves
½ teaspoon dried thyme leaves
3 tablespoons grated Cotija cheese

Calories: 279.97
Fat: 10.06 grams
Fat as % of calories: 32.3%
Carbohydrates: 32.95 grams
Fiber: 5.47 grams
Sodium: 482.72 mg
Vitamin A: 230% DV
Vitamin C: 10% DV
Calcium: 293.67 mg

INGREDIENTS

24 very large white mushrooms
1 tablespoon olive oil
1 onion, chopped
3 cloves garlic, minced
3 carrots, diced
2 cups frozen loose-pack
    spinach, thawed
1 cup shredded low-fat Gouda
    cheese
12 9" x 14" sheets phyllo dough,
    thawed
Olive oil cooking spray
2 tablespoons butter, melted

Stuffed Mushrooms in Phyllo

*This elegant dish is very delicious and not as difficult
as you may think. As long as you are gentle
and work quickly, phyllo dough is easy and fun to use.*

1. Remove stems from mushrooms and trim stem ends. Chop mushroom stems. Heat olive oil in large skillet over medium heat. Add mushroom caps to skillet, stem side up; cook for 4–5 minutes until bottoms are brown, shaking pan occasionally. Turn mushrooms stem side down; cook for 4–5 minutes or until liquid evaporates. Remove mushrooms to paper towels to drain, stem side down.

2. Add chopped mushroom stems, onion, garlic, and carrot to skillet; cook and stir until tender, about 7–8 minutes. Drain spinach well and add to skillet; cook and stir until liquid evaporates, about 5 minutes. Remove to large bowl and let cool for 20 minutes.

3. Preheat oven to 400°F. Stir cheese into spinach mixture. Stuff the mushroom caps with this mixture, using about 2 tablespoons per mushroom, rounding the tops.

4. Place a sheet of phyllo dough on work surface; spray with cooking spray. Top with second sheet. Cut in half to make two 7" x 9" rectangles. Arrange two stuffed mushrooms in a row on the phyllo, along the 7-inch side. Fold one end over, then fold in sides and roll up. Brush with butter and place stuffing side up on cookie sheet.

5. Repeat with remaining ingredients, making twelve rolls in all. Bake for 20–25 minutes or until phyllo is golden brown and crisp. Let cool for 10 minutes, then serve.

Stuffed Portobello Sandwiches

A savory combination of mushrooms, nuts, and cheese makes this elegant sandwich a dish your guests will remember for a long time.

1. In small bowl, combine rice and vegetable broth; bring to a boil over medium-high heat. Reduce heat to low, cover, and simmer for 35–45 minutes until rice is tender. Drain and place in large bowl; set aside.

2. In medium skillet heat olive oil over medium heat. Add onion and bell pepper; cook and stir until tender, about 6 minutes. Add to bowl with rice; stir in bread crumbs, salt, pepper, thyme, raisins, and walnuts. Stir in cheese.

3. Preheat oven to 350°F. Remove stems from mushrooms; discard stems. Carefully scrape out the mushroom's dark gills. Stuff mushrooms with the rice mixture and place on Silpat-covered cookie sheet. Bake for 20–30 minutes or until mushrooms are tender and filling starts to brown.

4. Spread butter on one side of each Bread slice; toast in oven until browned. Make sandwiches with Bread slices and stuffed mushrooms.

Raisins

Raisins contain a lot of boron, an essential trace mineral in our diets. They also have phenols, powerful antioxidants that are found in most fruits. Raisins have less phenol content than grapes because of the drying process, but they are still a good source. You can choose dark or golden raisins.

SERVES 6

Calories: 584.04
Fat: 18.83 grams
Fat as % of calories: 29.0%
Carbohydrates: 84.51 grams
Fiber: 9.20 grams
Sodium: 423.76 mg
Vitamin A: 30% DV
Vitamin C: 70% DV
Calcium: 240.75 mg

INGREDIENTS

½ cup brown rice
1 cup vegetable broth
1 tablespoon olive oil
1 onion, chopped
1 red bell pepper, chopped
¼ cup dry bread crumbs
¼ teaspoon salt
⅛ teaspoon pepper
½ teaspoon dried thyme leaves
½ cup golden raisins
¼ cup chopped walnuts
1 cup shredded low-fat Swiss
    cheese
6 large portobello mushrooms
3 tablespoons butter, softened
12 slices Cracked Wheat French
    Bread (page 139)

SERVES 10

Calories: 408.82
Fat: 11.86 grams
Fat as % of calories: 26.1%
Carbohydrates: 58.62 grams
Fiber: 7.57 grams
Sodium: 816.89 mg
Vitamin A: 20% DV
Vitamin C: 25% DV
Calcium: 246.53 mg

INGREDIENTS

½ cup medium pearl barley
1 cup vegetable stock
1 tablespoon olive oil
1 onion, chopped
3 cloves garlic, minced
1 jalapeño pepper, minced
1 15-ounce can black beans,
  drained
1 cup frozen corn
2 tomatoes, chopped
1 tablespoon chili powder
12 8-inch flour tortillas
1 cup shredded pepper jack
  cheese
1 cup shredded part-skim
  mozzarella cheese
1 16-ounce jar salsa
1 8-ounce can tomato sauce
¼ cup grated Cotija cheese

Barley and Black Bean Enchiladas

*These rich enchiladas are filled with parsley, vegetables, and black
beans, making them colorful and delicious.*

1. Preheat oven to 375°F. In small saucepan, combine barley and vegetable
    stock. Bring to a simmer. Cover and simmer until barley is tender, about
    35 minutes. Drain and set aside.

2. In large skillet, heat olive oil over medium heat. Add onion, garlic, and
    jalapeño pepper; cook and stir for 5 minutes. Stir in black beans, corn,
    tomatoes, chili powder, and cooked barley; simmer for 10 minutes.

3. Divide barley mixture among the tortillas; top with a mixture of pepper
    jack and mozzarella cheeses. Roll up and place in 9" x 13" baking dish.
    Pour salsa and tomato sauce over all; sprinkle with Cotija cheese. Bake
    for 45–55 minutes or until casserole is bubbling and cheese is melted and
    begins to brown.

Cotija Cheese

Cotija cheese is a hard Mexican grating cheese that is similar to Parmesan and
Romano but with a more intense flavor. You can find it in chunks or pregrated
at Mexican markets and usually in the big grocery stores. You can substitute
Parmesan or Romano for it, but there's nothing truly like it.

Vegetable Spanakopita

*Be sure to thaw the phyllo according to package directions
to make this classic Greek dish.*

SERVES 6

Calories: 297.39
Fat: 11.22 grams
Fat as % of calories: 33.9%
Carbohydrates: 27.81 grams
Fiber: 4.17 grams
Sodium: 522.47 mg
Vitamin A: 100% DV
Vitamin C: 15% DV
Calcium: 346.16 mg

INGREDIENTS

2 tablespoons olive oil, divided
1 onion, chopped
4 cloves garlic, minced
1 8-ounce package sliced
  mushrooms
1 10-ounce package frozen
  chopped spinach, thawed
1 cup chopped tomatoes
⅛ teaspoon pepper
2 tablespoons chopped fresh dill
½ cup part-skim ricotta cheese
3 egg whites
1 cup shredded part-skim
  mozzarella cheese
¼ cup crumbled feta cheese
1 tablespoon butter, melted
8 9" x 14" sheets frozen phyllo
  dough, thawed
6 tablespoons wheat germ

1. Preheat oven to 350°F. Spray a 9" x 9" baking pan with nonstick cooking spray and set aside. In large skillet heat 1 tablespoon olive oil over medium heat. Add onion and garlic; cook and stir for 3 minutes. Add mushrooms; cook and stir for 4 minutes longer. Add spinach and tomatoes; cook and stir until liquid evaporates, about 10–15 minutes longer. Remove from heat and place filling in large bowl; let cool.

2. Add pepper, dill, ricotta, egg whites, and mozzarella and feta cheeses to filling and mix well. In small bowl, combine 1 tablespoon olive oil with butter.

3. Place a sheet phyllo dough into prepared pan, letting edges hang over pan. Brush with some of the olive oil mixture and sprinkle with 1 tablespoon wheat germ. Layer four more sheets of phyllo on top, alternately spraying with cooking spray and brushing with olive oil mixture; top with wheat germ. Top with filling.

4. Fold edges of dough over filling. Top with remaining phyllo, brushing with olive oil mixture; tuck in edges. Bake for 35–45 minutes until golden brown.

Draining Frozen Spinach

Frozen spinach contains a large amount of water. Most recipes call for draining thawed frozen spinach. One way is to put the spinach in a kitchen towel, then squeeze over the sink until dry. You can also place the spinach between two plates; hold vertically and squeeze over the sink until dry.

INGREDIENTS

1 tablespoon olive oil
1 onion, chopped
5 cloves garlic, minced, divided
2 green bell peppers, chopped
2 tomatoes, chopped
¼ cup tomato paste
2 tablespoons lemon juice
¼ teaspoon salt
⅛ teaspoon cayenne pepper
1 teaspoon dried oregano
1 High-Fiber Pizza Crust (page 239), prebaked
1 cup shredded part-skim mozzarella cheese
¼ cup crumbled feta cheese
¼ cup minced parsley
2 teaspoons grated lemon zest

Greek Pizza

This fresh tasting pizza is topped with gremolata—the mixture of parsley, lemon zest, and garlic—to add a burst of flavor.

1. Preheat oven to 400°F. In large skillet, heat olive oil over medium heat. Add onion and 3 cloves garlic; cook and stir until crisp-tender, about 5 minutes. Add bell peppers, tomatoes, tomato paste, lemon juice, salt, pepper, and oregano and bring to a simmer. Simmer for 5 minutes, stirring frequently.

2. Place the Crust on a cookie sheet. Spread tomato mixture over all, and top with mozzarella and feta cheeses. Bake for 20–25 minutes or until Crust is very crisp and cheeses are melted and begin to brown. In small bowl, combine parsley, zest, and 2 cloves garlic and mix well. Sprinkle over the pizza and serve immediately.

Greek Flavors

Greek flavors and ingredients include feta cheese, oregano, olive oil, olives, lemons, sun-dried tomatoes, and fresh herbs. A Greek diet is part of the Mediterranean diet that is considered one of the healthiest in the world. Lots of fresh vegetables and fruits, along with healthy fats, make this diet not only healthy but delicious.

Baked Vegetable Egg Rolls

Spring roll wrappers are thinner than egg roll wrappers, allowing them to bake and crisp in the short baking time.

1. Preheat oven to 400°F. In large skillet, heat 1 tablespoon olive oil over medium-high heat. Add onion and garlic; stir-fry for 4 minutes. Add cabbage and gingerroot; stir-fry until vegetables are tender and liquid has evaporated.

2. Remove from heat and stir in cilantro, soy sauce, carrot, peas, and hoisin sauce. Let cool for 20 minutes.

3. Arrange spring roll wrappers on work surface. Place two tablespoons of the filling on a wrapper. Brush the edges with water and roll up, folding in sides to enclose filling. Brush with a bit of olive oil and place on baking sheet.

4. Repeat with remaining wrappers. Bake for 15 minutes, then turn and bake for 10 minutes or until rolls are browned and crisp. Cool and cut in half to serve.

SERVES 8

Calories: 254.97
Fat: 4.72 grams
Fat as % of calories: 16.6%
Carbohydrates: 44.96 grams
Fiber: 2.56 grams
Sodium: 530.36 mg
Vitamin A: 30% DV
Vitamin C: 10% DV
Calcium: 48.87 mg

INGREDIENTS

2 tablespoons olive oil, divided
1 onion, chopped
3 cloves garlic, minced
1 cup shredded red cabbage
1 tablespoon grated gingerroot
¼ cup minced cilantro
2 tablespoons low-sodium soy sauce
½ cup grated carrot
½ cup frozen baby peas, thawed
3 tablespoons hoisin sauce
16 spring roll wrappers

Asparagus–Spinach Frittata

Frittatas are delightful baked Italian omelets. Serve it for breakfast, brunch, or even dinner with a simple salad.

1. Snap ends off asparagus; discard ends. Cut spears into 2-inch lengths; set aside. In large, nonstick, ovenproof skillet, melt butter over medium heat. Add onion, garlic, and asparagus; cook and stir until crisp-tender, about 6–7 minutes. Preheat broiler.

2. Drain spinach well; add to skillet; cook and stir for 2 minutes. In food processor, combine eggs, cream cheese, cream, salt, and pepper; process until smooth. Pour into skillet; cook and stir, shaking pan occasionally, until bottom is browned.

3. Sprinkle frittata with cheese and place skillet 6 inches from broiler; broil for 6–8 minutes until light brown and puffy. Combine remaining ingredients in small bowl; use to garnish frittata.

SERVES 4

Calories: 499.98
Fat: 37.81 grams
Fat as % of calories: 68.0%
Carbohydrates: 13.64 grams
Fiber: 5.88 grams
Sodium: 860.07 mg
Vitamin A: 280% DV
Vitamin C: 30% DV
Calcium: 460.30 mg

INGREDIENTS

½ pound asparagus
2 tablespoons butter
1 onion, chopped
2 cloves garlic, minced
1 cup loose-pack frozen chopped spinach, thawed
8 eggs
1 3-ounce package cream cheese, softened
⅓ cup light cream
Salt and white pepper to taste
1 cup shredded Gouda cheese
1 cup chopped tomatoes
¼ cup chopped green onion
1 tablespoon chopped fresh basil leaves

INGREDIENTS

2 tablespoons butter
1 onion, chopped
4 cloves garlic, minced
1 teaspoon coriander seeds
1 tablespoon curry powder
1 teaspoon turmeric
½ teaspoon salt
⅛ teaspoon cayenne pepper
4 potatoes, diced
1 cup vegetable broth
4 cups fresh spinach leaves
¾ cup plain yogurt
⅓ cup mango chutney

INGREDIENTS

3 cups low-sodium vegetable stock
1½ cups bulgur, rinsed
2 tomatoes, chopped
2 cups grape tomatoes
1 zucchini, chopped
1 yellow summer squash, chopped
1 cucumber, peeled and chopped
1 red sweet onion, chopped
½ cup chopped fresh mint leaves
¼ cup chopped fresh basil leaves
¼ cup olive oil
¼ cup orange juice
¼ cup lemon juice
½ teaspoon salt
⅛ teaspoon white pepper

Potato–Spinach Curry

This mildly spicy curry has a wonderful blend of flavors and textures.

1. In large skillet, melt butter over medium heat. Add onion and garlic; cook and stir for 4 minutes. Add coriander, curry powder, turmeric, salt, and pepper; cook and stir for 3 minutes longer.

2. Add potatoes to skillet; cook and stir for 4 minutes. Add vegetable broth. Bring to a simmer, cover, and cook for 15–20 minutes or until potatoes are tender. Uncover skillet and simmer until liquid is absorbed.

3. Add spinach to skillet; cover and simmer until spinach wilts. Add yogurt and chutney and heat through.

Vegetable Tabbouleh

Tabbouleh is a salad made from cracked wheat or bulgur, vegetables, and a light dressing. It's an excellent light main dish for summer entertaining.

1. Bring the stock to a boil. Place bulgur in a large bowl, then pour stock over bulgur. Cover bowl with plate and let stand for 30 minutes. Drain well.

2. Add tomatoes, grape tomatoes, zucchini, squash, cucumber, and onion and toss to coat.

3. In food processor, combine remaining ingredients; process until smooth. Pour over bulgur mixture and toss to coat. Cover and chill for 2–3 hours before serving.

Chapter 9

Healthy Sides and Nutritious Breads

YIELDS 36 ROLLS

Calories: 135.16
Fat: 4.01 grams
Fat as % of calories: 26.6%
Carbohydrates: 20.30 grams
Fiber: 1.34 grams
Sodium: 157.39 mg
Vitamin A: 2% DV
Vitamin C: 2% DV
Calcium: 78.33 mg

INGREDIENTS

½ cup orange juice
1 cup water
½ cup skim milk
½ cup cornmeal
½ cup honey
2 tablespoons butter
2 cups whole wheat flour
1 cup bread flour
2–3 cups all-purpose flour
1½ teaspoons salt
1 0.25-ounce package active dry
 yeast
2½ cups diced sharp Cheddar
 cheese
2 tablespoons butter, melted

Melted Cheese Rolls

*Cornmeal and whole wheat flour add fiber to these delicious little
rolls. Be sure to serve them warm so the cheese is soft and melty.*

1. In medium saucepan, combine juice, water, and milk and bring to a
   boil. Stir in cornmeal; cook over medium heat, stirring constantly, until
   mixture thickens. Remove from heat and stir in honey and 2 tablespoons
   butter. Let cool for 30 minutes.

2. In large bowl, combine whole wheat flour, bread flour, ½ cup all-purpose
   flour, salt, and yeast and mix well. Add orange juice mixture; beat for 2
   minutes.

3. Gradually add enough remaining all-purpose flour to form a stiff dough.
   Knead dough on lightly floured surface until smooth and elastic, about
   8–9 minutes. Place in a greased bowl, turning to grease top.

4. Cover and let rise until doubled, about 1 hour. Punch down dough and
   divide into thirds. Knead ⅓ of the cheese cubes into each section of
   dough. Divide each third into 12 pieces; roll into smooth balls.

5. Place balls on greased cookie sheets about 2 inches apart. Cover and let
   rise until doubled, about 30–40 minutes. Preheat oven to 350°F. Bake
   rolls for 20–30 minutes until deep golden brown. Brush with the 2 tablespoons melted butter and remove to wire racks to cool; serve warm.

Citrus Juices

When you're making a recipe that has a lot of ingredients, you can use bottled lemon, orange, and lime juices. But when you're making a recipe where
the juices plays a primary role, please juice the actual fruit. The flavor will be
fresher and more intense, with a brightness you can't get from bottled juices.

Triple–Onion Scones

Chives are in the onion family, and they give these scones a nice zing. The whole wheat flour and wheat germ give the scones their heavenly texture.

1. Preheat oven to 400°F. In medium saucepan, melt butter and olive oil over medium heat. Add onion; cook and stir for 5 minutes. Add green onion; cook and stir for 3–4 minutes longer until tender. Remove from heat.

2. In large bowl combine flours, wheat germ, baking powder, baking soda, sugar, salt, and pepper and mix well. Add onion mixture, buttermilk, sour cream, and chives and stir just until combined.

3. Remove to lightly floured surface and knead dough 8 times. On ungreased cookie sheet, shape into a 9-inch circle. Cut into 10 wedges and separate slightly. Brush with the light cream.

4. Bake at 400°F for 16–20 minutes or until scones are light golden brown and set. Cool on wire racks for 10 minutes, then serve warm.

Whole Wheat Pastry Flour

Whole wheat pastry flour is made from whole wheat, but it's more finely ground so it acts more like all-purpose flour in recipes. It is made from soft wheat, while traditional whole wheat flour is made from hard wheat. This flour has less gluten and more starch, so it's a good choice for making cakes, cookies, and biscuits.

SERVES 10

Calories: 175.52
Fat: 7.24 grams
Fat as % of calories: 37.1%
Carbohydrates: 24.11 grams
Fiber: 2.54 grams
Sodium: 136.96 mg
Vitamin A: 4% DV
Vitamin C: 4% DV
Calcium: 83.85 mg

INGREDIENTS

2 tablespoons butter
3 tablespoons olive oil
1 large onion, finely chopped
¼ cup sliced green onion
1 cup all-purpose flour
1 cup whole wheat pastry flour
¼ cup wheat germ
1 teaspoon baking powder
½ teaspoon baking soda
1 tablespoon sugar
¼ teaspoon salt
¼ teaspoon white pepper
¾ cup low-fat buttermilk
⅓ cup nonfat sour cream
¼ cup minced chives
2 tablespoons nonfat light cream

SERVES 16

Calories: 98.14
Fat: 3.44 grams
Fat as % of calories: 31.4%
Carbohydrates: 15.41 grams
Fiber: 0.50 grams
Sodium: 260.51 mg
Vitamin A: 2% DV
Vitamin C: 0% DV
Calcium: 40.28 mg

INGREDIENTS

1 3-ounce package nonfat cream cheese
6 tablespoons grated Parmesan cheese
¼ teaspoon garlic powder
1 teaspoon dried thyme leaves
1 19-ounce tube refrigerated reduced-fat, whole wheat biscuit dough
2 tablespoons skim milk
3 tablespoons wheat germ

SERVES 12

Calories: 151.07
Fat: 5.84 grams
Fat as % of calories: 33.8%
Carbohydrates: 21.05 grams
Fiber: 1.77 grams
Sodium: 147.03 mg
Vitamin A: 2% DV
Vitamin C: 6% DV
Calcium: 60.44 mg

INGREDIENTS

2 heads Roasted Garlic (page 24)
2 tablespoons olive oil
2 tablespoons butter, softened
½ teaspoon lemon pepper
¼ cup grated Parmesan cheese
¼ cup grated Romano cheese
1 loaf Cracked Wheat French Bread (page 139)

Cheese-Filled Whole Wheat Biscuits

These crunchy biscuits are filled with a flavorful creamy cheese mixture. They are great with salads and soups and make a wonderful addition to entrées.

1. Preheat oven to 375°F. Line a cookie sheet with Silpat liner and set aside. In small bowl, combine cream cheese, Parmesan cheese, garlic powder, and thyme and mix well.

2. Divide biscuits into two layers each. Divide cream cheese mixture among the biscuits, leaving a ½-inch rim. Fold the dough around the filling, pressing to seal. Place seam side down on prepared cookie sheet. Brush with milk and sprinkle with wheat germ.

3. Bake for 12–15 minutes or until bread is deep golden brown. Let cool for 10 minutes, then serve.

The Best Light Garlic Cheese Bread

Mellow, roasted garlic along with cheese and lemon pepper makes crunchy French bread into a fabulous yet low-fat treat.

1. Preheat broiler. Remove Garlic from skins and place in small bowl. Mash with fork, then blend in remaining ingredients except the French Bread; mix well.

2. Cut Bread into 12 slices. Place on broiler pan; broil 6 inches from heat source for 3–5 minutes until brown on one side. Remove from oven and turn Bread over.

3. Spread evenly with garlic mixture. Return to broiler; broil for 3–4 minutes, watching carefully, until topping begins to bubble and brown. Remove from broiler and serve immediately.

Cracked Wheat French Bread

*You can find cracked wheat on the baking aisle of the supermarket;
other sources include your local co-op or health food store.*

2 LOAVES; SERVES 24

Calories: 137.67
Fat: 2.39 grams
Fat as % of calories: 15.6%
Carbohydrates: 24.59 grams
Fiber: 2.15 grams
Sodium: 116.95 mg
Vitamin A: 2% DV
Vitamin C: 4% DV
Calcium: 15.69 mg

INGREDIENTS

1 cup cracked wheat
3 tablespoons butter
1 teaspoon salt
1 cup water
1 egg
½ cup orange juice
½ cup buttermilk
*2 0.25-ounce packages active
    dry yeast*
2 cups whole wheat flour
3–4 cups bread flour
3 tablespoons wheat germ

1. Place cracked wheat, butter, and salt in a heatproof bowl. Place water in microwave-safe glass measuring cup. Microwave on high power for 2 minutes or until boiling. Pour over cracked wheat mixture; stir until butter melts. Let cool for 30 minutes.

2. Add egg, orange juice, and buttermilk to cracked wheat mixture and stir; mixture should be lukewarm. Add yeast and 1 cup whole wheat flour; beat to combine. Add remaining cup of whole wheat flour and 1 cup bread flour; beat well. Cover and let stand for 30 minutes.

3. Stir down dough and gradually add enough remaining bread flour to form a firm dough. Turn out onto floured surface and knead until elastic, about 6–7 minutes. Place in greased bowl, turning to grease top.

4. Cover and let rise for 1 hour. Punch down dough, turn out onto floured surface, cover with bowl, and let rest for 10 minutes. Divide dough in half. Roll or pat out each half into a 12" x 8" rectangle. Tightly roll up, starting with longer side.

5. Place on lightly greased cookie sheets. Slash top of dough with a sharp knife and sprinkle with wheat germ. Cover and let rise for 30–40 minutes until double.

6. Preheat oven to 375°F. Bake bread for 40–50 minutes or until golden brown and bread sounds hollow when tapped with finger. Let cool on wire rack.

Curried Cauliflower

Cauliflower is tender, sweet, and nutty. The curry powder and turmeric turn it a gorgeous yellow color as it roasts.

1. Preheat oven to 425°F. Rinse cauliflower and cut into florets; discard leaves. Dry cauliflower and combine with garlic in large shallow roasting pan.

2. In bowl, combine remaining ingredients except chutney and mix well. Drizzle over cauliflower; toss to coat. Roast for 40–50 minutes, stirring twice during roasting time, until cauliflower is tender. Drizzle with chutney and serve.

Cauliflower and Curry Powder

When cauliflower is combined with curry powder, it becomes a powerful antioxidant that can help protect against cancer. Researchers at Rutgers have found that turmeric, an ingredient in curry powder, contains curcumin, which, when combined with cruciferous vegetables, especially cauliflower, can halt development of prostate cancer.

Spicy Roasted Cauliflower

Roasting cauliflower makes it tender and sweet. Combine that with spicy ingredients and you have a low-carb side dish that won't be ignored!

1. Preheat oven to 425°F. Rinse cauliflower and remove leaves. Cut into florets, trimming the ends. Place cauliflower in shallow roasting pan.

2. In small saucepan, heat olive oil and butter over medium heat. Add garlic and jalapeño pepper; cook and stir until fragrant, about 3–4 minutes. Remove from heat and add chili powder and pepper.

3. Drizzle over cauliflower and toss to coat. Roast for 25–30 minutes or until cauliflower is tender when pierced with a fork. Sprinkle with cheese, then return to oven for 5–10 minutes longer until the cheese begins to brown. Serve immediately.

Buffalo Smashed Potatoes

Because you use the potato skins and add cauliflower, these potatoes have more fiber than traditional mashed potatoes.

1. Bring a large pot of water to a boil. Cook cauliflower florets for 5–6 minutes until tender; drain and place in large bowl. Cook potatoes for 10–12 minutes until tender; drain and add to bowl.

2. Meanwhile, in small skillet melt butter; add onion and garlic. Cook and stir until tender, about 7 minutes. When potatoes are done, immediately add butter mixture and mash with a potato masher, leaving some large pieces.

3. Preheat oven to 400°F. Add sour cream, ricotta, hot pepper sauce, salt, and pepper to potatoes and mix well. Pile into a 3-quart casserole and top with blue and Parmesan cheeses. Bake for 30–40 minutes or until potatoes are hot and top browns.

Garlic Roasted Potatoes

This lovely recipe is a great accompaniment to grilled chicken or a steak.

1. Preheat oven to 400°F. Scrub potatoes, then cut into 1-inch chunks. Combine with onions and garlic in large roasting pan. Drizzle with olive oil, sprinkle with salt, pepper, and thyme leaves and toss to coat.

2. Roast potatoes for 60–75 minutes, turning twice with a spatula during roasting time, until the potatoes are tender with crisp, brown skins. Sprinkle with lemon juice and mint and serve immediately.

Potato Skins

Keep the skins on potatoes when you slice or cube them. The skins have lots of fiber and help keep the vitamins inside the potatoes as they cook—but watch out for their color. A potato skin that has a greenish tinge should not be eaten. That green color is a chemical called solanine, which comes from exposure to light and can be toxic.

SERVES 6–8

Calories: 221.86
Fat: 7.42 grams
Fat as % of calories: 30.1%
Carbohydrates: 31.04 grams
Fiber: 3.63 grams
Sodium: 430.06 mg
Vitamin A: 6% DV
Vitamin C: 45% DV
Calcium: 162.03 mg

INGREDIENTS

2 cups cauliflower florets
4 russet potatoes, cubed
2 tablespoons butter
1 onion, chopped
6 cloves garlic, minced
½ cup nonfat sour cream
½ cup part-skim ricotta cheese
½ teaspoon hot pepper sauce
½ teaspoon salt
⅛ teaspoon white pepper
½ cup crumbled blue cheese
3 tablespoons grated Parmesan cheese

SERVES 12

Calories: 231.47
Fat: 4.78 grams
Fat as % of calories: 18.5%
Carbohydrates: 43.82 grams
Fiber: 4.59 grams
Sodium: 214.80 mg
Vitamin A: 0% DV
Vitamin C: 35% DV
Calcium: 39.71 mg

INGREDIENTS

5 pounds russet potatoes
2 onions, chopped
12 cloves garlic, minced
¼ cup olive oil
1 teaspoon salt
¼ teaspoon pepper
2 teaspoons dried thyme leaves
3 tablespoons lemon juice
2 tablespoons chopped fresh mint

SERVES 12

Calories: 271.84
Fat: 10.19 grams
Fat as % of calories: 33.7%
Carbohydrates: 33.12 grams
Fiber: 2.44 grams
Sodium: 648.81 mg
Vitamin A: 131% DV
Vitamin C: 10% DV
Calcium: 320.27 mg

INGREDIENTS

1 16-ounce package frozen hash
    brown potatoes, thawed
4 sweet potatoes, peeled
1 tablespoon butter
1 tablespoon olive oil
2 onions, chopped
6 cloves garlic, minced
1 16-ounce jar low-fat Alfredo
    sauce
1 8-ounce package nonfat cream
    cheese, cubed
1½ cups nonfat sour cream
2 cups shredded low-fat Swiss
    cheese
1 cup 1% milk
1 teaspoon dried basil leaves
1 teaspoon dried oregano leaves
½ teaspoon pepper

Good-For-You Creamy Cheesy Potatoes

Adding sweet potatoes to a classic, rich dish makes it more nutrient dense; the vitamin A content goes through the roof.

1. Drain the hash brown potatoes and place in a 5-quart slow cooker. Coarsely grate the sweet potatoes and add to the slow cooker; mix gently.

2. In large skillet, heat butter and olive oil over medium heat. Add onions and garlic; cook and stir until tender, about 6–7 minutes. Add to slow cooker and stir.

3. Add Alfredo sauce, cream cheese, sour cream, Swiss cheese, milk, basil, oregano, and pepper to skillet; cook and stir over medium-low heat until cream cheese melts. Pour over potatoes in slow cooker.

4. Cover and cook on low for 8–9 hours or until potatoes are tender and mixture is bubbling. Serve immediately.

Potatoes

Potatoes are a very healthy food, despite being denigrated in the low-carb craze. They contain lots of potassium and fiber, especially if you eat the skin. A chemical in potatoes called kukoamine may help reduce high blood pressure.

Orange-Glazed Carrots

The combination of orange, honey, and carrot is truly delicious, and it's also high in vitamins A and C.

1. In large saucepan, melt butter over medium heat. Add onion and garlic; cook and stir until tender, about 6 minutes. Add carrots to pan; cook and stir for 4 minutes until carrots are glazed.

2. Add orange juice concentrate, honey, salt, and pepper to saucepan. Bring to a simmer, then cover, reduce heat to low, and simmer for 4–5 minutes until carrots are tender and glazed. Serve immediately.

Baby Carrots

Baby carrots aren't actually immature carrots; they are cut down from a specialty carrot that is bred to be sweeter, grow longer, and ripen faster than regular carrots.

SERVES 6

Calories: 96.45
Fat: 2.16 grams
Fat as % of calories: 19.7%
Carbohydrates: 19.36 grams
Fiber: 1.85 grams
Sodium: 268.17 mg
Vitamin A: 210% DV
Vitamin C: 35% DV
Calcium: 38.57 mg

INGREDIENTS
1 tablespoon butter
1 onion, chopped
4 cloves garlic, minced
1 16-ounce bag baby carrots
½ cup frozen orange juice concentrate, thawed
2 tablespoons honey
½ teaspoon salt
⅛ teaspoon white pepper

Sweet and Spicy Carrots

The combination of sweet apricots and spicy mustard is the perfect complement to tender baby carrots. Serve this with roast chicken and rice pilaf.

1. In large saucepan, combine carrots and orange juice. Bring to a boil over high heat. Cover pan, reduce heat to low, and simmer for 8–10 minutes until carrots are crisp-tender. Drain, reserving ¼ cup of the liquid.

2. Combine cooked carrots, reserved juice, and remaining ingredients in the saucepan over medium heat. Cook and stir until sugar is dissolved and carrots are glazed and tender. Serve immediately.

Preserves

Read the labels on fruit preserves before you buy them. Some brands can offer a significant amount of vitamin C. You can find low-sugar or sugar-free brands if you're on a low-carb diet. Keep a good supply of them on hand, because they're delicious added to vegetables and a good way to flavor dips and fruit salads.

SERVES 8

Calories: 165.71
Fat: 3.27 grams
Fat as % of calories: 17.7%
Carbohydrates: 35.46 grams
Fiber: 2.33 grams
Sodium: 257.03 grams
Vitamin A: 320% DV
Vitamin C: 25% DV
Calcium: 50.20 mg

INGREDIENTS
2 16-ounce packages baby carrots
1 cup orange juice
2 tablespoons butter
¼ cup honey
2 tablespoons brown sugar
½ cup apricot preserves
3 tablespoons Dijon mustard
¼ teaspoon salt
⅛ teaspoon white pepper

SERVES 10

Calories: 151.63
Fat: 5.28 grams
Fat as % of calories: 34.4%
Carbohydrates: 17.61 grams
Fiber: 4.05 grams
Sodium: 290.72 mg
Vitamin A: 80% DV
Vitamin C: 60% DV
Calcium: 254.50 mg

INGREDIENTS

2 tablespoons butter
1 onion, chopped
3 cloves garlic, minced
3 tablespoons flour
½ teaspoon salt
⅛ teaspoon white pepper
½ teaspoon dried tarragon
    leaves
1½ cups skim milk
1 cup shredded low-fat Swiss
    cheese
½ cup low-fat sour cream
2 cups frozen sliced carrots,
    thawed
2 cups frozen baby peas, thawed
2 cups frozen cauliflower,
    thawed
2 cups frozen chopped broccoli,
    thawed
⅓ cup dried bread crumbs
2 tablespoons grated Parmesan
    cheese

Low-Fat Swiss Medley

You could use any combination of frozen vegetables you'd like in this colorful and hearty casserole. Just thaw and drain them well before adding to the sauce.

1. Preheat oven to 350°F. Spray a 2½-quart casserole with cooking spray and set aside.

2. In large saucepan, melt butter over medium heat. Add onion and garlic; cook and stir until tender, about 6 minutes. Add flour, salt, pepper, and tarragon and cook and stir until bubbly.

3. Add milk; bring to a simmer over medium heat, stirring constantly. Cook and stir until sauce thickens. Remove from heat and stir in cheese and sour cream.

4. Drain all vegetables well and stir into sauce. Pour into prepared casserole. In small bowl, combine bread crumbs and Parmesan cheese. Sprinkle over casserole. Bake for 35–45 minutes or until casserole is bubbling and crumbs are brown. Serve immediately.

Reducing Fat with Dairy Products

Dairy products are now available in many lower-fat and even nonfat versions. For best results, combine both low-fat products and nonfat products. Doing this lets you reduce the fat content while still maintaining the creamy texture, whether you're making a casserole or a quick bread.

Roasted Root Vegetables

Serve this mix of tender and sweet root vegetables as the side dish for a roasted chicken or a glazed spiral-sliced ham.

1. Preheat oven to 400°F. Cut the potatoes, rutabaga, parsnips, and carrots into 1-inch chunks. Leave the garlic cloves whole. Place in large roasting pan. Drizzle with olive oil and sprinkle with salt, pepper, and seasonings.

2. Roast vegetables for 70–80 minutes, turning twice with a spatula during roasting time, until the vegetables are tender and potatoes have crisp, brown skins.

Root Vegetables

Root vegetables are an excellent source of fiber and vitamin A. If you've never tried the more mundane varieties like parsnips and rutabaga, try this recipe.

SERVES 8–10

Calories: 232.58
Fat: 5.62 grams
Fat as % of calories: 21.7%
Carbohydrates: 43.07 grams
Fiber: 7.42 grams
Sodium: 350.78 mg
Vitamin A: 120% DV
Vitamin C: 70% DV
Calcium: 94.71 mg

INGREDIENTS
2 pounds russet potatoes
1 rutabaga, peeled
2 parsnips, peeled
4 large carrots, peeled
8 cloves garlic, peeled
3 tablespoons olive oil
1 teaspoon salt
¼ teaspoon white pepper
1 teaspoon dried basil leaves
1 teaspoon dried thyme leaves
1 teaspoon dried mint leaves

Rosemary Green Beans

This beautiful and festive dish is the perfect side dish for roast chicken or at Thanksgiving or Christmas dinner.

1. In large saucepan, melt butter over medium heat. Add garlic and red onion; cook and stir for 3 minutes. Add green beans; cook and stir for 3 minutes longer.

2. Add water and bring to a simmer. Cover saucepan, reduce heat, and simmer for 6–8 minutes or until beans are tender. Drain.

3. Return saucepan to medium heat and add salt, pepper, orange juice, honey, and rosemary. Bring to a simmer; simmer for 3–4 minutes until beans are glazed. Sprinkle with pine nuts and serve immediately.

SERVES 6

Calories: 111.15
Fat: 4.02 grams
Fat as % of calories: 32.5%
Carbohydrates: 18.64 grams
Fiber: 4.38 grams
Sodium: 215.71 mg
Vitamin A: 15% DV
Vitamin C: 40% DV
Calcium: 53.11 mg

INGREDIENTS
1 tablespoon butter
3 cloves garlic, minced
1 red onion, chopped
1½ pounds fresh green beans, trimmed
1 cup water
½ teaspoon salt
⅛ teaspoon white pepper
⅓ cup orange juice
2 tablespoons honey
1 tablespoon chopped fresh rosemary
2 tablespoons pine nuts, toasted

Calories: 218.38
Fat: 6.52 grams
Fat as % of calories: 26.9%
Carbohydrates: 33.56 grams
Fiber: 2.62 grams
Sodium: 302.33 mg
Vitamin A: 10% DV
Vitamin C: 15% DV
Calcium: 137.15 mg

INGREDIENTS

3 tablespoons butter
1 onion, chopped
2 cloves garlic, minced
3 tablespoons flour
⅛ teaspoon salt
⅛ teaspoon white pepper
1 teaspoon dried thyme leaves
1 cup skim milk
1 egg yolk
1 cup grated low-fat extra-sharp Cheddar cheese
2 cups frozen corn, thawed
2 15-ounce cans no-salt cream-style corn
4 egg whites
⅛ teaspoon cream of tartar

Fluffy Corn Soufflé

Soufflés will not wait for guests! Your guests must be ready and waiting for the soufflé. It will still taste good if it falls, but half the drama is in the presentation.

1. Preheat oven to 350°F. Spray the bottom of a 2-quart soufflé dish with nonstick cooking spray and set aside.

2. In large saucepan, melt butter over medium heat. Add onion and garlic; cook and stir until tender, about 6 minutes. Add flour, salt, pepper, and thyme leaves; cook and stir until bubbling.

3. Add milk; cook and stir until mixture comes to a simmer. Stir in egg yolk and remove from heat. Add cheese and both kinds of corn and set aside.

4. In medium bowl, combine egg whites and cream of tartar; beat until stiff peaks form. Stir a dollop of the egg whites into the corn mixture, then gently fold in remaining egg whites.

5. Pour into prepared soufflé dish. Bake for 45–55 minutes or until soufflé is puffed, golden brown on top, and set. Serve immediately.

Nutritious Eggs

Eggs are naturally nutritious. They are an excellent source of complete protein and contain vitamins B and A. You can also find eggs that have been enhanced with omega-3 fatty acids and more vitamins. One of the brand names is Eggland's Best. Read labels and pick the eggs that are right for you.

Grilled Asparagus with Garlic

When asparagus is roasted, it becomes tender and sweet. You can omit the dressing and serve the asparagus just with the drained, simmered garlic for 1.84 grams of fat.

1. Prepare and preheat grill. Rinse asparagus and snap off tough ends; discard ends. Place asparagus on cookie sheet.

2. In small saucepan, combine 1 tablespoon olive oil and whole cloves of garlic. Place over medium-low heat; cook until garlic begins to turn brown. Remove garlic from oil and place in food processor; reserve oil.

3. Drizzle asparagus with the reserved oil and sprinkle with seasoned salt and pepper; set aside.

4. Add remaining 2 tablespoons oil, vinegar, apple juice, and mustard to food processor; process until smooth.

5. Grill asparagus 6 inches from medium coals for 3–4 minutes, turning once, until tender and lightly browned. Place on serving plate and drizzle with mustard dressing. Serve immediately.

SERVES 6–8

Calories: 78.74
Fat: 5.40 grams
Fat as % of calories: 61.2%
Carbohydrates: 6.53 grams
Fiber: 2.63 grams
Sodium: 211.49 mg
Vitamin A: 15% DV
Vitamin C: 15% DV
Calcium: 37.82 mg

INGREDIENTS

2 pounds fresh asparagus
3 tablespoons olive oil, divided
8 cloves garlic, peeled
1 teaspoon seasoned salt
⅛ teaspoon white pepper
1 tablespoon balsamic vinegar
¼ cup apple juice
3 tablespoons Dijon mustard

INGREDIENTS

2 pounds Brussels sprouts
1 tablespoon lemon juice
2 tablespoons olive oil
1 teaspoon salt
¼ teaspoon white pepper
4 cloves garlic, minced
1 tablespoon butter
2 tablespoons brown sugar
2 tablespoons orange juice
2 tablespoons Dijon mustard

INGREDIENTS

1 butternut squash
1 acorn squash
2 onions, chopped
6 cloves garlic, minced
3 tablespoons olive oil
1 tablespoon curry powder
½ teaspoon salt
⅛ teaspoon pepper
2 apples, chopped
2 nectarines or peaches,
*   chopped*

Roasted Brussels Sprouts

Brussels sprouts are not the most popular, but these much-maligned vegetables are full of antioxidants and vitamins.

1. Preheat oven to 375°F. Trim the ends of the sprouts and remove any wilted or bruised leaves. Rinse them well, then dry in a kitchen towel. Place in large shallow roasting pan. Sprinkle with lemon juice, olive oil, salt, and pepper and toss to coat.

2. Roast for 40–50 minutes, turning the sprouts over with a spatula once during roasting time, until the sprouts are deep golden brown. Sprinkle garlic over the sprouts when you turn them with the spatula.

3. While the sprouts are roasting, melt butter in a small saucepan over low heat. Add sugar; cook and stir until a sauce forms. Remove from heat and stir in orange juice and mustard. Drizzle this mixture over the roasted sprouts and roast for 5 minutes longer, until the sprouts are glazed. Serve immediately.

Curried Roasted Squash with Fruit

Roasted squash is naturally sweet. When combined with apples and peaches, it makes an elegant and easy side dish.

1. Preheat oven to 375°F. Peel the squash and remove seeds; cut into 1-inch cubes. Combine with onions and garlic in a large shallow roasting pan. Drizzle with olive oil, curry powder, salt, and pepper and toss.

2. Roast for 35–40 minutes or until squash is almost tender. Add the apples; roast for 15 minutes longer. Then add nectarines or peaches; roast for 10 minutes longer or until tender. Serve immediately.

Three-Tomato Medley

Roasting tomatoes brings out their sweetness and concentrates the flavor. This dish can be served warm or cold.

1. Preheat oven to 400°F. Cut the plum and yellow tomatoes into 1-inch pieces and place in shallow baking dish. Drizzle with olive oil and sprinkle with salt, dried basil, and pepper.

2. Roast for 30 minutes, then add grape tomatoes and stir. Roast for another 10–15 minutes or until tomatoes are browned and caramelized. Sprinkle with fresh basil and serve.

SERVES 6

Calories: 92.04
Fat: 5.28 grams
Fat as % of calories: 56.5%
Carbohydrates: 10.75 grams
Fiber: 2.88 grams
Sodium: 248.28 mg
Vitamin A: 20% DV
Vitamin C: 60% DV
Calcium: 36.69 mg

INGREDIENTS
6 plum tomatoes
6 yellow tomatoes
2 tablespoons olive oil
½ teaspoon salt
1 teaspoon dried basil leaves
⅛ teaspoon white pepper
2 cups grape tomatoes
3 tablespoons chopped fresh basil

Light Cashew Rice Pilaf

Rice pilaf can be served with so many simple main dishes. This one is so hearty it can be a vegetarian main dish.

1. In large saucepan, combine wild rice and brown rice with vegetable broth, salt, pepper, and thyme. Bring to a boil over high heat, then cover, reduce heat to low, and simmer for 40–50 minutes or until rice is tender.

2. Meanwhile, in medium saucepan heat olive oil over medium heat. Add onion, garlic, and carrots; cook and stir for 4 minutes. Add mushrooms; cook and stir for 4–5 minutes longer until vegetables are tender. Remove from heat.

3. When the rice is tender, stir in the vegetables and cashews. Cook and stir over medium heat until mixture is blended. Sprinkle with parsley and serve.

SERVES 8–10

Calories: 230.54
Fat: 5.54 grams
Fat as % of calories: 21.6%
Carbohydrates: 36.15 grams
Fiber: 2.99 grams
Sodium: 266.20 mg
Vitamin A: 50% DV
Vitamin C: 5% DV
Calcium: 24.64 mg

INGREDIENTS
1 cup wild rice
1 cup long-grain brown rice
4 cups vegetable broth
½ teaspoon salt
⅛ teaspoon pepper
1 teaspoon dried thyme leaves
1 tablespoon olive oil
1 onion, chopped
4 cloves garlic, minced
3 carrots, sliced
1 8-ounce package sliced mushrooms
½ cup chopped toasted cashews
3 tablespoons chopped flat-leaf parsley

SERVES 6

Calories: 229.08
Fat: 6.59 grams
Fat as % of calories: 25.9%
Carbohydrates: 34.41 grams
Fiber: 7.99 grams
Sodium: 207.39 mg
Vitamin A: 15% DV
Vitamin C: 90% DV
Calcium: 143.61 mg

INGREDIENTS

1 tablespoon olive oil
1 onion, chopped
3 cloves garlic, minced
2 cups frozen lima beans
2 cups frozen soy beans
2 cups frozen cut green beans
2 tablespoons lemon juice
¼ cup vegetable broth
½ teaspoon dried thyme leaves
¼ teaspoon salt
⅛ teaspoon pepper

SERVES 8

Calories: 285.66
Fat: 8.05 grams
Fat as % of calories: 28.23%
Carbohydrates: 44.20 grams
Fiber: 3.01 grams
Sodium: 479.25 mg
Vitamin A: 50% DV
Vitamin C: 10% DV
Calcium: 92.81 mg

INGREDIENTS

1 cup brown rice
1 cup wild rice
4 cups vegetable broth
1 tablespoon butter
1 tablespoon olive oil
1 onion, chopped
3 cloves garlic, minced
1 cup shredded carrots
1 cup sliced celery
*1 10-ounce container low-fat
    Alfredo sauce*
¼ teaspoon salt
⅛ teaspoon white pepper
⅓ cup chopped flat-leaf parsley

Three-Bean Medley

*Soy beans, also known as edamame, are an excellent
source of protein, fiber, and B vitamins. This flavorful medley
is the perfect side dish for a grilled steak.*

1. In large saucepan, heat olive oil over medium heat. Add onion and garlic; cook and stir until crisp-tender, about 5 minutes. Add all three types of beans.

2. Cook and stir for 2–3 minutes. Add remaining ingredients and bring to a simmer. Cover, reduce heat to low, and simmer for 6–8 minutes or until all the beans are hot and tender. Serve immediately.

Mixed Rice Pilaf

*Read labels carefully and pick a brown rice and wild rice that need
the same amount of time to cook. Most are pretty close.*

1. In large saucepan, combine brown rice and wild rice with the vegetable broth. Bring to a simmer over medium-high heat. Cover, reduce heat to low, and simmer for 45–50 minutes or until the rice is tender.

2. Meanwhile, melt butter and olive oil in large saucepan over medium heat. Add onion and garlic; cook and stir until tender, about 7–8 minutes. Add carrots and celery; cook and stir for another 3–4 minutes. Remove from heat.

3. When rice is done, add the vegetable mixture to the rice along with the Alfredo sauce, salt, pepper, and parsley. Heat over medium-low heat, stirring frequently, until mixture begins to bubble. Serve immediately.

Chapter 10

Light Soups and Healthy Salads

SERVES 6

Calories: 272.58
Fat: 8.46 grams
Fat as % of calories: 27.9%
Carbohydrates: 37.09 grams
Fiber: 4.33 grams
Sodium: 823.28 mg
Vitamin A: 40% DV
Vitamin C: 70% DV
Calcium: 303.29 mg

INGREDIENTS

1 tablespoon butter
1 onion, chopped
4 cloves garlic, minced
4 tomatoes, chopped
½ teaspoon salt
⅛ teaspoon white pepper
½ teaspoon dried thyme leaves
½ teaspoon dried basil leaves
1 6-ounce can tomato paste
1 14.5-ounce can diced
   tomatoes, undrained
1 8-ounce can tomato sauce
3 cups chicken stock
1 13-ounce can low-fat
   evaporated milk
½ cup low-fat sour cream
3 tablespoons flour
⅓ cup crumbled bleu cheese

Tomato–Bleu Cheese Bisque

Adding fresh tomatoes to a mixture of canned tomatoes makes this soup fresh-tasting and rich. Serve with a spinach salad for a light lunch.

1. In large soup pot, melt butter over medium heat. Add onion and garlic; cook and stir for 5 minutes. Add tomatoes; cook and stir until liquid evaporates and mixture is thick.

2. Add salt, pepper, thyme, basil, tomato paste, diced tomatoes, and tomato sauce; cook and stir until mixture simmers. Add chicken stock; bring back to a simmer. Reduce heat to low and simmer for 10–15 minutes or until blended.

3. In medium bowl, combine milk, sour cream, and flour and mix well. Add ½ cup tomato mixture to milk mixture, stirring with a wire whisk to blend. Transfer all to the soup pot. Cook over low heat, stirring frequently, until soup is hot. Stir in bleu cheese and serve.

Onions

Frequently eating onions can help reduce cholesterol and lower blood pressure. The sulfur compounds that make you cry when you cut them also work their magic on your body. Onions also have quercitin, which has been found to have antitumor properties. In fact, eating lots of onions can reduce the risk of developing some types of cancer by up to 80 percent.

Lentil and Chicken Chili

This rich chili uses lentils instead of beans and adds brown rice.

1. Combine onion, garlic, and carrots in bottom of 4- to 5-quart slow cooker. Add chili powder, cumin, basil, salt, and peppers.

2. Top with lentils, rice, and chicken breasts. Pour diced tomatoes over all. In small bowl, combine tomato paste with 1 cup of the chicken stock; stir until tomato paste dissolves. Add to crockpot along with remaining chicken stock and water.

3. Cover and cook on low for 7–9 hours or until lentils and rice are tender and chicken is thoroughly cooked. Serve with sour cream and salsa, if desired.

Tomato Paste

Tomato paste is a very concentrated mixture of tomatoes and water that has been cooked until it's very thick. It adds a richness to soups, sauces, and stews that you can't get by just cooking down tomatoes. Look for low-salt varieties, since it can be quite salty. You can also find flavored varieties with onion, garlic, and herbs.

SERVES 6–8

Calories: 357.63
Fat: 3.72 grams
Fat as % of calories: 9.4%
Carbohydrates: 53.47 grams
Fiber: 15.87 grams
Sodium: 619.92 mg
Vitamin A: 70% DV
Vitamin C: 35% DV
Calcium: 78.84 mg

INGREDIENTS
2 onions, chopped
5 cloves garlic, minced
2 carrots, sliced
3 tablespoons chili powder
½ teaspoon cumin
1 teaspoon dried basil leaves
½ teaspoon salt
¼ teaspoon white pepper
⅛ teaspoon cayenne pepper
1½ cups dried lentils
½ cup brown rice
1 pound boneless, skinless
     chicken breasts, cubed
2 14.5-ounce cans diced
     tomatoes, undrained
½ cup tomato paste
4 cups low-sodium chicken
     stock
3 cups water

SERVES 6

Calories: 189.15
Fat: 6.73 grams
Fat as % of calories: 32.0%
Carbohydrates: 22.27 grams
Fiber: 4.47 grams
Sodium: 387.00 mg
Vitamin A: 40% DV
Vitamin C: 35% DV
Calcium: 104.85 mg

INGREDIENTS

1 tablespoon olive oil
1 onion, chopped
2 cloves garlic, minced
2 stalks celery, chopped
1 tablespoon curry powder
2 teaspoons sugar
¼ teaspoon salt
⅛ teaspoon pepper
1 16-ounce package frozen baby peas
2 cups vegetable broth
2 cups water
1 cup nonfat light cream
2 tablespoons lemon juice
½ cup low-fat sour cream
½ cup grated cucumber, drained
¼ cup chopped green onions
Pinch grated nutmeg

Curried Chilled Pea Soup

*This gorgeous soup has an intense spicy flavor from the curry powder,
and the sour cream topping provides a refreshing sweetness.*

1. In large soup pot, heat olive oil over medium heat. Add onion and garlic; cook and stir for 4 minutes. Add celery and curry powder; cook and stir for 4–5 minutes longer until tender.

2. Add sugar, salt, pepper, and peas; cook and stir for 2 minutes. Add broth and water; bring to a simmer. Reduce heat to low, cover pot, and simmer for 6–7 minutes until everything is tender.

3. Remove from heat and stir in light cream and lemon juice. Using an immersion blender, purée the soup. Pour into a large bowl, cover by placing plastic wrap directly on the soup, and refrigerate until cold, about 3–4 hours.

4. When ready to serve, combine sour cream, cucumber, green onion, and nutmeg in small bowl. Serve the soup in chilled bowls and top with sour cream mixture.

Curry Powder

You can easily make your own curry powder, although there are some good blends available. Combine teaspoons of cinnamon, cumin, coriander, turmeric, cloves, garlic, ginger and half teaspoons of pepper, cardamom, and onion powder. Store in a tightly sealed container in a cool, dry place, and use in everything from salad dressings to sandwiches.

Chilled Pesto Gazpacho

This simple cold soup is perfect for a hot summer's day.
Serve it on the porch with a fruit salad and
Strawberry Fudge Ice Cream Dessert (page 195) to finish.

1. Combine all ingredients except Pesto in large bowl. Cover and chill in refrigerator for 3–4 hours before serving.

2. To serve, spoon gazpacho into chilled soup bowls. Top each with a spoonful of Pesto.

SERVES 6

Calories: 177.30
Fat: 4.46 grams
Fat as % of calories: 22.6%
Carbohydrates: 32.68 grams
Fiber: 6.68 grams
Sodium: 275.87 mg
Vitamin A: 110% DV
Vitamin C: 220% DV
Calcium: 119.40 mg

INGREDIENTS

2 14.5-ounce cans diced
    tomatoes, undrained
2 cups spicy low-sodium V8 juice
1 green bell pepper, chopped
1 orange bell pepper, chopped
1 medium zucchini, chopped
2 garlic cloves, minced
½ cup chopped red onion
¼ cup chopped green onion
1 cup frozen corn, thawed
⅛ teaspoon pepper
⅓ cup orange juice
½ cup Roasted Garlic Pesto
    (page 32)

Slow Cooker Stroganoff Soup

Stroganoff made into soup makes a festive addition to any meal.
Serve in warmed soup bowls.

1. In 4-quart slow cooker, combine beef, onions, garlic, carrots, salt, thyme, pepper, beef stock, and water. Cover and cook on low for 7–8 hours or until beef and vegetables are tender.

2. In small bowl combine sour cream with flour. Add 1 cup of the hot liquid from slow cooker; mix with wire whisk. Add sour cream mixture to slow cooker. Cover and cook on high for 20–25 minutes or until soup thickens. Stir in egg noodles; cook for 6–7 minutes longer until noodles are tender.

3. Serve immediately, topped with chives.

SERVES 6

Calories: 392.62
Fat: 9.55 grams
Fat as % of calories: 21.9%
Carbohydrates: 38.00 grams
Fiber: 5.88 grams
Sodium: 471.03 mg
Vitamin A: 110%
Vitamin C: 10% DV
Calcium: 98.45 mg

INGREDIENTS

1½ pounds sirloin tip, cubed
2 onions, chopped
4 cloves garlic, minced
4 carrots, sliced
½ teaspoon salt
½ teaspoon dried thyme leaves
⅛ teaspoon pepper
4 cups low-sodium beef stock
3 cups water
1 cup low-fat sour cream
2 tablespoons flour
2 cups whole wheat egg noodles
¼ cup chopped chives

SERVES 6

Calories: 280.01
Fat: 9.62 grams
Fat as % of calories: 32.1%
Carbohydrates: 25.82 grams
Fiber: 2.75 grams
Sodium: 375.91 mg
Vitamin A: 10% DV
Vitamin C: 35% DV
Calcium: 80.09 mg

INGREDIENTS

1 tablespoon olive oil
1 onion, chopped
3 cloves garlic, minced
3 stalks celery, chopped
1 tablespoon curry powder
¼ teaspoon salt
⅛ teaspoon pepper
½ cup medium pearl barley
*1 48-ounce box low-sodium
   chicken broth*
1 green bell pepper, chopped
*1 pound medium raw shrimp,
   deveined*
½ cup nonfat light cream
½ cup coconut milk
1 tablespoon cornstarch

Curried Shrimp and Barley Soup

*This elegant soup is perfect as a first course in small portions
or as the main dish for lunch.*

1. In large soup pot, heat olive oil over medium heat. Add onion and garlic; cook and stir for 5 minutes. Add celery, curry powder, salt, and pepper; cook and stir for 2 minutes.

2. Add barley and chicken broth; bring to a simmer over medium heat. Reduce heat to low, cover, and simmer for 20 minutes. Add bell pepper and shrimp; bring back to a simmer. Simmer for 3–4 minutes or until shrimp curl and turn pink.

3. In small bowl combine cream, coconut milk, and cornstarch and mix well. Add to soup; cook and stir until soup steams; do not let it boil. Serve immediately.

Barley

Barley is packed full of fiber, which can help lower cholesterol levels and reduce LDL cholesterol (the bad cholesterol). It is delicious and slightly chewy with a nutty flavor, and it makes a perfect addition to soups and salads. Barley can also reduce the risk of developing type 2 diabetes.

Low-Fat French Onion Soup

Making this classic soup in the slow cooker helps reduce the fat. All you have to do at the end is ladle it into bowls and top with cheese toasts.

1. In 4- to 5-quart slow cooker, combine olive oil, onions, garlic, and sugar. Cover and cook on high for 1–2 hours, stirring occasionally, until the onions are deep golden brown. Halfway through cooking time, add the red wine. Do not let this burn.

2. Add carrots, Beef Stock, Chicken Stock, salt, pepper, and marjoram. Cover and cook on low for 4–5 hours. Meanwhile, in small bowl, combine cream cheese, Havarti, and Parmesan cheeses.

3. Preheat broiler. Spread cheese mixture on Bread slices and broil until cheese begins to brown. Spoon soup into hot bowls and top with Bread.

Slow-Cooking Onions

Because the onions won't fill the slow cooker at least halfway, you'll need to stir them occasionally to prevent burning. For this reason, in the first step you can't just set the slow cooker and walk away. The method used in this recipe causes the onions to become very sweet and caramelized, and they add great flavor to this classic soup.

SERVES 8

Calories: 338.85
Fat: 12.08 grams
Fat as % of calories: 32.1%
Carbohydrates: 36.99 grams
Fiber: 4.33 grams
Sodium: 462.92 mg
Vitamin A: 100% DV
Vitamin C: 15% DV
Calcium: 176.55 mg

INGREDIENTS

1 tablespoon olive oil
5 onions, chopped
4 cloves garlic, minced
1 teaspoon sugar
½ cup dry red wine
4 carrots, sliced
4 cups Healthy Beef Stock (page 160)
4 cups Healthy Chicken Stock (page 160)
½ teaspoon salt
⅛ teaspoon pepper
½ teaspoon dried marjoram leaves
1 3-ounce package low-fat cream cheese, softened
1 cup shredded Havarti cheese
2 tablespoons grated Parmesan cheese
8 slices Cracked Wheat French Bread (page 139)

SERVES 6

Calories: 366.30
Fat: 11.55 grams
Fat as % of calories: 28.4%
Carbohydrates: 45.58 grams
Fiber: 3.97 grams
Sodium: 934.82 mg
Vitamin A: 90% DV
Vitamin C: 30% DV
Calcium: 325.90 mg

INGREDIENTS

3 slices turkey bacon
1 leek, chopped
3 cloves garlic, minced
3 carrots, chopped
4 potatoes, diced
2 cups chicken stock
1 cup water
2 tablespoons butter
1 onion, chopped
3 tablespoons flour
½ teaspoon salt
¼ teaspoon white pepper
½ teaspoon dried marjoram leaves
1 13-ounce can evaporated nonfat milk
¼ cup nonfat light cream
1 cup shredded extra-sharp low-fat Cheddar cheese
¼ cup grated Parmesan cheese
¼ cup minced chives

Light Potato–Cheese Chowder

A chowder is a thicker soup, usually with added milk or cream for richness and smoothness. This light version is very flavorful.

1. In large soup pot, cook turkey bacon over medium heat until crisp. Drain bacon on paper towels, crumble, and set aside in refrigerator. Drain fat from pan; do not wipe out.

2. Cook leek, garlic, and carrots in fat remaining in pan for 5–6 minutes or until crisp-tender. Add potatoes; cook and stir for 3 minutes longer. Add chicken stock and water; bring to a boil. Reduce heat to low, cover pan, and simmer until vegetables are tender, about 13–18 minutes.

3. In another large saucepan, melt butter over medium heat. Add onion; cook and stir until tender, about 6 minutes. Add flour, salt, pepper, and marjoram to onion mixture; cook and stir until bubbly. Add milk and cream; cook and stir until mixture is thickened and starts to bubble. Remove from heat.

4. Add milk mixture to the potato mixture and stir thoroughly until combined. Add both types of cheese; cook and stir until melted. Garnish with bacon and chives and serve immediately.

Buffalo Chicken Chowder

Flavored like Buffalo chicken wings, this delicious soup is full of vitamins and minerals, and it's low fat!

1. Toss chicken with flour, salt, and pepper. Heat oil in large soup pot over medium heat. Add chicken; cook and stir until chicken is light brown; remove from pan.

2. Add butter to pot and melt. Add onion, garlic, 1½ cups celery, mushrooms, and carrots; cook and stir, scraping up drippings, until vegetables are crisp-tender, about 7–8 minutes. Return chicken to pot and add Chicken Stock.

3. Bring to a simmer, cover, reduce heat to low, and simmer for 15–20 minutes until chicken is thoroughly cooked. Stir in evaporated milk, cream, Swiss cheese, feta, and hot pepper sauce; cook and stir until cheese melts and soup is creamy.

4. In small bowl, combine tomatoes, ½ cup chopped celery, and dressing and stir well. Ladle soup into warmed bowls and top with tomato mixture; serve immediately.

SERVES 6–8

Calories: 321.03
Fat: 11.22 grams
Fat as % of calories: 31.4%
Carbohydrates: 19.86 mg
Fiber: 2.99 grams
Sodium: 658.55 mg
Vitamin A: 150% DV
Vitamin C: 20% DV
Calcium: 442.27 mg

INGREDIENTS

1½ pounds boneless, skinless chicken breasts, cubed
3 tablespoons flour
½ teaspoon salt
⅛ teaspoon cayenne pepper
1 tablespoon olive oil
1 tablespoon butter
1 onion, chopped
4 cloves garlic, minced
2 cups sliced celery, divided
1 8-ounce package sliced mushrooms
2 cups baby carrots
4 cups Healthy Chicken Stock (page 160)
1 13-ounce can nonfat evaporated milk
½ cup light cream
1½ cups shredded low-fat Swiss cheese
½ cup crumbled feta cheese
¼ teaspoon hot pepper sauce
1½ cups chopped tomatoes
⅓ cup low-fat blue cheese dressing

YIELDS 12 CUPS

Calories: 46.08
Fat: 1.56 grams
Fat as % of calories: 30%
Carbohydrates: 0.71 grams
Fiber: 0.02 grams
Sodium: 135.73 mg
Vitamin A: 10% DV
Vitamin C: 2% DV
Calcium: 6.11 mg

INGREDIENTS

2 pounds chicken bones
2 onions
4 whole cloves
3 cloves garlic, minced
4 carrots, chopped
2 stalks celery, chopped
2 teaspoons dried basil leaves
1 teaspoon dried thyme leaves
10 cups water
1 teaspoon salt
¼ teaspoon pepper

Healthy Chicken Stock

Buy whole chickens and bone-in chicken breasts and freeze the bones and skin after you've cooked the meat. When you have enough, make this recipe.

1. Place chicken bones in 6- to 7-quart slow cooker. Chop one onion and add to slow cooker; cut one onion in half. Push the whole cloves into one onion half and add to slow cooker. Add remaining ingredients.

2. Cover and cook on low for 10–12 hours or until stock tastes rich. Strain into large bowl, pressing on ingredients to remove as much juice as possible. Refrigerate stock overnight. In the morning, discard the fat. Freeze stock in 1-cup portions.

YIELDS 12 CUPS

Calories: 44.04
Fat: 1.39 grams
Fat as % of calories: 28.4%
Carbohydrates: 2.01 grams
Fiber: 0.17 grams
Sodium: 85.97 mg
Vitamin A: 10% DV
Vitamin C: 3% DV
Calcium: 7.31 mg

INGREDIENTS

3 pounds beef bones
2 onions, halved
4 carrots, pared
5 tomatoes, halved
1 8-ounce package button
    mushrooms
10 cups water
4 cloves garlic, peeled
½ teaspoon salt
¼ teaspoon pepper
1 bay leaf
1 tablespoon dried parsley leaves
1 teaspoon dried marjoram
    leaves
1 teaspoon lemon peel

Healthy Beef Stock

Making your own stock is such a satisfying enterprise, and it's easy. Ask your butcher for beef bones, and strain the stock by slowly pouring it through a large strainer into a clean stock pot.

1. Place bones, onions, carrots, tomatoes, and mushrooms in large roasting pan. Place in oven and turn to 400°F. Roast for 2½ hours, turning with spatula halfway through cooking time, until bones and vegetables are browned.

2. Place bones in 6-quart slow cooker. Chop vegetables and add to slow cooker along with water, garlic, salt, pepper, bay leaf, parsley, marjoram, and lemon peel. Cover and cook on low for 9–10 hours or until liquid tastes rich.

3. Strain liquid into large container. Press on ingredients to extract as much juice as possible. Cover and refrigerate stock overnight. The next day, remove layer of fat from top. Refrigerate up to 3 days. Freeze in 1-cup portions for longer storage.

Mixed-Berry and Greens Salad

Beautiful fresh berries are marinated in a tangy fruit vinaigrette and tossed with special lettuces in this gorgeous salad.

1. Two hours before serving, in small bowl combine strawberries and blueberries with the Vinaigrette. Toss to coat, cover, and refrigerate.

2. When ready to serve, combine lettuce, endive, and spinach in serving bowl. Top with strawberry mixture, then sprinkle with raspberries. Toss to coat and serve immediately.

Fresh Berries

Fresh berries are very perishable; buy only what you can use within two days. Do not prepare berries before you're ready to use them. Rinsing berries in advance will make them soggy and may hasten mold development. Store berries in their original container, and rinse and slice or chop berries just before serving.

Raspberry Vinaigrette

This pink vinaigrette is delicious on any plain green salad, or try it drizzled over a mixed fruit salad for lunch.

1. In food processor or blender, combine all ingredients. Process or blend until mixture is smooth.

2. Pour into small jar with tight lid. Cover and refrigerate up to 1 week, shaking the dressing vigorously before you use it.

Homemade Flavored Vinegar

It's easy to make vinegars at home. Just select any fresh herbs, spices, or fruits and rinse and dry them well. Add them to good-quality wine vinegars, cover tightly, and let stand for about a week before using. However, do not make homemade flavored oils; the risk of botulism is simply too great, even when they're refrigerated.

SERVES 8

Calories: 170.27
Fat: 5.58 grams
Fat as % of calories: 25.5%
Carbohydrates: 30.61 grams
Fiber: 4.52 grams
Sodium: 84.77 mg
Vitamin A: 40% DV
Vitamin C: 70% DV
Calcium: 43.55 mg

INGREDIENTS

2 cups strawberries, sliced
1 cup blueberries
¾ cup Raspberry Vinaigrette
   (page 161)
4 cups butter lettuce, torn
2 cups curly endive, chopped
2 cups baby spinach leaves
1 cup raspberries

YIELDS 1 CUP; SERVES 8

Calories: 168.33
Fat: 6.87 grams
Fat as % of calories: 36.7%
Carbohydrates: 27.20 grams
Fiber: 1.57 grams
Sodium: 98.49 mg
Vitamin A: 0% DV
Vitamin C: 10% DV
Calcium: 10.01 mg

INGREDIENTS

¼ cup extra-virgin olive oil
½ cup raspberry vinegar
1 cup frozen raspberries, thawed
¼ cup honey
2 tablespoons sugar
¼ teaspoon salt
⅛ teaspoon white pepper
½ teaspoon dried tarragon
   leaves
¼ cup raspberry jam
1 tablespoon Dijon mustard

**YIELDS 2 CUPS; SERVING
SIZE 2 TABLESPOONS**

Calories: 48.74
Fat: 1.75 grams
Fat as % of calories: 32.3%
Carbohydrates: 7.77 grams
Fiber: 0.16 grams
Sodium: 208.07 mg
Vitamin A: 5% DV
Vitamin C: 5% DV
Calcium: 28.72 mg

INGREDIENTS
⅔ cup ketchup
½ cup plain low-fat yogurt
⅓ cup low-fat sour cream
1 3-ounce package low-fat
   cream cheese, softened
2 tablespoons lemon juice
½ cup sweet pickle relish
1 cup baby sweet pickles, chopped
⅛ teaspoon white pepper
1 tablespoon white wine
   Worcestershire sauce

Hundred Island Dressing

*This dressing has just as much taste and much fewer calories than
Thousand Island dressing, which is usually about 70 percent fat.*

1. In blender or food processor, combine ketchup, yogurt, sour cream, cream cheese, and lemon juice and blend or process until smooth. Spoon into medium bowl.

2. Add pickle relish, pickles, pepper, and Worcestershire sauce. Mix well, cover, and refrigerate up to 1 week.

SERVES 6

Calories: 122.08
Fat: 4.22 grams
Fat as % of calories: 31.3%
Carbohydrates: 17.76 grams
Fiber: 4.25 grams
Sodium: 174.88 mg
Vitamin A: 80% DV
Vitamin C: 40% DV
Calcium: 56.62 mg

INGREDIENTS
4 cups baby spinach
2 cups butter lettuce
2 cups frozen baby peas, thawed
1 cup chopped celery
1 Granny Smith apple, chopped
½ cup Healthy Creamy
   Vinaigrette (page 163)

Simple Green Salad

*The combination of soft lettuce and spinach with crunchy celery and
apples, bathed in a sweet and spicy salad dressing, is sublime.*

In large serving bowl, combine spinach and lettuce; toss gently. Add peas, celery, and apple. Pour Vinaigrette over all and toss to coat; serve immediately.

Green Salads

Green salads are a great source of fiber. Eating a salad before dinner—as long as the dressing is used sparingly—will help fill you up so you don't eat as much of the more calorie-heavy foods. Salad greens should be prepared a couple of hours before serving. Rinse them well and wrap in a kitchen towel; roll up and store in the fridge.

Healthy Creamy Vinaigrette

Most salad dressings are at least 80 percent fat,
so they should be used in moderation.

Combine all ingredients in food processor or blender. Process or blend until smooth. Transfer to small jar with screw-top lid and refrigerate for up to 4 days. Before serving, shake vigorously to re-emulsify.

Salad Dressings

Because of the low-calorie nature of most salad dressing ingredients like fruit juices and vinegars, the oil provides most of the calories. If you include nutrient-dense ingredients like apricots and orange juice, dressings can also provide lots of vitamin C and fiber. Also choose heart-healthy fats like olive oil.

French Salad Dressing

Your own homemade salad dressing is a real treat for guests. French
dressing that contains tomato products is also called Catalina Dressing.

Combine all ingredients in food processor or blender; process or blend until smooth. Transfer to small jar with tight lid and refrigerate for up to 3 days. Shake well before using.

Chili Sauce

Look for lower-fat and low-sodium varieties of chili sauce in the supermarket. If you can't find them, you can make your own by combining ½ cup ketchup with 1–2 tablespoons horseradish, 2 tablespoons grated onion, 1 clove of minced garlic, some different types of pepper, and a tablespoon or two of mustard.

YIELDS 1½ CUPS; SERVING SIZE 3 TABLESPOONS

Calories: 93.93
Fat: 7.09 grams
Fat as % of calories: 67.9%
Carbohydrates: 7.63 grams
Fiber: 0.77 grams
Sodium: 148.23 mg
Vitamin A: 15% DV
Vitamin C: 20% DV
Calcium: 17.98 mg

INGREDIENTS
4 tablespoons extra-virgin olive oil
½ cup orange juice
¼ cup apricot nectar
½ cup chopped canned apricots
1 teaspoon grated orange zest
3 tablespoons Dijon mustard
¼ cup nonfat light cream
1 tablespoon fresh thyme leaves
½ teaspoon dried basil leaves
¼ teaspoon salt
⅛ teaspoon pepper

YIELDS 1 CUP; SERVING SIZE 2 TABLESPOONS

Calories: 43.58
Fat: 0.15 grams
Fat as % of calories: 3.1%
Carbohydrates: 11.63 grams
Fiber: 0.38 grams
Sodium: 66.57 mg
Vitamin A: 5% DV
Vitamin C: 15% DV
Calcium: 8.25 mg

INGREDIENTS
½ cup low-sodium chili sauce
2 tablespoons ketchup
½ cup chopped tomato
2 tablespoons honey
3 tablespoons lemon juice
½ teaspoon paprika
2 tablespoons minced onion
1 tablespoon Dijon mustard

SERVES 8

Calories: 317.79
Fat: 9.38 grams
Fat as % of calories: 26.5%
Carbohydrates: 49.75 grams
Fiber: 14.57 grams
Sodium: 665.88 mg
Vitamin A: 110% DV
Vitamin C: 160% DV
Calcium: 129.62 mg

INGREDIENTS

1 head cauliflower
1 head broccoli
1 cup medium pearl barley
2 15-ounce cans black beans, drained
2 cups grated carrots
1 pint grape tomatoes
¼ cup extra-virgin olive oil
½ cup orange juice
3 tablespoons Dijon mustard
1 teaspoon dried oregano leaves
Salt and cayenne pepper to taste
⅓ cup crumbled feta cheese

SERVES 6

Calories: 117.58
Fat: 4.33 grams
Fat as % of calories: 33.1%
Carbohydrates: 18.53 grams
Fiber: 2.89 grams
Sodium: 214.15 mg
Vitamin A: 45% DV
Vitamin C: 100% DV
Calcium: 63.25 mg

INGREDIENTS

3 cucumbers
½ teaspoon salt
2 15-ounce cans mandarin oranges, drained
⅓ cup sliced green onion
½ cup sour cream
¼ cup orange juice
½ teaspoon dried dill weed
⅛ teaspoon pepper

High-Fiber Barley Veggie Salad

Raw cauliflower has a delicious crunch and nutty taste. Raw broccoli has a sharper taste, so it's blanched in this easy recipe.

1. Bring a large pot of water to a boil. Remove the florets from the cauliflower; divide into 1-inch pieces and set aside. Remove the florets from the broccoli and divide into 1-inch pieces. Add to the boiling water; cook for 2 minutes, then plunge into ice water. Remove from ice water when cool. Combine with cauliflower in large bowl.

2. Cook barley as directed on package. Add to broccoli mixture along with rinsed and drained black beans and carrots. Top with grape tomatoes.

3. In small bowl, combine olive oil, orange juice, mustard, oregano, salt, cayenne pepper, and feta cheese; blend until combined. Pour over salad and toss gently. Cover and refrigerate for 3–4 hours to blend flavors.

Cucumber–Orange Salad

This refreshing salad is a great addition to grilled steak or salmon. The cucumber is sprinkled with salt to help remove some of the liquid so the finished product is creamy.

1. Peel cucumbers and cut in half; remove seeds with spoon. Slice ¼-inch thick and place in large bowl; sprinkle with salt and set aside. Let stand for 30 minutes, then drain cucumbers thoroughly. Add mandarin oranges and green onions.

2. In small bowl, combine remaining ingredients and mix well. Pour over cucumber mixture and stir to coat. Cover and chill for 2–3 hours before serving.

Creamy Apricot Gelatin Salad

This creamy salad makes a perfect side to a cold soup, or serve it alongside waffles for a great brunch.

1. In small saucepan, combine 1 cup apricot nectar with egg, ⅓ cup sugar, and flour; beat well with wire whisk. Cook over low heat, stirring constantly, until mixture boils and thickens. Remove from heat and chill until cold.

2. In large bowl, combine gelatin and ⅓ cup sugar; set aside. Drain apricot halves, discarding juice. Chop apricots into small pieces; set aside. Pour 1 cup orange juice over gelatin mixture; stir to combine.

3. Combine 1 cup orange juice and 1 cup apricot nectar in microwave-safe glass measuring cup. Microwave on full power until boiling, about 5 minutes. Immediately pour into gelatin mixture; stir until sugar and gelatin are completely dissolved. Add chopped apricots, then chill in refrigerator for 1½ hours, or until syrupy.

4. When apricot mixture is syrupy, beat the chilled flour mixture until smooth. Fold into the apricot mixture along with whipped topping. Pour into 1½-quart casserole dish, cover, and chill until set, about 4–5 hours. Cut into squares to serve.

SERVES 8

Calories: 192.86
Fat: 2.13 grams
Fat as % of calories: 9.9%
Carbohydrates: 41.31 grams
Fiber: 1.55 grams
Sodium: 31.24 mg
Vitamin A: 50% DV
Vitamin C: 90% DV
Calcium: 29.24 mg

INGREDIENTS

2 cups apricot nectar, divided
1 egg, beaten
⅔ cup sugar, divided
3 tablespoons flour
2 0.25-ounce packages
    unflavored gelatin
2 15-ounce cans apricot halves
2 cups orange juice, divided
1 cup frozen low-fat whipped
    topping, thawed

SERVES 12

Calories: 283.94
Fat: 7.67 grams
Fat as % of calories: 24.3%
Carbohydrates: 48.18 grams
Fiber: 6.19 grams
Sodium: 364.21 mg
Vitamin A: 170% DV
Vitamin C: 45% DV
Calcium: 97.08 mg

INGREDIENTS

6 russet potatoes, cubed
2 sweet potatoes, peeled and cubed
3 carrots, sliced
1 onion, chopped
6 cloves garlic, minced
2 tablespoons olive oil
1 cup plain yogurt
¼ cup lemon juice
¼ cup skim milk
½ cup low-fat mayonnaise
¼ cup Dijon mustard
¼ cup chopped fresh dill weed
2 cups frozen baby peas, thawed
1 8-ounce package sliced
    mushrooms

SERVES 6

Calories: 178.73
Fat: 3.15 grams
Fat as % of calories: 15.9%
Carbohydrates: 37.18 grams
Fiber: 4.92 grams
Sodium: 206.95 mg
Vitamin A: 15% DV
Vitamin C: 70% DV
Calcium: 102.11 mg

INGREDIENTS

3 cups shredded green cabbage
2 cups shredded red cabbage
⅓ cup chopped green onion
3 Granny Smith apples, diced
1 cup halved red grapes
1 cup chopped celery
½ cup plain yogurt
½ cup light cream
2 tablespoons sugar
2 tablespoons honey
2 tablespoons mustard
¼ teaspoon salt
1 teaspoon dried thyme leaves
⅛ teaspoon white pepper
2 tablespoons lemon juice

Potato–Vegetable Salad

*Roasting sweet potatoes, russet potatoes, carrots, onions, and garlic
makes a sweet and caramelized base for a fabulous salad.*

1. Preheat oven to 400°F. In large roasting pan, combine potatoes, carrots, onion, and garlic and toss. Drizzle with olive oil and toss again. Roast for 60–75 minutes, turning once during cooking time, until vegetables are tender and brown on the edges.

2. Meanwhile, in large bowl combine yogurt, lemon juice, milk, mayonnaise, mustard, and dill; mix well. When vegetables are tender, immediately add to yogurt mixture. Add peas and mushrooms; stir gently to coat.

3. Cover and chill for 4–5 hours before serving.

Mom's Healthy Apple Coleslaw

*Coleslaw is a wonderful accompaniment to any grilled meat, from
hamburgers to sirloin steak to chicken. The fresh taste and crunch
adds to the meal.*

1. In large bowl combine cabbages, green onion, apples, grapes, and celery and toss to mix.

2. In small bowl, combine remaining ingredients and stir until blended. Drizzle over cabbage mixture and toss to coat. Cover and chill for 2–3 hours before serving.

Chapter 11

Cookies, Brownies, and Candies You Won't Regret Eating

**YIELDS 5 DOZEN
COOKIES**

Calories: 68.02
Fat: 2.72 grams
Fat as % of calories: 35.9%
Carbohydrates: 10.53 grams
Fiber: 0.76 grams
Sodium: 36.17 mg
Vitamin A: 5% DV
Vitamin C: 2% DV
Calcium: 5.76 mg

INGREDIENTS

⅔ cup butter, softened
1 cup powdered sugar
½ teaspoon salt
1 teaspoon cinnamon
¼ teaspoon cardamom
2 egg whites
¼ cup orange juice
1½ cups all-purpose flour
¾ cup whole wheat flour
¾ cup chopped dried cherries
½ cup chopped hazelnuts
¾ cup chopped dried apricots
½ cup finely chopped dates
⅓ cup orange juice
Granulated sugar

Fruit and Spice Cookies

These cookies are filled with good things.
You could use any type of chopped dried fruits that you'd like:
raisins or dried currants would be delicious too.

1. In large bowl, beat butter with powdered sugar, salt, cinnamon, and cardamom until fluffy. Add egg whites and ¼ cup orange juice and mix well.

2. Stir in all-purpose flour and whole wheat flour until a dough forms. Add cherries, hazelnuts, apricots, and dates. Cover and chill dough for 2–3 hours.

3. Preheat oven to 350°F. Form dough into ¾-inch balls and place on ungreased cookie sheets. Bake for 12–15 minutes or until cookies are set and very light golden brown on the bottoms.

4. Immediately roll in orange juice, then in granulated sugar to coat. Cool on wire racks.

Dried Cherries

Cherries and dried cherries are very nutritious. These little fruits have beta carotene and flavonoids, including anthocyanins, which can help improve heart health by reducing bad cholesterol. Tart cherries contain compounds called SODs, which are superantioxidants. They are very effective at ridding your body of aging and dangerous free radicals.

Cranberry Meringue Drops

Meringues are the perfect nonfat cookie for any party. Folding in dried cranberries and two kinds of chocolate chips elevates them to decadent status!

1. Preheat oven to 300°F. Line two large cookie sheets with parchment paper or Silpat liners; set aside.

2. In large bowl, combine egg whites with lemon juice and salt. Beat until soft peaks form. Gradually add sugar, beating until very stiff peaks form.

3. Fold in cranberries and both kinds of chocolate. Drop by teaspoons onto prepared cookie sheets. Bake for 25–30 minutes or until cookies are set. Cool for 10 minutes, then place on wire racks to cool completely. Store in airtight containers.

YIELDS 36 COOKIES

Calories: 43.63
Fat: 1.12 grams
Fat as % of calories: 2.31%
Carbohydrates: 8.39 grams
Fiber: 0.42 grams
Sodium: 14.06 mg
Vitamin A: 2% DV
Vitamin C: 2% DV
Calcium: 3.92 mg

INGREDIENTS

3 egg whites
2 teaspoons lemon juice
⅛ teaspoon salt
⅔ cup sugar
1 cup chopped dried sweetened cranberries
½ cup mini semisweet chocolate chips
¼ cup white chocolate chips, chopped

Lemon Truffle Meringue Cookies

These little cookies are airy, creamy, dense, and light all at the same time.

1. Preheat oven to 200°F. In large bowl, combine egg whites, lemon juice, and salt; beat until foamy. Gradually add sugar, beating at high speed until sugar dissolves and meringue holds stiff peaks. Beat in vanilla.

2. Line cookie sheets with parchment paper. Drop by tablespoons onto the parchment paper. Using your finger, make an indentation in the center of each meringue. Bake for 35–45 minutes until the meringues are dry.

3. Make the Truffle mixture while the meringues are baking. Chill the filling until cold. When meringues are done, remove to wire rack to cool.

4. When the Truffle mixture is cold, beat on high speed with electric mixer until fluffy. Spoon or pipe into the indentation in the meringues. Sprinkle the Truffle mixture with some crushed candy. Store in refrigerator.

YIELDS 36 COOKIES

Calories: 84.53
Fat: 1.98 grams
Fat as % of calories: 21.1%
Carbohydrates: 15.17 grams
Fiber: 0.02 grams
Sodium: 53.09 mg
Vitamin A: 2% DV
Vitamin C: 2% DV
Calcium: 56.10 mg

INGREDIENTS

3 egg whites
2 teaspoons lemon juice
⅛ teaspoon salt
¾ cup sugar
1 teaspoon vanilla
1 recipe Low-Fat Lemon Truffles (page 170)
½ cup finely crushed lemon candy

YIELDS 36 PIECES

Calories: 151.15
Fat: 5.57 grams
Fat as % of calories: 33.1%
Carbohydrates: 24.22 grams
Fiber: 0.62 grams
Sodium: 53.57 mg
Vitamin A: 10% DV
Vitamin C: 0% DV
Calcium: 25.61 mg

INGREDIENTS

1 cup brown sugar
1 cup granulated sugar
½ cup powdered sugar
1 cup skim milk
⅓ cup corn syrup
*1 10-ounce bag large
     marshmallows*
1½ cups peanut butter
2 teaspoons vanilla

Low-Fat Peanut Butter Fudge

*Three kinds of sugar give a depth of flavor and smoothness to this easy
microwave peanut butter fudge.*

1. Grease a 13" x 9" pan with unsalted butter and set aside. In large micro-wave-safe bowl, combine brown sugar, granulated sugar, powdered sugar, skim milk, and corn syrup; mix well. Microwave on high for 2 minutes, remove and stir. Rinse spoon. Microwave for 2 minutes longer, remove, and stir. Microwave for 2 minutes, then remove.

2. Stir in marshmallows until melted. Add peanut butter and vanilla and mix well. Spoon into prepared pan and refrigerate until set. Cut into squares.

YIELDS 36 TRUFFLES

Calories: 66.90
Fat: 1.98 grams
Fat as % of calories: 26.6%
Carbohydrates: 10.96 grams
Fiber: 0.02 grams
Sodium: 40.45 mg
Vitamin A: 2% DV
Vitamin C: 2% DV
Calcium: 55.94 mg

INGREDIENTS

*1 13-ounce can low-fat
     sweetened condensed milk*
⅓ cup lemon juice
*1 8-ounce package low-fat
     cream cheese, softened*
1 cup white chocolate chips
*2 teaspoons finely grated lemon
     peel*
Powdered sugar

Low-Fat Lemon Truffles

*You can serve these lemony and creamy truffles as is or use as a filling
in Lemon Truffle Meringue Cookies (page 169).*

1. In small bowl, combine milk with lemon juice and mix until smooth. Set aside. In large bowl, beat cream cheese until soft and fluffy. Gradually beat in milk mixture until smooth.

2. Place white chocolate chips and lemon peel in small microwave-safe bowl. Microwave on 30 percent power for 2 minutes, then remove and stir. Continue microwaving for 30-second intervals on 30 percent power, stirring after each interval, until chips are melted.

3. Gradually beat the chocolate mixture into the cream cheese mixture. Cover and chill until firm, about 4–5 hours.

4. Form mixture into ¾-inch balls and roll in powdered sugar to coat. Store in refrigerator.

Fruity Chocolate Shortbread

Shortbread is traditionally very high in fat. This version adds egg whites to lower the fat content while maintaining the crisp texture.

1. Preheat oven to 325°F. Spray a 13" x 9" baking pan with nonstick baking spray containing flour and set aside.

2. In large bowl, combine butter with brown sugar and beat until fluffy. Add egg whites, vanilla, and salt and mix well. Add 1¼ cups all-purpose flour and ¾ cup whole wheat flour and stir until a dough forms.

3. Toss apricots, cherries, and cranberries with remaining ¼ cup all-purpose flour and mix into dough. Press dough into prepared baking pan. Bake for 20–25 minutes or until shortbread is set. Cool completely on wire rack.

4. Microwave chocolate chips in a microwave-safe bowl on 50 percent power for 2 minutes, then remove and stir until smooth. Stir cherries and blueberries into chocolate.

5. Cut shortbread into 36 pieces. Dip the bottom third of each piece into chocolate mixture to coat. Place on waxed paper until chocolate sets.

Cranberries

Cranberries can promote health in a number of ways. They are high in compounds called proanthocyanidins, which can help ward off infection by destroying E. coli bacteria in the stomach. They may also help prevent ulcers and are naturally high in fiber, vitamin C, and vitamin A. When dried and sweetened, they are an excellent snack food.

SERVES 36

Calories: 147.31
Fat: 4.92 grams
Fat as % of calories: 30.0%
Carbohydrates: 25.50 grams
Fiber: 1.72 grams
Sodium: 45.77 mg
Vitamin A: 10% DV
Vitamin C: 2% DV
Calcium: 15.03 mg

INGREDIENTS

10 tablespoons butter, softened
1 cup brown sugar
2 egg whites
2 teaspoons vanilla
¼ teaspoon salt
1½ cups all-purpose flour, divided
¾ cup whole wheat pastry flour
½ cup chopped dried apricots
½ cup chopped dried cherries
½ cup chopped dried cranberries
1 cup dark chocolate chips
⅓ cup chopped dried cherries
⅓ cup chopped dried blueberries

SERVES 24

Calories: 176.75
Fat: 6.71 grams
Fat as % of calories: 34.1%
Carbohydrates: 27.90 grams
Fiber: 2.39 grams
Sodium: 107.36 mg
Vitamin A: 4% DV
Vitamin C: 0% DV
Calcium: 39.83 mg

INGREDIENTS

½ cup water
⅓ cup butter
1 cup cocoa powder
1 cup sugar
¾ cup brown sugar
½ cup low-fat sour cream
1 cup all-purpose flour
1 cup whole wheat pastry flour
1 teaspoon baking powder
½ teaspoon baking soda
¼ teaspoon salt
2 teaspoons vanilla
2 eggs
4 egg whites
1 cup mini marshmallows
½ cup chopped toasted
    hazelnuts
½ cup dark chocolate chips

New and Improved Rocky Road Brownies

*These rich and fudgy brownies have less fat and
more fiber than traditional brownies.*

1. Preheat oven to 325°F. In a large microwave-safe bowl, combine water, butter, and cocoa powder. Microwave on high for 1 minute, then remove and stir. Continue microwaving on high at 30-second intervals until mixture boils.

2. Remove from microwave and add sugar and brown sugar; mix well. Add sour cream, all-purpose flour, whole wheat pastry flour, baking powder, baking soda, salt, and vanilla and mix until combined.

3. Stir in eggs and egg whites until blended. Pour into prepared pan. Bake for 22–26 minutes or until brownies are set.

4. Immediately sprinkle with marshmallows; return to oven. Bake for 3–4 minutes longer until marshmallows puff. Remove from oven and sprinkle with hazelnuts and dark chocolate chips. Cool on wire rack, then cut into squares.

Rocky Road

Rocky road is traditionally a combination of milk chocolate, marshmallows, and nuts. By using dark chocolate, egg whites, and heart-healthy nuts, you get almost the same taste with less sugar and fat, including more healthy fats. Toasting the nuts intensifies the flavor and lets you use less.

Low-Fat Cream Cheese Frosting

You can spread this frosting on any simple cookie or cake or use it to make a quick snack for your kids by spreading it between graham crackers.

1. In a large bowl, combine butter, all of the cream cheese, and sour cream; beat well until fluffy.

2. Add half of the powdered sugar; beat until fluffy. Stir in vanilla and salt and beat well. Add remaining powdered sugar, beating constantly until frosting reaches desired spreading consistency.

Frostings

You can flavor frosting in many different ways. This frosting, even though it has cream cheese and sour cream, can be transformed into a chocolate frosting by beating in 2 ounces of melted unsweetened chocolate. Or create a caramel frosting by stirring in ½ cup caramel ice cream topping.

High-Fiber Ginger Creams

These soft and slightly chewy cookies have a subtle crunch from the wheat germ and flaxseed. They're delicious with the Cream Cheese Frosting.

1. Preheat oven to 375°F. In a large bowl, combine butter, brown sugar, and egg and beat until fluffy. Add molasses, honey, orange juice, and vanilla and beat until smooth.

2. In a medium bowl, combine flours, wheat germ, flaxseed, ginger, cinnamon, salt, and baking soda and mix well. Add to butter mixture and stir until a batter forms.

3. Drop batter by teaspoons onto ungreased cookie sheets. Bake for 9–12 minutes or until cookies are set and light golden brown. Cool on sheet for 4 minutes, then remove to wire racks to cool completely.

4. When cookies are cool, frost with the Frosting. Store covered at room temperature.

YIELDS 2 CUPS; SERVING SIZE 2 TABLESPOONS

Calories: 139.27
Fat: 3.15 grams
Fat as % of calories: 20.4%
Carbohydrates: 26.10 grams
Fiber: 0.0 grams
Sodium: 104.38 mg
Vitamin A: 4% DV
Vitamin C: 0% DV
Calcium: 31.55 mg

INGREDIENTS

2 tablespoons butter, softened
1 3-ounce package low-fat cream cheese, softened
2 3-ounce packages nonfat cream cheese, softened
⅓ cup low-fat sour cream
4 cups powdered sugar
2 teaspoons vanilla
⅛ teaspoon salt

YIELDS 24 COOKIES

Calories: 157.56
Fat: 4.46 grams
Fat as % of calories: 25.5%
Carbohydrates: 27.67 grams
Fiber: 1.18 grams
Sodium: 71.92 mg
Vitamin A: 4% DV
Vitamin C: 4% DV
Calcium: 29.41 mg

INGREDIENTS

⅓ cup butter, softened
½ cup brown sugar
1 egg
¼ cup molasses
¼ cup honey
½ cup orange juice
1 teaspoon vanilla
1 cup whole wheat pastry flour
1 cup all-purpose flour
¼ cup wheat germ
2 tablespoons flaxseed, ground
2 teaspoons ground ginger
½ teaspoon cinnamon
¼ teaspoon salt
1 teaspoon baking soda
½ recipe Low-Fat Cream Cheese Frosting (page 173)

SERVES 24

Calories: 259.42
Fat: 11.00 grams
Fat as % of calories: 38.4%
Carbohydrates: 41.44 grams
Fiber: 3.34 grams
Sodium: 16.06 mg
Vitamin A: 30% DV
Vitamin C: 0% DV
Calcium: 58.19 mg

INGREDIENTS

*8-ounce milk chocolate bar,
    chopped
2 8-ounce dark chocolate bars,
    chopped
1 cup toasted slivered almonds
1½ cups mini marshmallows
1½ cups chopped dried apricots
1½ cups chopped dried cherries
1 cup dried currants*

Rocky Road Fruit Bark

This chewy, crunchy, and sweet candy is a real treat that everyone will love. You can use your own favorite dried fruits to make it your own.

1. Combine milk chocolate and all but ⅓ cup of the dark chocolate in large microwave-safe bowl. Microwave on 50 percent power for 2 minutes, then remove and stir. Continue microwaving on 50 percent power for 30-second intervals, stirring after each interval, until chocolate is melted and smooth.

2. Remove from microwave and stir in reserved chocolate until melted and smooth. Add remaining ingredients, stirring gently just to combine.

3. Spoon mixture onto prepared pan and spread evenly. Chill in refrigerator until set. Break candy into pieces, then store in airtight container at room temperature.

YIELDS 36

Calories: 86.68
Fat: 8.20 grams
Fat as % of calories: 85.1%
Carbohydrates: 7.01 grams
Fiber: 0.73 grams
Sodium: 18.19 mg
Vitamin A: 2% DV
Vitamin C: 0% DV
Calcium: 12.03 mg

INGREDIENTS

*12 ounces bittersweet chocolate,
    chopped
4 ounces semisweet chocolate,
    chopped
3 tablespoons butter
1 cup heavy cream
2 teaspoons vanilla
⅛ teaspoon salt
⅓ cup sifted cocoa powder*

Low-Carb Truffles

Do not use baking chocolate in this recipe; use a high-quality brand, like Callebaut or Scharffen Berger.

1. Place the chocolates in a large bowl. In small saucepan, combine butter and cream; heat over low heat until steam begins to rise and bubbles form around the edges. Pour over chocolate.

2. Immediately begin stirring the mixture; stir until chocolate melts and mixture is smooth. Add vanilla and salt and mix well.

3. Cover and chill mixture for 4–5 hours until firm. Then beat mixture at high speed until fluffy, about 3–5 minutes. Return to refrigerator to chill until firm, about 1 hour.

4. Shape mixture into 36 truffles. Roll truffles in the cocoa powder, shaking off excess. Store tightly covered at room temperature.

Light Peanut Butter and Cherry Cookies

The dried cherries have the flavor of jelly with more fiber and less sugar. These little cookies are pretty and elegant too.

1. Preheat oven to 350°F. In large bowl, combine peanut butter with butter; beat until smooth. Add brown sugar; beat until fluffy. Add egg whites and beat until combined. Stir in vanilla.

2. Add baking soda and flours and mix until a dough forms. Stir in dried cherries. Form into ¾-inch balls and place on ungreased cookie sheets. Flatten with a drinking glass dipped into sugar.

3. Bake for 9–13 minutes or until cookies are set. Remove from cookie sheets and cool on wire rack. Drizzle cooled cookies with melted chocolate. Store tightly covered at room temperature.

YIELDS 36 COOKIES

Calories: 99.35
Fat: 3.40 grams
Fat as % of calories: 30.8%
Carbohydrates: 16.18 grams
Sodium: 63.07 mg
Fiber: 0.77 grams
Vitamin A: 15% DV
Vitamin C: 0% DV
Calcium: 15.49 mg

INGREDIENTS
½ cup peanut butter
¼ cup butter, softened
1¼ cups brown sugar
3 egg whites
1 teaspoon vanilla
1 teaspoon baking soda
1 cup all-purpose flour
¾ cup whole wheat pastry flour
1 cup chopped dried cherries
¼ cup dark chocolate chips, melted

Butterscotch Chocolate Brownies

These brownies are nice and chewy because of all of the brown sugar and the egg whites. You can glaze them with dark chocolate if you'd like.

1. Preheat oven to 350°F. In medium saucepan, melt butter over medium heat. Reduce heat to low and cook butter, watching carefully, until butter turns brown, about 9–10 minutes. Remove from heat and pour into large bowl; stir in cocoa.

2. Stir in brown sugar and granulated sugar, then beat in egg, egg whites, and vanilla. Stir in all-purpose flour, whole wheat flour, baking powder, baking soda, and salt and mix just until combined.

3. Spoon and spread in prepared pan. Bake for 25–30 minutes or until brownies are just set and begin to pull away from sides of pan. Cool completely on wire rack, then store in airtight container at room temperature.

SERVES 24

Calories: 167.92
Fat: 5.60 grams
Fat as % of calories: 30.0%
Carbohydrates: 28.16 grams
Fiber: 0.91 grams
Sodium: 145.98 mg
Vitamin A: 4% DV
Vitamin C: 0% DV
Calcium: 32.43 mg

INGREDIENTS
⅔ cup butter
⅓ cup cocoa powder
1½ cups brown sugar
¾ cup granulated sugar
1 egg
4 egg whites
2 teaspoons vanilla
1½ cups all-purpose flour
½ cup whole wheat pastry flour
1 teaspoon baking powder
1 teaspoon baking soda
¼ teaspoon salt

Calories: 129.26
Fat: 4.23 grams
Fat as % of calories: 29.5%
Carbohydrates: 21.05 grams
Fiber: 1.78 grams
Sodium: 57.37 mg
Vitamin A: 4% DV
Vitamin C: 4% DV
Calcium: 12.94 mg

INGREDIENTS

⅓ cup canola oil
¼ cup butter, softened
¼ cup low-fat sour cream
1 cup brown sugar
¾ cup granulated sugar
2 tablespoons honey
2 teaspoons vanilla
4 egg whites
3 tablespoons orange juice
1 cup all-purpose flour
1 cup whole wheat pastry flour
1 teaspoon baking soda
½ teaspoon salt
2 cups oatmeal
¼ cup oat bran
1 cup chopped walnuts
1½ cups chopped dried
    blueberries

Blueberry Oatmeal Cookies

Oatmeal cookies should be crisp when you bite into them, then chewy as you eat them. These, despite being low fat, are just perfect.

1. Preheat oven to 350°F. In large bowl, combine oil, butter, sour cream, brown sugar, granulated sugar, honey, and vanilla and beat well. Add egg whites and orange juice and mix until combined.

2. Add all-purpose flour, whole wheat flour, baking soda, and salt and mix until a dough forms. Stir in remaining ingredients.

3. Drop by teaspoonfuls onto ungreased cookie sheets. Bake for 10–14 minutes or until cookies are light brown and set. Cool on wire racks.

Dried Blueberries

Dried blueberries, especially those made from wild blueberries, have some of the highest levels of antioxidants of any food. They're chewy and delicious and perfect for folding into everything from simple cookies to cakes to chicken salad. They're also great for kid's snacking, especially when combined with granola and nuts.

Blueberry Cream Cheese Bars

These pretty bars have a creamy filling and intense blueberry topping.

1. Preheat oven to 350°F. In medium bowl, combine flours, brown sugar, and oatmeal and mix well. Cut in butter until particles are fine. Stir in orange juice until crumbly. Press into 13" x 9" pan. Bake for 12 minutes, then cool.

2. In large bowl, beat cream cheese until fluffy. Add condensed milk, then add egg and egg whites and beat until smooth. Pour over crust. Bake for 25–35 minutes until filling is set. Cool completely.

3. In small bowl, combine pie filling, dried blueberries, and lemon juice. Spoon and spread over bars; cover and chill for 4–6 hours before serving.

Dried Fruit

Dried fruits are very good for you but relatively high in calories. Because the water has been evaporated, the sugars are concentrated, making them sweeter than their fresh counterparts. Dried fruits are high in fiber, potassium, and anti-oxidants. In fact, dried wild blueberries have the highest antioxidant count of any fruit or vegetable.

SERVES 36

Calories: 181.95
Fat: 4.78 grams
Fat as % of calories: 23.6%
Carbohydrates: 28.22 grams
Fiber: 1.65 grams
Sodium: 78.45 mg
Vitamin A: 5% DV
Vitamin C: 20% DV
Calcium: 181.95 mg

INGREDIENTS

¾ cup all-purpose flour
½ cup whole wheat flour
⅓ cup brown sugar
1 cup regular oatmeal
⅓ cup butter, softened
¼ cup orange juice
2 8-ounce packages low-fat cream cheese, softened
1 8-ounce package nonfat cream cheese, softened
1 14-ounce can low-fat sweetened condensed milk
1 egg
3 egg whites
1 15-ounce can blueberry pie filling
1 cup dried blueberries
2 tablespoons lemon juice

YIELDS 36 BARS

Calories: 149.82
Fat: 5.04 grams
Fat as % of calories: 30.3%
Carbohydrates: 23.88 grams
Fiber: 1.92 grams
Sodium: 59.13 mg
Vitamin A: 5% DV
Vitamin C: 3% DV
Calcium: 26.81 mg

INGREDIENTS

1½ cups brown sugar, divided
1 cup all-purpose flour
½ cup whole wheat flour
½ teaspoon baking powder
¼ teaspoon salt
1 cup regular oatmeal
⅓ cup butter, softened
¼ cup orange juice
2 eggs
2 egg whites
1 teaspoon vanilla
2 cups Mixed Nut Granola (page 51)

YIELDS 48 COOKIES

Calories: 85.38
Fat: 6.52 grams
Fat as % of calories: 68.7%
Carbohydrates: 6.49 grams
Fiber: 0.73 grams
Sodium: 51.79 mg
Vitamin A: 2% DV
Vitamin C: 2% DV
Calcium: 15.52 mg

INGREDIENTS

1 cup butter, softened
½ cup almond paste
1 cup brown sugar Splenda
2 tablespoons orange juice
1 teaspoon vanilla
½ teaspoon almond extract
1½ cups almond flour
½ cup whole wheat pastry flour
½ teaspoon xanthan gum
½ teaspoon salt
½ cup ground almonds

Granola Chews

These chewy bars are filled with goodness, including nuts and dried fruit.

1. Preheat oven to 350°F. In large bowl combine ½ cup brown sugar, flours, baking powder, salt, and oatmeal. Cut in butter, then add orange juice and stir until crumbly. Press into a 13" x 9" pan. Bake for 12–15 minutes until set.

2. In same bowl, combine eggs, egg whites, 1 cup brown sugar, and vanilla and beat until combined. Stir in Granola. Pour over the crust and spread evenly.

3. Bake for 20–30 minutes until the filling is just set and golden brown on top. Cool completely on wire rack, then cut into bars to serve.

Low-Carb Caramel Cookies

These flavorful cookies are crumbly and tender. Handle them carefully, because they're fragile.

1. In large bowl, combine butter, almond paste, and Splenda and beat until well mixed. Add orange juice, vanilla, and almond extract and beat well.

2. Stir in flours, xanthan gum, salt, and ground almonds and mix well. Form into two 12-inch rolls, about 1½ inches in diameter, and wrap well in plastic wrap. Chill for at least 6 hours.

3. When ready to bake, preheat oven to 350°F. Slice dough into ¼-inch thick rounds and place on ungreased cookie sheets. Bake for 8–12 minutes or until cookies are light golden brown. Cool on cookie sheets for 3 minutes, then remove to wire racks to cool.

Soft Frosted Apricot Cookies

These beautiful cookies are soft and tender with
a wonderful apricot flavor—yum!

1. Preheat oven to 350°F. In large bowl, combine ⅓ cup butter and 3 ounces cream cheese; beat until fluffy. Add brown sugar and granulated sugar; beat until smooth. Add apricot nectar, egg whites, and 1 teaspoon vanilla and mix.

2. In medium bowl, stir together flours, salt, baking powder, baking soda, and cardamom. Add to butter mixture and mix until a dough forms. Stir in dried apricots.

3. Drop cookies by tablespoons onto greased baking sheets. Bake for 12–16 minutes or until cookies are golden brown. Remove to wire racks to cool.

4. In small saucepan, melt 3 tablespoons butter over low heat. Cook until butter turns brown, about 4–5 minutes. Remove to large bowl and cool. Beat in 8 ounces cream cheese, then add powdered sugar, apricot preserves, and 1 teaspoon vanilla; beat well. Frost cooled cookies.

YIELDS 36 COOKIES

Calories: 182.54
Fat: 4.39 grams
Fat as % of calories: 21.6%
Carbohydrates: 34.89 grams
Fiber: 1.62 grams
Sodium: 112.61 mg
Vitamin A: 15% DV
Vitamin C: 3% DV
Calcium: 35.82 mg

INGREDIENTS

⅓ cup butter, softened
1 3-ounce package low-fat cream cheese
1 cup brown sugar
½ cup granulated sugar
⅓ cup apricot nectar
2 egg whites
2 teaspoons vanilla, divided
1½ cups all-purpose flour
1 cup whole wheat pastry flour
½ teaspoon salt
1 teaspoon baking powder
½ teaspoon baking soda
¼ teaspoon cardamom
2 cups chopped dried apricots
3 tablespoons butter, softened
1 8-ounce package low-fat cream cheese, softened
3 cups powdered sugar
¼ cup apricot preserves

Calories: 140.85
Fat: 4.19 grams
Fat as % of calories: 26.8%
Carbohydrates: 24.80 grams
Fiber: 1.08 grams
Sodium: 85.35 mg
Vitamin A: 3% DV
Vitamin C: 3% DV
Calcium: 34.37 mg

INGREDIENTS

⅓ cup butter
1⅓ cups brown sugar
¼ cup honey
¼ cup orange juice
1 egg
2 egg whites
2 teaspoons vanilla
1 cup all-purpose flour
½ cup whole wheat flour
2 tablespoons flaxseed, ground
1 teaspoon baking powder
¼ teaspoon salt
½ cup sliced almonds, toasted
½ cup toffee bits

Healthy Norwegian Brownies

*These blond brownies are chewy, sweet,
and nutty—all at the same time.*

1. Preheat oven to 350°F. Spray a 9-inch square pan with nonstick baking spray containing flour and set aside.

2. In large bowl, combine butter, brown sugar, honey, and orange juice and mix well. Add egg, egg whites, and vanilla and beat until combined.

3. Stir in flours, flaxseed, baking powder, and salt, then add almonds and toffee bits. Spread into prepared pan. Bake for 19–23 minutes or until brownies are just set. Cool completely, then cut into bars.

Toasting Nuts

To toast nuts, spread them evenly on a cookie sheet and bake them in a preheated 350°F oven for 10–15 minutes, shaking once during baking time, until the nuts are fragrant and turn a deeper brown. If you toast nuts before chopping them, let them cool completely first or they could become mushy.

Coco-Mocha Divinity

Divinity is a nonfat candy; add some cocoa powder, coconut, and coffee and it becomes a decadent treat with very little fat.

1. In small bowl, combine cocoa powder, espresso powder, melted butter, and 1 tablespoon water and mix well; set aside.

2. Put the egg whites in a large mixing bowl and let stand at room temperature. In a large saucepan, combine sugar, salt, corn syrup, ⅓ cup water, and vanilla; stir over medium heat until sugar dissolves. When it comes to a boil, reduce heat to medium low and cover for 3 minutes.

3. Uncover saucepan and cook candy, without stirring, until it reaches 246°F on a candy thermometer.

4. When syrup reaches 246°F, start beating egg whites in a stand mixer. Beat until stiff peaks form. When the syrup reaches 250°F, slowly beat the syrup into the egg whites in a thin stream, beating constantly.

5. Beat until mixture begins to look slightly dull, not glossy. When it begins to firm, beat in the cocoa mixture, then fold in the coconut. Quickly drop by tablespoons onto waxed paper and let stand until firm. Store in airtight container at room temperature.

Coconut

Coconut is a whole food; it's high in fiber and healthy fats, including lauric acid, an essential fatty acid. To toast it, spread on a small cookie sheet and bake in a preheated 350°F toaster oven until golden brown, about 8–10 minutes, stirring twice during baking time.

YIELDS 36 CANDIES

Calories: 71.00
Fat: 1.50 grams
Fat as % of calories: 19.0%
Carbohydrates: 14.83 grams
Fiber: 0.46 grams
Sodium: 8.34 mg
Vitamin A: 0% DV
Vitamin C: 0% DV
Calcium: 2.34 mg

INGREDIENTS
⅓ cup cocoa powder
1 tablespoon instant espresso powder
2 tablespoons butter, melted
⅓ cup plus 1 tablespoon water
2 egg whites
2½ cups sugar, divided
¼ teaspoon salt
½ cup corn syrup
1½ teaspoons vanilla
1 cup toasted coconut

**YIELDS 4 DOZEN
COOKIES**

Calories: 194.38
Fat: 7.01 grams
Fat as % of calories: 32.4%
Carbohydrates: 30.41 grams
Fiber: 2.42 grams
Sodium: 94.91 mg
Vitamin A: 15% DV
Vitamin C: 2% DV
Calcium: 27.91 mg

INGREDIENTS

½ cup butter, softened
1½ cups peanut butter
1 cup brown sugar
½ cup powdered sugar
⅓ cup honey
1 egg
4 egg whites
2 teaspoons vanilla
1 cup all-purpose flour
⅓ cup whole wheat pastry flour
½ teaspoon baking powder
½ teaspoon baking soda
½ teaspoon salt
2½ cups regular oatmeal
½ cup oat bran
1 cup dried currants
1 cup dried cherries
1 cup dried cranberries
½ cup cherry jelly

Oatmeal PBJ Cookies

*Peanut butter, oatmeal, and lots of dried fruit
make this cookie hearty and delicious.*

1. Preheat oven to 325°F. In large bowl, combine butter and peanut butter; beat until smooth. Add brown sugar and beat well. Then stir in powdered sugar, honey, egg, egg whites, and vanilla.

2. Add the flours, baking powder, baking soda, and salt and stir until a dough forms. Stir in oatmeal and oat bran, then add the dried fruit.

3. Drop dough by tablespoons onto a Silpat-lined cookie sheet. Using your thumb, make an indentation in each cookie and top with ½ teaspoon of jelly. Bake for 12–16 minutes or until cookies are set. Cool for 5 minutes on cookie sheets, then remove to wire rack to cool.

Xanthan Gum

When you're baking with nongluten flours, which are also lower-carb flours, you have to add something to give the cookies structure. Xanthan gum, which is easily found in health food stores and online, provides the structure just as gluten does. It's a dense powder; measure it carefully and be sure it's well mixed into the dough.

Chapter 12

Cakes, Pies, and Other Desserts You Can Indulge In

INGREDIENTS

7 Granny Smith apples
2 tablespoons lemon juice
½ cup brown sugar
⅓ cup orange juice
¼ cup flour
¼ teaspoon salt
1 teaspoon cinnamon
¼ teaspoon nutmeg
⅛ teaspoon cardamom
*10 9" x 14" sheets frozen phyllo
  dough, thawed*
2 tablespoons butter, melted
2 tablespoons honey
5 tablespoons ground almonds
5 tablespoons granulated sugar
1 tablespoon butter, melted

Mom's Lighter Apple Pie

*This gorgeous pie uses a butter, honey, and
almond mixture to layer between the sheets of phyllo dough.
Serve it warm with a scoop of raspberry sorbet.*

1. Preheat oven to 375°F. Spray a 9-inch pie pan with butter-flavored non-stick cooking spray and set aside. Peel, core, and slice apples ½-inch thick, sprinkling with lemon juice as you work.

2. In large saucepan, combine apples, brown sugar, orange juice, flour, salt, cinnamon, nutmeg, and cardamom. Bring to a simmer over medium heat, then reduce heat to low and simmer until apples are crisp-tender, about 8–10 minutes. Remove from heat and set aside.

3. Place 1 sheet of the phyllo dough on work surface. In small bowl, combine melted butter and honey and mix well. Brush butter mixture over dough and sprinkle with 1 tablespoon almonds and 1 tablespoon granulated sugar. Top with another layer of dough. Repeat this process until you have five stacks of dough, each two layers thick.

4. Place dough in prepared pan, starting from just below the lip of the pan, letting the dough fall across the bottom and over the other edge. Spray with butter-flavored nonstick cooking spray and layer another stack on top, turning it slightly so about ⅓ of the pie plate is covered. Continue in this manner until the pan is covered with the dough stacks.

5. Spoon in the apple filling. Gently pull the overhanging edges of phyllo dough over the filling, pleating to fit. Brush with 1 tablespoon butter. Bake for 23–30 minutes or until dough is golden brown and crisp and apples are bubbling and tender. Let cool for 1 hour, then serve.

Low-Fat Brownie Pie

This pie, because it has a crust based on egg whites, has less fat than traditional dessert pies. You can fill it with whatever you'd like. A combination of fruit and chocolate sorbet is low-fat and sublime.

1. Preheat oven to 325°F. Spray a 9-inch pie plate with nonstick baking spray containing flour and set aside. In large bowl, beat egg whites with salt and cream of tartar until soft peaks form. Gradually add sugar, beating until very stiff peaks form. Beat in cocoa, then fold in crushed cookies and vanilla.

2. Spread mixture into prepared pie plate. Bake for 20–30 minutes or until the crust is set. Cool completely on wire rack.

3. When crust is cool, let sorbet stand at room temperature for 15 minutes to soften. Fold in strawberries. Pile into pie crust, cover, and freeze for at least 4 hours or until firm. Let pie stand at room temperature for 20 minutes before serving for easier slicing.

SERVES 10

Calories: 215.69
Fat: 5.89
Fat as % of calories: 24.6%
Carbohydrates: 39.53 grams
Fiber: 2.04 grams
Sodium: 208.72 mg
Vitamin A: 2% DV
Vitamin C: 25% DV
Calcium: 64.66 mg

INGREDIENTS
3 egg whites
⅛ teaspoon salt
⅛ teaspoon cream of tartar
½ cup sugar
2 tablespoons cocoa powder
1 cup crushed plain chocolate wafer cookies
1 teaspoon vanilla
3 cups sugar-free chocolate sorbet
1 cup chopped strawberries

Light 'n Creamy Orange Eggnog Pie

This festive pie could be garnished with some Candied Citrus Peel (page 198) or grated dark chocolate for a beautiful finish.

1. In small bowl, combine gelatin and ⅓ cup orange juice; mix well and set aside. Drain the mandarin oranges on a paper towel, discarding juice; set aside.

2. In large saucepan, combine sugar, flour, salt, and orange zest and mix well with wire whisk. Gradually stir in ½ cup orange juice and eggnog. Cook over medium heat, stirring constantly, until mixture thickens.

3. Remove from heat and stir in softened gelatin; mix until dissolved. Stir in vanilla. Cut orange segments into 3 pieces each; fold into eggnog mixture along with 1¼ cups of the whipped topping.

4. Spoon mixture into Pie Crust. Top with remaining ¾ cup whipped topping. Cover and chill for 4–6 hours or until set. Cut into wedges to serve.

SERVES 8

Calories: 368.42
Fat: 13.69 grams
Fat as % of calories: 33.3%
Carbohydrates: 55.59 grams
Fiber: 2.59 grams
Sodium: 157.60 mg
Vitamin A: 20% DV
Vitamin C: 50% DV
Calcium: 103.66 mg

INGREDIENTS
1 0.25-ounce envelope unflavored gelatin
⅓ cup orange juice
1 15-ounce can mandarin oranges
½ cup sugar
3 tablespoons flour
⅛ teaspoon salt
2 teaspoons orange zest
½ cup orange juice
1½ cups low-fat eggnog
2 teaspoons vanilla
2 cups frozen nondairy low-fat whipped topping, thawed, divided
1 recipe Crunchy Whole Wheat Pie Crust (page 188), cooled

Calories: 344.41
Fat: 10.76 grams
Fat as % of calories: 28.1%
Carbohydrates: 60.83 grams
Fiber: 5.01 grams
Sodium: 143.43 mg
Vitamin A: 6% DV
Vitamin C: 15% DV
Calcium: 71.56 mg

INGREDIENTS

*1 0.25-ounce package
   unflavored gelatin*
¾ cup orange juice, divided
2 cups finely chopped dates
¼ cup brown sugar
¼ teaspoon salt
⅛ teaspoon cardamom
½ cup skim milk
1 egg
1½ teaspoons vanilla
*1 cup nonfat frozen whipped
   topping, thawed*
*1 Whole Wheat Pie Crust (page
   188), baked and cooled*
*3 tablespoons Candied Citrus
   Peel (page 198)*

Fluffy Date Pie

*Don't use the prechopped dates packaged in the supermarket;
they are too hard and stiff for this recipe.*

1. In small bowl combine gelatin and ¼ cup orange juice; set aside. In large saucepan combine remaining ½ cup orange juice, dates, brown sugar, salt, cardamom, and milk. Cook and stir over medium heat for 8 minutes until dates begin to melt.

2. Beat egg in small bowl; stir in ½ cup of the hot date mixture, beating well. Add to mixture in saucepan. Continue to cook and stir over medium heat until mixture thickens, about 3–4 minutes. Remove from heat.

3. Stir in softened gelatin mixture and vanilla and mix until gelatin dissolves. Cover and chill until mixture begins to set, about 1 hour.

4. Beat date mixture well, then fold in the whipped topping. Spoon into Pie Crust, then top with Candied Citrus Peel. Cover and chill pie for 3–4 hours, then serve.

Dates

Dates are a very sweet fruit, but they are naturally sweet. They are cholesterol free and rich in iron, calcium, potassium, and vitamins A, B, and C. They're great for eating out of hand, and they melt beautifully into many recipes. Try to find Medjool dates; they are large and very soft and sweet.

Apricot Rice Pudding Tart

*A creamy rice pudding, studded with apricots,
is layered with chocolate in a crisp pie crust.*

1. When the crumbs for the Pie Crust have baked, press them into the bottom and up sides of a 10-inch tart pan with removable sides. Cool completely.

2. Place chocolate chips in a small microwave-safe bowl. Microwave on 50 percent power for 1 minute, then remove and stir. Continue microwaving on 50 percent power for 30-second intervals, stirring after each interval, until chips are melted and mixture is smooth. Spread on bottom of cooled pie shell.

3. Prepare Rice Pudding and cool, then chill in refrigerator until thick. Fold in chopped apricots and spoon over chocolate in Pie Crust. Cover and chill for 3–4 hours before serving.

SERVES 12

Calories: 352.21
Fat: 13.09 grams
Fat as % of calories: 33.4%
Carbohydrates: 53.81 grams
Fiber: 2.63 grams
Sodium: 132.68 mg
Vitamin A: 20% DV
Vitamin C: 15% DV
Calcium: 148.27 mg

INGREDIENTS
1 Crunchy Whole Wheat Pie
    Crust (page 188)
½ cup semisweet chocolate
    chips
3 cups Creamy Ginger Rice
    Pudding (page 195)
1 cup chopped canned apricots,
    drained

Crunchy Whole Wheat Pie Crust

*Get some fiber and vitamins even in your pie crust!
This one is not only delicious, but it is super simple to make.*

1. Preheat oven to 375°F. In medium bowl, combine flours, salt, nuts, and brown sugar and mix until blended.

2. In small bowl combine orange juice and melted butter. Add to flour mixture and stir until crumbly. Crumble mixture into a 9-inch square pan.

3. Bake for 14–16 minutes, stirring twice during cooking time, until crumbs are golden brown and fragrant. Remove from oven and cool for 10 minutes, then press crumbs firmly onto bottom and up sides of a 9-inch pie pan. Cool completely and fill with filling or use as directed in recipe.

SERVES 8

Calories: 211.81
Fat: 12.55 grams
Fat as % of calories: 53.0%
Carbohydrates: 22.25 grams
Fiber: 1.77 grams
Sodium: 77.34 mg
Vitamin A: 4% DV
Vitamin C: 2% DV
Calcium: 17.59 mg

INGREDIENTS
¾ cup all-purpose flour
½ cup whole wheat flour
Pinch salt
⅓ cup finely chopped walnuts
¼ cup brown sugar
2 tablespoons orange juice
⅓ cup butter, melted

Calories: 144.62
Fat: 7.41 grams
Fat as % of calories: 45.9%
Carbohydrates: 17.48 grams
Fiber: 2.53 grams
Sodium: 73.84 mg
Vitamin A: 2% DV
Vitamin C: 4% DV
Calcium: 34.51 mg

INGREDIENTS
1 cup whole wheat pastry flour
½ cup all-purpose flour
2 tablespoons flaxseed, ground
⅛ teaspoon salt
2 tablespoons brown sugar
3 tablespoons coconut oil
2 tablespoons butter
2 tablespoons buttermilk
3 tablespoons orange juice

Whole Wheat Pie Crust

Coconut oil isn't bad for you! It has antifungal and antiviral properties, and the saturated fat is medium-chain, which means it's easily processed by the body.

1. In medium bowl, combine flours with flaxseed, salt, and brown sugar; mix well with your fingers to combine completely.

2. Cut in the coconut oil and butter, using two knives or a pastry blender until particles are fine and even. Sprinkle in the buttermilk, tossing crumbs with a fork, then sprinkle in enough orange juice so the dough will stick together when you press it.

3. Form dough into a ball, wrap in plastic wrap, and chill for 2 hours. Then place on lightly floured surface and whack with a rolling pin until malleable. Roll out into an 11-inch circle. Ease into a 9-inch pie pan, fold edges under, and crimp. You can now fill the crust and bake according to a recipe or prebake it.

4. To prebake, preheat oven to 400°F. Prick the bottom and sides of the pie crust. Bake for 13–17 minutes or until crust is light brown and set. Cool completely before filling.

Pie Crust Uses

If you have a pie crust or two in the freezer, you're 80 percent on your way to dessert. Fill it with canned pie filling, revved up with complementary canned, drained fruits, and bake until bubbly. Bake and cool the crust and fill it with layers of sorbet and ice cream sauces, then freeze until firm. Use your imagination!

Orange and Lemon Olive Oil Cake

Olive oil is so good for you, it almost makes this cake a health food! All the orange and lemon really boosts the vitamin C content too.

1. Preheat oven to 325°F. Spray a 12-cup Bundt pan with nonstick baking spray containing flour; set aside. In large bowl, combine flour, sugar, baking powder, baking soda, and salt and mix well; set aside.

2. In medium bowl, combine orange juice, ⅓ cup lemon juice, buttermilk, olive oil, vanilla, and 1 egg; beat until combined. Stir into flour mixture; beat until blended.

3. In small bowl, beat egg whites until stiff. Fold into the batter until combined. Pour into prepared pan. Bake for 40–50 minutes or until cake is dark golden brown and a toothpick inserted in center comes out clean.

4. In small bowl, combine powdered sugar and ¼ cup lemon juice; mix well. Spoon half over the cake in the pan. Loosen edges of cake and turn out onto serving plate. Spoon remaining powdered sugar mixture over cake; let cool completely.

SERVES 12

Calories: 388.30
Fat: 14.28 grams
Fat as % of calories: 33.0%
Carbohydrates: 61.36
Fiber: 0.77 grams
Sodium: 250.72 mg
Vitamin A: 2% DV
Vitamin C: 15% DV
Calcium: 73.51 mg

INGREDIENTS

2½ cups flour
1¾ cups sugar
2 teaspoons baking powder
1 teaspoon baking soda
¼ teaspoon salt
⅓ cup orange juice
⅓ cup lemon juice
⅓ cup buttermilk
¾ cup light olive oil
2 teaspoons vanilla
1 egg
5 egg whites
1 cup powdered sugar
¼ cup lemon juice

INGREDIENTS

*1 16-ounce can pear halves in
    light syrup, undrained*
*1 16-ounce package angel food
    cake mix*
½ cup pear nectar
1 teaspoon vanilla

Pear Angel Food Cake

*Believe it or not, no one has thought of this angel food cake flavor
before! It has lots of flavor; you can also use it in other recipes.*

1. Preheat oven to 350°F. Place pear halves with juice in a food processor;
   process until smooth. Combine with angel food cake mix, pear nectar,
   and vanilla in large bowl.

2. Beat on low speed for 1 minute, then increase speed to medium-high
   and beat for 1 minute longer, until batter is smooth. Pour into ungreased
   10-inch tube pan.

3. Bake for 40–50 minutes or until cake is dark golden brown. Immediately
   turn pan upside down onto a funnel and let stand until cool. Run knife
   around edges and remove from pan.

INGREDIENTS

1 recipe Fruit Salsa (page 26)
*8 (2-inch thick) slices Pear
    Angel Food Cake*

Grilled Pear Angel Food Cake with Fruit Salsa

This gorgeous and healthy dessert is perfect for summer entertaining.

1. Prepare and preheat grill. Prepare and chill Fruit Salsa.

2. When ready to eat, place slices of Angel Food Cake on grill 6 inches from
   heat source. Grill for 30–50 seconds on each side, turning once, until the
   cake develops grill marks and is hot. Place on serving plates and top with
   salsa. Serve immediately.

Angel Food Cake Tips

Because the structure of angel food cake is so delicate, there are rules to follow. First, don't grease the pan. Cool it upside down for best results. To remove
the cake, you need to run a knife around the sides of the pan, then push the
bottom out of the tube pan. Cut around the center hole and the bottom, then
carefully remove the cake.

Apricot–Pear Angel Cake

The fruit in this dish bolsters the nutritional value, and the pears and apricots complement each other nicely.

1. In large saucepan, combine sugar with cornstarch and salt and mix with wire whisk. Drain apricot halves, reserving juice. Add enough apricot nectar to juice to equal 1¾ cups.

2. Stir nectar and lemon juice into sugar mixture. Cook over medium heat, stirring frequently, until mixture boils and thickens. Stir in butter and vanilla.

3. Drain apricot halves on paper towel and coarsely chop. Fold into nectar mixture, cover, and chill until thick, about 2–3 hours.

4. Slice Angel Food Cake into 3 sections. Spread the apricot filling in between the layers. Sprinkle cake with powdered sugar. Store in refrigerator.

SERVES 12

Calories: 259.49
Fat: 2.13 grams
Fat as % of calories: 7%
Carbohydrates: 58.57 grams
Fiber: 1.60 grams
Sodium: 295.77 mg
Vitamin A: 20% DV
Vitamin C: 40% DV
Calcium: 51.64 mg

INGREDIENTS
½ cup sugar
¼ cup cornstarch
⅛ teaspoon salt
1 16-ounce can apricot halves
1 cup apricot nectar
¼ cup lemon juice
2 tablespoons butter
1 teaspoon vanilla
1 recipe Pear Angel Food Cake (page 190)
3 tablespoons powdered sugar

Mini Strawberry Baked Alaska

Read labels when you are purchasing the sorbet. Some varieties don't have much nutrition. Others offer 30% vitamin C per ½ cup serving.

1. Let sorbet stand at room temperature for 10–15 minutes to soften. Place cookies on cookie sheet covered with parchment paper. Top each cookie with ¼ cup of sorbet, rounding the sorbet top. Freeze until hard, about 3–4 hours.

2. When sorbet is frozen, combine egg whites with lemon juice in large bowl; beat until soft peaks form. Gradually add the marshmallow creme, beating until stiff peaks form.

3. Top each mound of sorbet with a thick layer of egg whites, sealing the whites to the paper. Freeze until hard, about 3–4 hours.

4. When ready to serve, preheat oven to 450°F. Bake the solidly frozen desserts for 5–7 minutes or until meringues are browned. Serve immediately.

SERVES 8–10

Calories: 196.12
Fat: 2.62 grams
Fat as % of calories: 12%
Carbohydrates: 40.78 grams
Fiber: 2.30 grams
Sodium: 115.23 mg
Vitamin A: 5% DV
Vitamin C: 16% DV
Calcium: 36.30 mg

INGREDIENTS
4 cups strawberry sorbet
16 chocolate wafer cookies
3 egg whites
2 teaspoons lemon juice
1 7-ounce jar marshmallow creme

INGREDIENTS

*1 16-ounce package baby
    carrots*
*¼ cup chopped crystallized
    ginger*
1 cup granulated sugar
1 cup brown sugar
½ cup honey
¾ cup vegetable oil
2 eggs
4 egg whites
⅔ cup orange juice
1 tablespoon ground ginger
1 teaspoon cinnamon
½ teaspoon cloves
½ teaspoon salt
1½ cups all-purpose flour
*1½ cups whole wheat pastry
    flour*
2 teaspoons baking powder
½ teaspoon baking soda
*1 recipe Low-Fat Cream Cheese
    Frosting (page 173)*

Gingerbread Carrot Cake

*A combination of gingerbread and carrot cake is simply inspired. You
can serve it without the frosting for 266 calories and 9 grams of fat.*

1. Preheat oven to 350°F. Spray a 13" x 9" pan with nonstick baking spray
   containing flour and set aside. Place carrots in food processor. Process
   until finely ground; remove half of the carrots to large bowl. Add the
   crystallized ginger to food processor; process until finely ground. Add to
   large bowl.

2. Add granulated sugar, brown sugar, honey, oil, eggs, egg whites, and
   orange juice and mix well. Stir in ginger, cinnamon, cloves, salt, flours,
   baking powder, and baking soda and stir until combined. Spread in prepared pan.

3. Bake for 45–55 minutes or until cake is dark golden brown and begins to
   pull away from sides of pan. Cool completely on wire rack.

4. Spread cooled cake with the Cream Cheese Frosting. Store leftovers covered at room temperature.

Banana–Orange Cupcakes

You can frost these cupcakes with a cream cheese frosting or a chocolate frosting if you'd like. They're perfect for a children's birthday party.

1. Preheat oven to 375°F. Spray 18 muffin cups with nonstick baking spray containing flour; set aside.

2. In large bowl, combine all-purpose flour, whole wheat flour, baking powder, baking soda, salt, cinnamon, granulated sugar, and brown sugar and mix well.

3. In medium bowl, combine oil, eggs, ⅓ cup orange juice, and vanilla and mix well. Add to flour mixture and stir until combined; beat for 1 minute. Spoon into prepared muffin cups.

4. Bake for 20–25 minutes or until cupcakes spring back when lightly touched. Remove to wire rack. In small bowl, combine ¼ cup orange juice and powdered sugar and mix well; spoon over cupcakes. Cool completely, then serve.

YIELDS 18

Calories: 228.34
Fat: 8.82 grams
Fat as % of calories: 34.7%
Carbohydrates: 35.97 grams
Fiber: 1.11 grams
Sodium: 99.46 mg
Vitamin A: 0% DV
Vitamin C: 7% DV
Calcium: 33.98 mg

INGREDIENTS

1½ cups all-purpose flour
½ cup whole wheat flour
1 teaspoon baking powder
½ teaspoon baking soda
¼ teaspoon salt
1 teaspoon cinnamon
½ cup granulated sugar
¾ cup brown sugar
⅔ cup vegetable oil
2 eggs
⅓ cup orange juice
1¼ cups mashed bananas
1 teaspoon vanilla
¼ cup orange juice
1 cup powdered sugar

Calories: 254.54
Fat: 6.35 grams
Fat as % of calories: 22.4%
Carbohydrates: 46.50 grams
Fiber: 1.43 grams
Sodium: 187.76 mg
Vitamin A: 50% DV
Vitamin C: 5% DV
Calcium: 39.88 mg

INGREDIENTS
1 16-ounce bag baby carrots
1 8-ounce can crushed
    pineapple, undrained
½ cup canola oil
1 cup granulated sugar
1 cup brown sugar
1 egg
3 egg whites
2 teaspoons vanilla
1¾ cups all-purpose flour
1¼ cups whole wheat flour
3 tablespoons cornstarch
1 teaspoon baking powder
1 teaspoon baking soda
1 teaspoon cinnamon
½ teaspoon salt
2 3-ounce packages low-fat
    cream cheese, softened
1 3-ounce package nonfat cream
    cheese, softened
⅓ cup nonfat sour cream
2½ cups powdered sugar
1 tablespoon orange juice

Low-Fat Carrot Cupcakes

*Be sure to use baby carrots when you make these cupcakes.
They are sweeter and more tender than regular carrots,
so they keep the cupcakes moist.*

1. Preheat oven to 350°F. Spray 24 muffin cups with nonstick baking spray containing flour; set aside. In food processor, process the baby carrots until ground; remove from food processor and place in large bowl. In same food processor bowl, process the pineapple with liquid until smooth. Add to bowl with carrots.

2. Add oil, granulated sugar, brown sugar, egg, egg whites, and vanilla and beat well. Add flours, cornstarch, baking powder, baking soda, cinnamon, and salt and mix until well blended. Spoon mixture into prepared muffin cups, filling each ⅔ full.

3. Bake for 20–25 minutes or until cupcakes spring back when lightly touched with finger. Remove to wire rack to cool completely.

4. For frosting, combine remaining ingredients in medium bowl. Beat on low speed until blended, then beat on high speed until fluffy. Frost cooled cupcakes.

Baby Vegetables

Baby vegetables are usually immature versions of the original vegetable. But baby carrots are simply trimmed large carrots, and grape tomatoes are a different variety of tomato altogether. Kids love these small veggies and will probably at least try them. And they look so cute on a serving tray!

Strawberry Fudge Ice Cream Dessert

This elegant dessert is perfect for a warm summer evening.

1. Let the sorbet stand at room temperature for 10–15 minutes to soften. Spoon and pack into a 13" x 9" glass baking dish. Freeze for 1 hour. Pack the ice cream on top of the sorbet. Freeze for 4 hours.

2. Meanwhile, combine chocolate chips, powdered sugar, milk, and butter in large saucepan. Bring to a boil over medium heat, stirring frequently. Reduce heat to medium-low and cook, stirring frequently with a wire whisk, until mixture thickens and is smooth, about 8–10 minutes.

3. Remove sauce from heat and stir in vanilla. Cool completely, stirring occasionally, about 2 hours.

4. Pour cooled sauce over the ice cream mixture. Return to freezer and freeze until firm, about 5–6 hours. Cut into squares to serve.

SERVES 16

Calories: 343.40
Fat: 10.68 grams
Fat as % of calories: 24%
Carbohydrates: 61.45 grams
Fiber: 1.98 grams
Sodium: 123.11 mg
Vitamin A: 10% DV
Vitamin C: 25% DV
Calcium: 244.08 mg

INGREDIENTS

3 1-pint containers strawberry sorbet
6 cups low-fat vanilla ice cream
1 12-ounce package semisweet chocolate chips
2½ cups powdered sugar
1 13-ounce can evaporated skim milk
¼ cup butter
1 teaspoon vanilla

Creamy Ginger Rice Pudding

Apricot nectar adds a sweet and tart flavor to this recipe. You can serve it as is or save some to make Apricot Rice Pudding Tart (page 187).

1. Combine rice, both kinds of milk, apricot nectar, ginger, and salt in large saucepan. Bring to a simmer over medium-high heat, stirring frequently. Reduce heat to low and simmer for 25–30 minutes, stirring frequently, until rice is tender and mixture is thickened. Stir in vanilla.

2. Let cool for 30 minutes, then serve, or chill until cold, then serve.

Rice for Pudding

You can use any type of rice you'd like in this pudding recipe. If you use brown rice, the texture won't be as creamy and the flavor will be stronger, but each serving will provide you with twice the fiber as white rice. Basmati or arborio rice can also be used for a thicker pudding.

SERVES 8

Calories: 355.39
Fat: 5.86 grams
Fat as % of calories: 14.8%
Carbohydrates: 66.47 grams
Fiber: 0.87 grams
Sodium: 177.11 mg
Vitamin A: 10% DV
Vitamin C: 20% DV
Calcium: 291.20 mg

INGREDIENTS

1½ cups uncooked long-grain rice
1 13-ounce can nonfat sweetened condensed milk
1½ cups skim milk
½ cup apricot nectar
1 teaspoon ground ginger
¼ teaspoon salt
1½ teaspoons vanilla

SERVES 12

Calories: 316.98
Fat: 4.77 grams
Fat as % of calories: 13.5%
Carbohydrates: 63.57 grams
Fiber: 3.42 grams
Sodium: 227.39 mg
Vitamin A: 35% DV
Vitamin C: 35% DV
Calcium: 100.03 mg

INGREDIENTS

*8 cups cubed Cracked Wheat
    French Bread (page 139)*
1 cup diced dried apricots
*1 15-ounce can apricot halves,
    drained and chopped*
3 tablespoons butter
2 cups skim milk
2 cups apricot nectar
*1½ cups granulated sugar,
    divided*
½ cup brown sugar
½ teaspoon salt
2 teaspoons vanilla
2 eggs
6 egg whites, divided
1 tablespoon lemon juice
½ cup sugar

Apricot Bread Pudding

*A flavorful bread pudding topped with an airy meringue makes this
dessert healthy and very special.*

1. Preheat oven to 350°F. Spray a 13" x 9" glass baking dish with nonstick cooking spray containing flour and set aside. In large bowl, combine cubed Bread, dried apricots, and chopped apricots; toss and set aside.

2. In large saucepan, combine butter, milk, and apricot nectar and heat until steaming. Pour over bread mixture and stir.

3. In medium bowl, combine 1 cup granulated sugar, brown sugar, salt, vanilla, eggs, and 2 egg whites and beat well. Stir into bread mixture. Pour into prepared baking dish. Place dish in a larger pan; place in oven and add water to larger pan to come ½-inch up sides of glass baking dish. Bake for 35 minutes.

4. In medium bowl, combine remaining 4 egg whites with lemon juice; beat until soft peaks form. Gradually add ½ cup sugar, beating until stiff peaks form.

5. Remove casserole from oven and spread meringue over hot mixture, carefully sealing to edges. Return to oven and bake for 15–20 minutes longer or until meringue is browned. Let cool for 30 minutes, then serve.

Fruit in Desserts

You can make almost any dessert healthier by adding fruit. Combine seasonal chopped fresh fruits with a bit of sugar and orange juice or Grand Marnier liqueur and use it to top cakes, pies, sorbets, and sherbets. In fact, for the healthiest dessert, serve this fruit mixture over more fruit!

Strawberry Fluff

Make sure you use meringue powder, not egg white powder, in this recipe. Since the egg whites in the powder are dehydrated, there's less of a concern for food poisoning.

1. Mash strawberries with potato masher or purée in food processor. Place in medium saucepan with lemon juice and cornstarch. Bring to a simmer over medium-high heat, then reduce heat to low and simmer, stirring constantly until thickened, about 4–5 minutes. Cool completely.

2. In large bowl, combine meringue powder and water and beat together until powder dissolves. Add sugar and salt and beat until stiff peaks form. Using same beaters, beat strawberry mixture until smooth.

3. Fold strawberry mixture and whipped topping into meringue. Spoon into six dessert cups and sprinkle with dark chocolate. Cover and chill for 3–4 hours until set.

SERVES 6

Calories: 141.46
Fat: 2.40 grams
Fat as % of calories: 15.3%
Carbohydrates: 24.28 grams
Fiber: 1.19 grams
Sodium: 146.73 mg
Vitamin A: 0% DV
Vitamin C: 35% DV
Calcium: 24.10 mg

INGREDIENTS

1 10-ounce package frozen
   strawberries, thawed
2 tablespoons lemon juice
3 tablespoons cornstarch
3 tablespoons meringue powder
9 tablespoons water
⅓ cup sugar
⅛ teaspoon salt
1 cup frozen nonfat whipped
   topping, thawed
½ cup grated dark chocolate

Peach and Blueberry Floating Islands

A rich fruity pudding topping with airy and soft meringues.

1. Preheat oven to 250°F. Line a cookie sheet with Silpat liner and set aside. In large bowl, combine pudding mix, milk, nectar, and vanilla and mix well. Let stand for 10 minutes until mixture starts to thicken. Fold in peaches and blueberries; pour into large shallow serving bowl and refrigerate.

2. An hour before serving time, combine egg whites, cream of tartar, lemon juice, and salt in a large bowl; beat until foamy. Gradually add 1¼ cups sugar, beating until stiff peaks form and sugar is almost dissolved. Spoon meringue onto prepared cookie sheets in eight mounds.

3. Bake for 25–30 minutes or until toothpick inserted in center comes out clean and meringues are lightly browned. Let cool for 20 minutes, then spoon on top of pudding and serve immediately.

SERVES 8

Calories: 284.25
Fat: 0.98 grams
Fat as % of calories: 3.1%
Carbohydrates: 65.32 grams
Fiber: 1.80 grams
Sodium: 285.24 mg
Vitamin A: 10% DV
Vitamin C: 25% DV
Calcium: 86.40 mg

INGREDIENTS

2 3.5-ounce packages instant
   banana pudding mix
2 cups cold 1% milk
1 cup peach nectar
1 teaspoon vanilla
3 peaches, peeled and chopped
1½ cups blueberries
6 egg whites
¼ teaspoon cream of tartar
1 tablespoon lemon juice
Pinch salt
1¼ cups sugar

Easy Sweet Crepes

Fill these crepes with fruit marinated in Grand Marnier or orange juice.

1. In large bowl, combine egg, egg substitute, and egg whites; beat until frothy. Add orange juice, skim milk, and melted butter and beat well.

2. Add flours, sugar, salt, and vanilla and beat until smooth. Let batter stand for 30 minutes.

3. Spray a 7-inch crepe pan or with nonstick cooking spray. Place over medium heat. Using a ¼ cup measure, pour 3 tablespoons of the batter onto the hot pan. Immediately lift the pan and swirl so the batter evenly coats the bottom.

4. Cook for 60–70 seconds or until you can pick up the crepe. Carefully flip the crepe and cook for 45 seconds. Invert onto a kitchen towel. Repeat with remaining batter. Do not stack crepes when cool; separate each with some waxed paper.

Candied Citrus Peel

Mix some of this sweet and chewy candy into some vanilla ice milk and top with Low-Fat Fudge Sauce (page 199) for a healthy sundae.

1. Cut the peels off the fruit—remove as little of the white pith as possible. Cut the peel into 1" x ⅓" strips. Continue until you have about 1 cup of peel.

2. Place peel in medium saucepan and cover with water. Bring to a boil over high heat, then reduce heat to low and simmer for 8 minutes. Drain peel, then repeat this process two times. Drain peel and place in small bowl.

3. In same saucepan, combine sugar, ⅓ cup water, and juice and bring to a simmer. Add peel to saucepan and simmer for 15 minutes or until mixture is thick and peel is tender.

4. Remove peel from saucepan with slotted spoon and place on wire rack. Let dry, uncovered, overnight. You can roll the cooled peel in some more granulated sugar. Store at room temperature in airtight container.

Low-Fat Fudge Sauce

This delicious sauce only has 1 gram of saturated fat per serving.
It's so rich and creamy, you won't miss the fat!

1. In medium saucepan, combine sugar, skim milk, salt, and vegetable oil and mix well with wire whisk. Bring to a boil over medium heat, stirring constantly, until sugar dissolves. Stir in cocoa powder and sweetened condensed milk.

2. Bring to a simmer over low heat, stirring frequently, until sauce is thick and smooth. Remove from heat and stir in vanilla. Cool completely, stirring occasionally.

3. Pour mixture into a clean glass jar and seal. Store at room temperature for 3–4 days, or in refrigerator for up to 2 weeks. Heat before serving.

Sweetened Condensed Milk

Sweetened condensed milk can be found in several varieties. The regular type is everywhere. You can also find low-fat and fat-free versions. And there is a type found on Mexican food shelves that is called dulce de leche—a caramel version that is ultra rich. Any of them would work in this simple recipe.

YIELDS 1½ CUPS;
SERVING SIZE 2
TABLESPOONS

Calories: 159.10
Fat: 5.34 grams
Fat as % of calories: 30.2%
Carbohydrates: 28.81 grams
Fiber: 1.78 grams
Sodium: 80.59 mg
Vitamin A: 2% DV
Vitamin C: 2% DV
Calcium: 134.95 mg

INGREDIENTS
3 tablespoons sugar
¼ cup skim milk
⅛ teaspoon salt
3 tablespoons vegetable oil
¾ cup cocoa powder
1 13-ounce can low-fat
sweetened condensed milk
1 teaspoon vanilla

Chapter 13

Fun (and Nutritious!) Party Recipes for Kids

**YIELDS 28 SNACKS;
SERVES 10**

Calories: 157.51
Fat: 6.07 grams
Fat as % of calories: 34.7%
Carbohydrates: 14.01 grams
Fiber: 1.01 grams
Sodium: 410.97 mg
Vitamin A: 20% DV
Vitamin C: 15% DV
Calcium: 18.34 mg

INGREDIENTS

14 cooked Healthy Meatballs
   (page 84), cooled
6 9" x 14" sheets frozen phyllo
   dough, thawed
3 tablespoons butter, melted
Nonstick olive oil spray
¾ cup ketchup
¼ cup tomato paste
3 tablespoons tomato juice
1 tomato, chopped

Turtles in Blankets

*Meatballs, cut in half to resemble turtles, are healthier than cocktail
franks, and kids love them just as much.*

1. Preheat oven to 400°F. Cut the Meatballs in half and set aside.

2. Place a sheet of phyllo dough on work surface and brush with butter. Top
   with a second sheet and spray with the olive oil spray. Top with a third
   sheet. Cut into fourteen 1" x 9" strips. Place half a meatball at the end of
   each strip and roll up. Brush finished turtles with more butter and place
   on cookie sheet.

3. Repeat with remaining phyllo dough, butter, spray, and meatballs. Bake
   for 13–18 minutes or until meatballs are hot and pastry is browned and
   crisp. Remove from oven and remove to wire racks to cool for about 20
   minutes.

4. While turtles are cooling, mix ketchup, tomato paste, tomato juice, and
   tomato in small bowl and mix well. Serve with turtles for dipping.

Kids and Appetite

Kids don't have as big an appetite as adults think. Their stomachs are only
about the size of their fist. Kids really do like to snack, and as long as they
snack on healthy foods like fruits and vegetables and whole grains, that's the
best way to feed them. So give your kids lots of choices and don't force food
on them.

Sneaky Spaghetti Sauce

This delicious and mild recipe sneaks shredded carrots into the sauce, where they dissolve. The carrots also help thicken the sauce.

1. In large saucepan, heat olive oil and butter over medium heat. Add onion; cook and stir for 6 minutes. Add carrot; cook and stir for 3 minutes longer.

2. Add remaining ingredients and bring to a simmer. Reduce heat to low and simmer, partially covered, for 30–40 minutes or until sauce is blended. Serve over hot cooked pasta.

SERVES 8

Calories: 134.76
Fat: 3.76 grams
Fat as % of calories: 25.1%
Carbohydrates: 25.62 grams
Fiber: 4.21 grams
Sodium: 772.22 mg
Vitamin A: 80% DV
Vitamin C: 50% DV
Calcium: 46.07 mg

INGREDIENTS
1 tablespoon olive oil
1 tablespoon butter
1 onion, finely chopped
1 cup finely shredded carrot
2 14.5-ounce cans diced tomatoes, undrained
1 cup ketchup
4 tomatoes, chopped
1 8-ounce can no-salt tomato sauce
⅛ teaspoon pepper
1 teaspoon dried Italian seasoning

Mexican Black Bean Tartlets

These little tartlets are cute and easy for kids to eat. You can tell them that black beans are also called turtle beans.

1. Preheat oven to 400°F. Soften tortillas, one at a time, as directed on package. Using a biscuit cutter, cut four 3½-inch circles out of each tortilla. Immediately press into a nonstick muffin cup. Repeat, making 24 cups in all; set aside.

2. In medium bowl, beat egg and egg white with ricotta cheese. Stir in shredded Cheddar and Monterey jack cheeses, then gently fold in remaining ingredients except Cotija cheese and salsa.

3. Spoon mixture into muffin cups using a ¼ cup measure, scooping about 3 tablespoons of the mixture into each cup. Sprinkle with Cotija cheese. Bake for 14–19 minutes or until filling is set and lightly browned. Top with salsa and serve.

YIELDS 24 TARTLETS

Calories: 114.43
Fat: 4.56 grams
Fat as % of calories: 35.8%
Carbohydrates: 11.77 grams
Fiber: 2.48 grams
Sodium: 234.48 mg
Vitamin A: 10% DV
Vitamin C: 10% DV
Calcium: 126.63 mg

INGREDIENTS
6 8-inch corn tortillas
1 egg
1 egg white
½ cup part-skim ricotta cheese
½ cup shredded Cheddar cheese
½ cup shredded low-fat Monterey jack cheese
1 cup canned black beans, drained
1 cup grape tomatoes, halved
½ cup frozen corn, thawed
2 tablespoons grated Cotija cheese
½ cup mild salsa

Calories: 206.32
Fat: 7.13 grams
Fat as % of calories: 31.3%
Carbohydrates: 23.89 grams
Fiber: 3.30 grams
Sodium: 428.21 mg
Vitamin A: 5% DV
Vitamin C: 15% DV
Calcium: 236.24 mg

INGREDIENTS
1½ cups cauliflower florets
1 cup whole wheat elbow
    macaroni
1 cup whole wheat small shell
    pasta
2½ cups 2% milk
¼ cup flour
2 tablespoons butter
¼ teaspoon salt
Pinch white pepper
1 3-ounce package low-fat
    cream cheese, softened
1 cup shredded low-fat
    American cheese
1 cup shredded low-fat Colby
    cheese
¼ cup whole wheat bread
    crumbs

Sneaky Mac 'n Cheese

Cauliflower is the secret ingredient in this recipe.
Odds are good the kids won't even notice it with the two kinds of
pasta and three kinds of cheese.

1. Preheat oven to 400°F. Spray a 2-quart casserole with nonstick cooking spray and set aside. Cut the florets into small pieces about the size of the shell pasta. Bring a large pot of water to a boil. Cook the cauliflower pieces for 2–3 minutes or until tender. Remove cauliflower with slotted spoon and set aside; keep water boiling. Cook pasta in the water until al dente according to package directions.

2. In large saucepan, combine milk, flour, butter, salt, and pepper. Stir well with wire whisk, then bring to a boil. Boil, stirring constantly, until thickened. Remove from heat and stir in cream cheese, American cheese, and Colby cheese; set aside.

3. Add pasta and cauliflower to sauce; stir gently and pour into casserole. Top with bread crumbs. Bake for 15–20 minutes or until sauce is bubbling and bread crumbs are browned.

Whole Wheat Pasta

Look carefully in the pasta aisle of your supermarket. It's possible to find whole wheat pastas and whole grain pastas that are very close to the color, taste, and consistency of plain white pasta. If your kids still look askance, start with half whole wheat and half white and gradually increase the proportion.

Creamy Low-Fat Turkey Tartlets

These tartlets are filled with kid-friendly ingredients.

1. Preheat oven to 325°F. Spray 36 mini muffin cups with nonstick cooking spray and set aside.

2. In small bowl, combine cracker crumbs with butter and Parmesan cheese; mix well. Divide crumb mixture among muffin cups and press down gently. Top with Colby cheese; set aside.

3. In medium saucepan, cook turkey until almost done, stirring to break up meat. Drain well, then add carrots; cook for 3 minutes longer. Stir in peas and remove from heat.

4. In small bowl, combine egg, egg whites, sour cream, and milk. Beat until smooth. Divide turkey mixture among the muffin cups and spoon egg mixture over. Bake for 12–17 minutes or until tartlets are puffed and set.

YIELDS 36 TARTLETS; SERVES 12

Calories: 179.15
Fat: 7.03 grams
Fat as % of calories: 35.3%
Carbohydrates: 8.48 grams
Fiber: 0.59 grams
Sodium: 260.95 mg
Vitamin A: 20% DV
Vitamin C: 5% DV
Calcium: 120.73 mg

INGREDIENTS

¾ cup crushed soda crackers
3 tablespoons butter, melted
3 tablespoons grated Parmesan cheese
1 cup grated low-fat Colby cheese
½ pound ground turkey breast
⅓ cup grated carrots
⅓ cup baby peas
1 egg
2 egg whites
⅓ cup nonfat sour cream
1 cup buttermilk

Turkey Meatball Sliders

These little meatballs look just like tiny hamburgers. You can also serve these on split miniature sandwich buns instead of crackers.

1. Preheat oven to 350°F. In large bowl, crumble bread into fine pieces. Add apple juice, carrot, egg, salt, and pepper and beat well. Add turkey breast; work with your hands just until combined.

2. Form mixture into 18 meatballs; flatten slightly. Place on cookie sheet with sides. Bake for 17–23 minutes or until internal temperature registers 165°F.

3. Meanwhile, in small bowl combine ketchup and mustard and mix well. When meatballs are done, transfer briefly to paper towels to drain. Then put a dab of the mustard mixture onto each cracker and top with a meatball. Serve immediately.

YIELDS 18 SLIDERS; SERVES 6–8

Calories: 174.85
Fat: 5.04 grams
Fat as % of calories: 25.9%
Carbohydrates: 12.03 grams
Fiber: 1.70 grams
Sodium: 308.93 mg
Vitamin A: 15% DV
Vitamin C: 6% DV
Calcium: 28.94 mg

INGREDIENTS

2 slices whole wheat bread
¼ cup apple juice
⅓ cup finely grated carrot
1 egg
¼ teaspoon salt
Pinch pepper
1¼ pounds ground turkey breast
2 tablespoons ketchup
2 tablespoons mustard
18 whole-grain crackers

SERVES 12

Calories: 281.74
Fat: 12.41 grams
Fat as % of calories: 39.6%
Carbohydrates: 20.10 grams
Fiber: 1.47 grams
Sodium: 293.08 mg
Vitamin A: 2% DV
Vitamin C: 5% DV
Calcium: 37.68 mg

INGREDIENTS

1 tablespoon olive oil
1 onion, finely chopped
⅓ cup tomato sauce
3 tablespoons honey
2 eggs, beaten
1 tablespoon mustard
*1 tablespoon Worcestershire
    sauce*
*2 cups whole wheat bread
    crumbs*
2 pounds ground turkey
⅓ cup ketchup
2 tablespoons brown sugar

Mini Turkey Meatloaves

*These mini meatloaves are very fun for kids to eat. Serve with Healthy
Mashed Potato Balls (page 211) for a great birthday lunch.*

1. Preheat oven to 375°F. Spray 12 muffin cups with nonstick cooking spray
   and set aside.

2. In small saucepan, heat olive oil over medium heat. Add onion; cook and
   stir until very tender, about 7–8 minutes. Remove from heat and place in
   large bowl. Add tomato sauce, honey, eggs, mustard, and Worcestershire
   sauce and mix well. Add bread crumbs and stir to combine; let stand for
   10 minutes.

3. Add ground turkey, working gently with hands until just combined.
   Divide mixture among the muffin cups, using a scant ⅓ cup for each.

4. In small bowl combine ketchup and brown sugar and mix well. Spoon
   on top of each mini meatloaf. Bake for 17–23 minutes or until internal
   temperature registers 165°F. Let cool for 10 minutes, then serve.

Ground Turkey

You can find both ground turkey breast and mixed ground turkey, which is white
and dark meat combined. Either one will work in recipes; it's just a matter of
taste. The mixed ground turkey will have more flavor just because the dark
meat has more fat. Use either one within two days of purchase; freeze for longer storage.

Crisp Baked Chicken Nuggets

Kids love anything small, because, well, they're small! Cut meat into small portions and they'll be more likely to eat it.

1. Cut chicken into 1½" pieces and place in large baking dish. Pour buttermilk over all, stir to coat, cover, and refrigerate for 8–24 hours.

2. Preheat oven to 400°F. Spray a 15" x 10" jelly roll pan with nonstick cooking spray and set aside.

3. Remove chicken from refrigerator. Remove chicken from buttermilk; discard buttermilk.

4. On a plate, combine bread crumbs, cheese, parsley, basil, salt, and pepper; mix well. Roll chicken in bread crumb mixture to coat and place in single layer on jelly roll pan.

5. Bake for 18–23 minutes or until chicken registers 165°F on a meat thermometer and coating is brown and crisp. Serve with Sauce for dipping.

Panko

Panko bread crumbs are very crisp, dry bread crumbs from Japan. They are very low in fat and make an extremely crisp crust on any food. Store tightly covered in the refrigerator for longest life. You can find them in Asian markets or in the international foods aisle of larger supermarkets.

SERVES 8

Calories: 225.55
Fat: 4.24 grams
Fat as % of calories: 16.9%
Carbohydrates: 17.52 grams
Fiber: 2.03 grams
Sodium: 562.97 mg
Vitamin A: 30% DV
Vitamin C: 25% DV
Calcium: 94.04 mg

INGREDIENTS

2 pounds boneless, skinless chicken breasts
1 cup buttermilk
1 cup panko bread crumbs
¼ cup grated Parmesan cheese
1 tablespoon dried parsley flakes
1 teaspoon dried basil leaves
¼ teaspoon salt
⅛ teaspoon pepper
1 cup Sneaky Spaghetti Sauce (page 203), warmed

SERVES 8

Calories: 308.67
Fat: 11.29 grams
Fat as % of calories: 32.9%
Carbohydrates: 35.25 grams
Fiber: 4.10 grams
Sodium: 296.80 mg
Vitamin A: 8% DV
Vitamin C: 8% DV
Calcium: 137.52 mg

INGREDIENTS

3 Slow-Cooked Chicken Breasts
    (page 100)
½ cup raspberry yogurt
2 tablespoons honey
2 Granny Smith apples, sliced
1 tablespoon lemon juice
2 tablespoons butter, softened
8 slices whole wheat bread
4 1-ounce slices deli Colby
    cheese

Whole Wheat Sandwich Kebabs

Read labels carefully; you can find whole wheat bread that looks and tastes just like white bread. Your kids will never know.

1. Cut chicken into thin slices. In a small bowl, combine yogurt and honey and mix well.

2. Toss sliced apples with lemon juice. Spread butter onto one side of each slice of bread. Make sandwiches with the bread, sliced chicken, yogurt mixture, apples, and cheese.

3. Cut each sandwich into four pieces. Skewer the pieces onto eight wooden skewers. Serve immediately, or cover and refrigerate up to 2 hours before serving.

SERVES 4–6

Calories: 216.48
Fat: 9.08 grams
Fat as % of calories: 37.7%
Carbohydrates: 23.76 grams
Fiber: 1.35 grams
Sodium: 460.49
Vitamin A: 8% DV
Vitamin C: 6% DV
Calcium: 178.00 mg

INGREDIENTS

4 slices whole wheat bread
4 teaspoons butter, softened
6 tablespoons strawberry
    preserves
1 3-ounce package low-fat
    cream cheese, softened
2 1-ounce slices American
    cheese
3 1-ounce slices low-fat
    American cheese

Kids' Favorite Healthy Toasted Cheese

You can use any flavor preserves you'd like in this delicious recipe; choose your child's favorite. The combination of sweet preserves with salty cheese is really good.

1. Spread one side of each slice of bread with butter. Place in toaster oven, buttered side up, and toast until bread is light golden brown. Remove from toaster oven and place on work surface, unbuttered side up.

2. In small bowl, combine preserves and cream cheese; mix well. Spread over unbuttered side of bread. Tear American cheese into small pieces and mix; cover cream cheese mixture with cheese pieces.

3. Return to toaster oven; turn to broil. Broil sandwiches until the cheese melts and is bubbly. Remove from toaster oven and let cool for 5 minutes. Cut in half diagonally and serve.

Mini Vegetable Pot Stickers

Pot stickers get their name from their preparation. First fried in a bit of oil, they are then simmered in broth or water until tender and hot.

1. In medium skillet, heat 2 teaspoons olive oil over medium heat. Add onion; cook and stir for 2 minutes. Add chicken breast; cook and stir until almost done, about 5 minutes longer. Add carrots; cook and stir for 2 minutes. Stir in corn and remove from heat.

2. Add soy sauce and 3 tablespoons ketchup; let mixture cool for 20 minutes. Place 5 pot sticker wrappers on work surface. Place about a teaspoon of filling on each. Moisten the edges with water and lift the edges to seal together at the top. Repeat with remaining wrappers and filling.

3. Heat 2 teaspoons olive oil in a large nonstick skillet over medium-high heat. Add half of the pot stickers and fry until bottoms are browned, about 3–4 minutes. Then add ¼ cup water to skillet, cover, and steam until pot stickers are hot and water has evaporated. Let cool for 10 minutes, then serve with more ketchup. Repeat with remaining olive oil and pot stickers.

Kids and Fat

Children need more fat than adults do. In fact, children under the age of four should get about 35 percent of their calories from fat. Kids older than four should have that amount reduced to 25 to 35 percent of their calories. Fat is needed for proper brain growth and development. Children should never be fed an ultra low-fat diet unless directed by a doctor and a nutritionist.

YIELDS 32; SERVING SIZE 4 POT STICKERS

Calories: 229.05
Fat: 4.29 grams
Fat as % of calories: 16.9%
Carbohydrates: 40.37 grams
Fiber: 1.48 grams
Sodium: 468.89 mg
Vitamin A: 20% DV
Vitamin C: 6% DV
Calcium: 34.01 mg

INGREDIENTS

2 tablespoons olive oil, divided
⅓ cup finely chopped onion
⅓ cup ground chicken breast
⅓ cup grated carrots
⅓ cup frozen corn
1 tablespoon low-sodium soy sauce
½ cup plus 3 tablespoons ketchup, divided
32 pot sticker or wonton wrappers

SERVES 6–8

Calories: 185.31
Fat: 6.47 grams
Fat as % of calories: 31.4%
Carbohydrates: 22.79 grams
Fiber: 3.35 grams
Sodium: 704.78 mg
Vitamin A: 35% DV
Vitamin C: 35% DV
Calcium: 142.19 mg

INGREDIENTS

1 cup Sneaky Spaghetti Sauce
   (page 203)
1 tablespoon chopped parsley
⅓ cup turkey pepperoni slices,
   chopped
½ cup chopped green bell
   pepper
½ cup sliced fresh mushrooms
6 4-inch whole wheat pita breads
1 cup shredded part-skim
   mozzarella cheese
2 tablespoons grated Parmesan
   cheese

SERVES 8

Calories: 98.61
Fat: 4.41 grams
Fat as % of calories: 40.0%
Carbohydrates: 12.92 grams
Fiber: 3.23 grams
Sodium: 286.80 mg
Vitamin A: 15% DV
Vitamin C: 15% DV
Calcium: 42.08 mg

INGREDIENTS

1 pound frozen whole green
   beans
½ cup orange juice
1 tablespoon butter
2 tablespoons honey
½ teaspoon salt
⅓ cup chopped peanuts

Pita Pizzas

*You could leave off the chopped bell peppers or mushrooms
if you think your kids won't let you get away with it.
That will reduce the vitamin C content, though.*

1. Preheat oven to 400°F. In small bowl, combine Sauce, parsley, turkey pepperoni, bell pepper, and mushrooms; mix well to combine. Divide among the pita breads and top with mozzarella and Parmesan cheeses.

2. Place on cookie sheet and bake for 12–18 minutes or until pizzas are hot and cheese melts and begins to brown. Remove to wire racks; let cool for 10 minutes. Place on serving platter and cut each pizza into quarters.

Nutty Green Beans

*Make sure that no one at your child's party has a nut
allergy before serving these beans. They're sweet and tender,
with a nice crunch from the peanuts.*

1. Place green beans in microwave-safe baking dish. Top with orange juice and cover with microwave-safe plastic wrap, venting a corner.

2. Microwave the beans as directed on package until tender. Drain well, then add butter, honey, and salt. Stir to coat beans. Sprinkle with peanuts and serve.

Candy Carrots

Baby carrots are naturally sweet, but the addition of brown sugar and honey makes them a side dish your kids will gobble up.

1. Combine carrots and water in a large saucepan; bring to a boil over high heat. Reduce heat to low and simmer carrots for 8–9 minutes until almost tender. Drain well and return to saucepan.

2. Add salt, butter, orange juice, honey, and brown sugar. Bring to a simmer over medium heat, then reduce heat to low and simmer for 3–5 minutes or until carrots are glazed and tender. Let cool for 10 minutes, then serve.

SERVES 6

Calories: 84.27
Fat: 2.07 grams
Fat as % of calories: 28.8%
Carbohydrates: 16.97 grams
Fiber: 2.29 grams
Sodium: 153.39 mg
Vitamin A: 260% DV
Vitamin C: 10% DV
Calcium: 28.14 mg

INGREDIENTS

1 16-ounce package baby carrots
2 cups water
½ teaspoon salt
1 tablespoon butter
2 tablespoons orange juice
2 tablespoons honey
2 tablespoons brown sugar

Healthy Mashed Potato Balls

The cheese will disguise the color of the carrots in these little potato balls.

1. Bring a large pot of water to a boil. Add cauliflower; cook for 2–3 minutes until tender; remove with slotted spoon and place in bowl. Add carrots to water; cook for 4–5 minutes until tender; remove with slotted spoon to bowl.

2. Add potatoes to water; cook for 10–12 minutes or until tender. Drain well and add to bowl with vegetables. Add butter, salt, pepper, and lemon juice; mash until well combined. Stir in Cheddar cheese to blend, then add whole milk and beat well. Cover and chill until cold, about 3–4 hours.

3. Preheat oven to 375°F. Spray a large cookie sheet with nonstick baking spray and set aside. Stir egg into cold mashed potatoes. Form into 1½-inch balls. On a plate, combine Parmesan cheese and bread crumbs. Roll potato balls in crumb mixture to coat. Place on cookie sheets. Bake for 19–24 minutes or until crisp and golden brown.

SERVES 12

Calories: 136.63
Fat: 6.34 grams
Fat as % of calories: 41.7%
Carbohydrates: 13.12 grams
Fiber: 1.53 grams
Sodium: 318.93 mg
Vitamin A: 25% DV
Vitamin C: 15% DV
Calcium: 125.11 mg

INGREDIENTS

1 cup chopped cauliflower florets
½ cup chopped carrots
2 potatoes, peeled and chopped
2 tablespoons butter
½ teaspoon salt
Pinch white pepper
1 tablespoon lemon juice
1 cup shredded low-fat Cheddar cheese
2 tablespoons whole milk
1 egg
¼ cup grated Parmesan cheese
1 cup dried bread crumbs

SERVES 8

Calories: 129.44
Fat: 7.87 grams
Fat as % of calories: 54.7%
Carbohydrates: 9.31 grams
Fiber: 1.36 grams
Sodium: 196.02 mg
Vitamin A: 60% DV
Vitamin C: 20% DV
Calcium: 99.95 mg

INGREDIENTS

1 3-ounce package cream
    cheese, softened
1 cup low-fat sour cream
¼ cup apple juice
⅓ cup grated Parmesan cheese
1 cup baby carrots
1 cup small button mushrooms
1 cup celery sticks
1 cup grape tomatoes
1 8-ounce jar baby corn, drained

Baby Veggie Dip

A slightly sweet, cheesy dip is the perfect
complement to tender baby vegetables.

1. In small bowl, beat cream cheese until soft and fluffy. Gradually add sour cream, beating until smooth. Slowly add apple juice, beating again until smooth. Stir in Parmesan cheese. Cover and chill for 2–3 hours before serving.

2. When ready to eat, arrange the vegetables on a serving plate. Place a small bowl with the dip in the center; serve immediately.

YIELDS 30 POPSICLES

Calories: 28.86
Fat: 0.07 grams
Fat as % of calories: 2.1%
Carbohydrates: 7.28 grams
Fiber: 0.48 grams
Sodium: 0.97 mg
Vitamin A: 5% DV
Vitamin C: 20% DV
Calcium: 4.12 mg

INGREDIENTS

2 mangoes
2 peaches
1 8-ounce can crushed
    pineapple, undrained
3 6-ounce cans pineapple-
    orange juice
2 tablespoons honey

Fruity Popsicles

Wow, these popsicles have lots of flavor! You could make them from all
peaches or all mangoes if you'd like; or use nectarines.

1. Peel mangoes and cut into chunks. Peel peaches and cut into chunks. Combine in food processor or blender with remaining ingredients and process or blend until smooth.

2. You can use commercial popsicle molds or small paper drink cups. Divide mixture among the molds or cups. Freeze for about 30 minutes, or until mixture starts to freeze, then insert wooden sticks. Freeze until solid, about 3–4 hours.

3. To unmold, run cold water over the molds or gently peel the drink cups off the food. Store in the freezer up to 2 weeks.

Cherry Pie Cones

*Using ice cream cones to hold cherry pie filling helps cut down
on the fat and makes pie easier for little ones to eat.*

1. In medium bowl, combine pie filling, cherries, and miniature chocolate chips; set aside.

2. Place milk chocolate chips in a small microwave-safe bowl. Microwave on 50 percent power for 2 minutes, then stir until melted.

3. Using a small pastry brush, brush the melted chocolate inside the ice cream cones. Let stand until hardened, about 20 minutes. Fill each with ¼ cup pie filling mixture, then cover and refrigerate up to 4 hours.

4. When ready to serve, top with the frozen whipped topping.

SERVES 12

Calories: 203.75
Fat: 7.41 grams
Fat as % of calories: 32.7%
Carbohydrates: 33.26 grams
Fiber: 1.57 grams
Sodium: 30.98 mg
Vitamin A: 2% DV
Vitamin C: 5% DV
Calcium: 41.19 mg

INGREDIENTS

1 21-ounce can cherry pie filling
1 cup bing cherries, pitted and
    halved
½ cup miniature semisweet
    chocolate chips
1 cup milk chocolate chips
12 flat-bottomed ice cream
    cones
1 cup frozen whipped topping,
    thawed

Caramel Fruit Dip

*You can add orange juice to just about anything! It adds a depth of
flavor to this delicious caramel sauce.*

1. Combine caramels and orange juice in small microwave-safe bowl. Microwave on 50 percent power for 3–4 minutes. Remove and stir. Continue microwaving for 1-minute intervals, stirring after each interval, until caramels are melted and mixture is smooth.

2. In medium bowl, beat cream cheese with sugars and vanilla. Gradually beat in the caramel mixture, beating until smooth. Cover and refrigerate up to 8 hours.

3. When ready to serve, place dip in a serving bowl and drizzle with caramel ice cream topping. Serve with sliced fruit that has been sprinkled with lemon juice to prevent browning.

SERVES 8–10

Calories: 250.33
Fat: 5.82 grams
Fat as % of calories: 20.9%
Carbohydrates: 48.82 grams
Fiber: 2.95 grams
Sodium: 158.10 mg
Vitamin A: 5% DV
Vitamin C: 15% DV
Calcium: 72.19 mg

INGREDIENTS

20 caramels, unwrapped
¼ cup orange juice
1 8-ounce package low-fat
    cream cheese, softened
¼ cup powdered sugar
¼ cup brown sugar
1 teaspoon vanilla
⅓ cup caramel ice cream
    topping
3 apples, sliced
2 pears, sliced
2 tablespoons lemon juice

YIELDS 36 BARS

Calories: 139.42
Fat: 4.35 grams
Fat as % of calories: 28.1%
Carbohydrates: 23.30 grams
Fiber: 2.15 grams
Sodium: 40.39 mg
Vitamin A: 2% DV
Vitamin C: 5% DV
Calcium: 15.56 mg

INGREDIENTS

1 cup quick-cooking oatmeal
1½ cups regular oatmeal
½ cup brown sugar
⅓ cup oat bran
2 tablespoons ground flaxseed
1 teaspoon cinnamon
1 cup whole wheat pastry flour
¼ teaspoon salt
½ teaspoon baking soda
⅓ cup honey
⅓ cup applesauce
1 egg
⅓ cup vegetable oil
1½ teaspoons vanilla
½ cup chopped walnuts
1 cup cherry preserves
1 cup chopped sweet cherries
½ cup mini semisweet chocolate
    chips

High-Fiber Cherry Oatmeal Bars

*A sweet cherry and chocolate filling adds great flavor
to these chewy bar cookies.*

1. Preheat oven to 350°F. Spray a 9" x 13" baking pan with nonstick baking spray that contains flour and set aside.

2. In large bowl, combine both kinds of oatmeal, brown sugar, oat bran, flaxseed, cinnamon, flour, salt, and baking soda and mix well. In small bowl, combine honey, applesauce, egg, oil, and vanilla and beat until smooth.

3. Add honey mixture to dry ingredients and mix until crumbly. Stir in walnuts. Press half of this mixture into prepared pan. In small bowl, combine preserves, cherries, and chocolate chips. Spread over crust in pan. Top with remaining oat mixture.

4. Bake for 18–23 minutes or until bars turn light golden brown around the edges. Cool completely, then cut into bars.

Honey

Honey is a great choice as a sweetener in all sorts of recipes. But never feed honey to a child under one year of age; there are some toxins in honey that can make infants sick. Eating honey can be a good way to help prevent and reduce allergies to plants in your area. Look for honey that is produced as close to your home as possible.

American Cheese Fondue with Fruit Dippers

*Use an electric fondue pot if you can find one;
they are safer than the type that use canned heat.*

1. In medium saucepan, combine apple juice, milk, flour, and salt; bring to a boil over medium heat. Cook, stirring, until mixture bubbles and thickens. Add American cheese; reduce heat to low. Cook and stir until melted.

2. Brush pear and apple slices with lemon juice. Pour fondue mixture into fondue pot. Serve with fruits.

Fresh Fruit

As with any recipe using fresh fruit, you can use your favorite types. If you're going to use pears or apples, don't peel them because the peel adds fiber. Sprinkle with lemon juice as you chop them. Kiwi should be peeled, but include the seeds. Delicate fruits like raspberries and blueberries should be added at the last minute.

SERVES 8

Calories: 188.59
Fat: 7.45 grams
Fat as % of calories: 35.5%
Carbohydrates: 24.14 grams
Fiber: 3.23 grams
Sodium: 445.08 mg
Vitamin A: 15% DV
Vitamin C: 25% DV
Calcium: 208.29 mg

INGREDIENTS
½ cup apple juice
1 cup 2% milk
3 tablespoons flour
¼ teaspoon salt
2 cups diced American cheese
2 pears, sliced
2 apples, sliced
2 tablespoons lemon juice
1 cup cherry tomatoes

Chapter 14

Healthy and Happy Holidays

INGREDIENTS

20 Gingersnaps (page 231),
    crushed
2 tablespoons butter, melted
⅓ cup plus 2 tablespoons honey
1 tablespoon olive oil
1 onion, chopped
2 pears, peeled and diced
1 cup diced cooked ham
3 tablespoons orange juice
⅓ cup orange marmalade
½ cup shredded low-fat Swiss
    cheese

Glazed Ham and Fruit Tartlets

*These beautiful little tartlets are an elegant main dish for a winter
lunch during the holiday season.*

1. In medium bowl, combine cookie crumbs with butter and ⅓ cup honey;
    mix well. Divide among six 4-inch tartlet pans; press onto bottom and
    ½-inch up sides; set aside.

2. In medium saucepan, heat olive oil over medium heat. Add onion; cook
    and stir for 4 minutes. Add pears; cook and stir for 3 minutes longer.
    Add ham and orange juice; cook and stir until liquid evaporates, about 5
    minutes longer. Remove from heat. Preheat oven to 350°F.

3. Stir orange marmalade into ham mixture; divide mixture among the
    tartlet shells. Top with cheese and drizzle each with half of the remaining
    honey. Place shells on cookie sheet and bake for 25–35 minutes or until
    tartlets are glazed. Drizzle with rest of the honey. Cool for 20 minutes,
    then serve.

Meat with Fruit

Meats, with their robust, full texture and flavor, pair perfectly with many fruits,
which add a sweet and tangy edge to the dish. Adding fruits to meat dishes is
an excellent way to add more vitamins and fiber. It tastes wonderful, too. Think
about pairing beef with oranges, ham with cherries or cranberries, and chicken
with apples.

Perfect Roast Turkey

Cooking turkey from the frozen state is the safest method. This flavorful fruit stuffing is full of vitamins and minerals.

1. Slice the two unpeeled onions and the oranges into ½-inch thick slices and arrange in large shallow roasting pan. Unwrap turkey and place on slices. Place in oven and turn oven to 325°F. Roast the turkey for 3½ hours.

2. Remove turkey from oven and remove the gizzards and neck from the turkey cavities. Pour 1 cup orange juice and chicken stock into roasting pan.

3. In small saucepan, melt butter over medium heat. Add chopped onion and garlic; cook and stir until tender, about 5 minutes. Cube toasted bread and place in large bowl. Add onion mixture, cranberries, apple, raisins, salt, and pepper and toss to coat. Drizzle with ⅓ cup orange juice and toss again.

4. Stuff this mixture into the turkey cavity and neck cavity; use toothpicks to secure skin. Return to oven.

5. Roast turkey for another 1¼ to 2 hours, until the temperature in the thigh registers 180°F, basting turkey occasionally with pan drippings. Remove stuffing from turkey, then slice turkey to serve.

SERVES 12–14

Calories: 485.32
Fat: 12.41 grams
Fat as % of calories: 23.0%
Carbohydrates: 27.77 grams
Fiber: 3.29 grams
Sodium: 357.88 mg
Vitamin A: 5% DV
Vitamin C: 25% DV
Calcium: 81.01 mg

INGREDIENTS

2 onions
3 oranges
1 12- to 14-pound frozen turkey
1⅓ cup orange juice, divided
1 cup chicken stock
2 tablespoons butter
1 onion, chopped
3 cloves garlic, minced
8 slices whole wheat bread, toasted
½ cup dried cranberries
2 apples, chopped
½ cup golden raisins
½ teaspoon salt
⅛ teaspoons pepper

INGREDIENTS

4 12-ounce turkey tenderloins
½ teaspoon salt
⅛ teaspoon pepper
1 tablespoon olive oil
1 tablespoon butter
1 onion, chopped
*½ cup whole-berry cranberry
    sauce*
1 cup dried cranberries
*1 teaspoon dried marjoram
    leaves*
1 egg
*4 slices Cracked Wheat French
    Bread (page 139), toasted*
½ cup chopped hazelnuts
⅓ cup orange juice
1 cup dried bread crumbs

Cranberry–Turkey Tenderloins

*Turkey tenderloins are juicy and tender, and there's no waste at all
since they're skinless and boneless. The flavorful cranberry stuffing
makes this a quintessential holiday recipe.*

1. Cut turkey tenderloins in half crosswise. Butterfly each tenderloin half,
   cutting to within ½ inch of the opposite side. Open up the tenderloin
   halves and sprinkle with salt and pepper.

2. Heat olive oil and butter in a medium saucepan over medium heat. Add
   onion; cook and stir until very tender, about 7 minutes. Remove from
   heat and stir in cranberry sauce, dried cranberries, and marjoram. Let
   cool for 10 minutes, then add egg.

3. Crumble the French Bread into ¼-inch pieces and add to cranberry mixture along with hazelnuts. Divide mixture among the turkey tenderloin
   halves. Fold turkey over filling to enclose; secure with toothpicks.

4. Dip turkey tenderloins into orange juice; roll in bread crumbs to coat.
   Place in shallow roasting pan. Preheat oven to 325°F. Bake tenderloins
   for 20 minutes, then turn over with a spatula and bake for 20–25 minutes longer until turkey registers 165°F on a meat thermometer. Remove
   toothpicks and serve.

Hazelnuts

Hazelnuts, along with most other nuts, are very good for you. The hazelnut,
or filbert, has special fatty acids, including oleic acid, that can actually help
reduce cholesterol levels, including the bad LDL cholesterol. To remove the
tough brown skin, toast the hazelnuts, then rub the warm nuts in a kitchen
towel; discard the skins.

Crispy Nutty Chicken with Cherry Salsa

Because the chicken is baked there is less fat and fewer calories. The cherry salsa is the perfect sweet and tart complement.

1. Preheat oven to 400°F. On plate, combine walnuts, bread crumbs, flour, salt, and pepper; mix well. In shallow bowl, combine egg white with orange juice; beat well.

2. Dip chicken into egg white mixture, then into walnut mixture, pressing to coat. Place chicken on wire rack in shallow roasting pan. Bake for 15–23 minutes or until chicken registers 165°F. Serve with Cherry Salsa.

SERVES 8

Calories: 411.26
Fat: 16.12 grams
Fat as % of calories: 35.3%
Carbohydrates: 33.40 grams
Fiber: 3.03 grams
Sodium: 523.20 mg
Vitamin A: 10% DV
Vitamin C: 15% DV
Calcium: 56.22 mg

INGREDIENTS
¾ cup ground walnuts
½ cup dried bread crumbs
¼ cup flour
1 teaspoon salt
¼ teaspoon pepper
1 egg white
⅓ cup orange juice
8 boneless, skinless chicken
   breasts
2 cups Cherry Salsa (page 224)

Angel Biscuits

Biscuits are usually very high in fat. Using cream cheese cuts the fat while adding flavor, and using both yeast and baking powder makes the biscuits very light and fluffy.

1. In small bowl, combine yeast and water; set aside. In large bowl, combine whole wheat flour, all-purpose flour, sugar, baking powder, baking soda, and salt and mix well. Add cream cheese and butter; cut in using two knives or pastry blender until coarse crumbs form.

2. Add yeast mixture, buttermilk, orange juice, and egg white; mix just until a dough forms. Cover and let stand for 30 minutes.

3. Preheat oven to 400°F. Drop dough by tablespoons onto parchment-paper-lined cookie sheets. Let stand for 15 minutes, then bake for 10–15 minutes or until biscuits are light golden brown. Remove to wire rack to cool for 10 minutes, then serve.

YIELDS 16 BISCUITS

Calories: 113.76
Fat: 3.67 grams
Fat as % of calories: 29.0%
Carbohydrates: 17.23 grams
Fiber: 1.33 grams
Sodium: 139.33 mg
Vitamin A: 2% DV
Vitamin C: 2% DV
Calcium: 42.85 mg

INGREDIENTS
1 0.25-ounce package active dry
   yeast
¼ cup water
1 cup whole wheat pastry flour
1½ cups all-purpose flour
2 tablespoons sugar
1 teaspoon baking powder
½ teaspoon baking soda
¼ teaspoon salt
1 3-ounce package cream
   cheese, softened
2 tablespoons butter
½ cup buttermilk
1 egg white
3 tablespoons orange juice

SERVES 8

Calories: 300.50
Fat: 9.48 grams
Fat as % of calories: 28.4%
Carbohydrates: 20.54 grams
Fiber: 1.65 grams
Sodium: 367.88 mg
Vitamin A: 6% DV
Vitamin C: 20% DV
Calcium: 180.14 mg

INGREDIENTS

1 tablespoon butter
1 onion, chopped
3 cloves garlic, minced
1 Granny Smith apple, finely chopped
½ teaspoon dried thyme leaves
1½ cups shredded Muenster cheese
½ teaspoon salt
⅛ teaspoon pepper
8 boneless, skin-on chicken breasts
Olive oil for coating
3 Granny Smith apples, peeled and sliced
1¼ cups apple juice, divided
½ cup orange juice
2 tablespoons lemon juice
½ teaspoon ground ginger
2 tablespoons cornstarch

Apple-Stuffed Chicken Breasts

A cheesy apple mixture is stuffed between the chicken and skin, then the roasted chicken is served with a rich sauce made with apple slices.

1. In medium saucepan, melt butter over medium heat. Add onion and garlic; cook and stir for 4 minutes. Add chopped apple; cook and stir until tender, about 4–5 minutes longer. Remove from heat and place in small bowl. Let cool for 30 minutes.

2. Preheat oven to 375°F. When apple mixture is cool, stir in thyme, cheese, salt, and pepper. Loosen the skin from flesh of chicken, leaving the skin attached at one side. Divide apple mixture among chicken breasts, stuffing under the skin. Smooth skin back over chicken.

3. Place chicken, skin side up, in roasting pan. Brush with olive oil. Bake for 25–35 minutes or until meat thermometer registers 165°F.

4. While chicken is baking, combine sliced apples, 1 cup apple juice, orange juice, lemon juice, and ginger in a large skillet. Bring to a boil over medium heat. Simmer for 5–6 minutes or until apples are tender. Remove from heat.

5. When chicken is done, return skillet with apples to heat. In small bowl combine remaining ¼ cup apple juice with cornstarch; add to apple mixture and bring just to a simmer. Serve the apple sauce with the chicken.

Baking Crisp Chicken

You don't have to fry chicken to get a crisp coating. First, consider the ingredients you'll use for the coating. Ground nuts and bread crumbs add great crunch and won't become soggy. Place the coated chicken on a sturdy wire rack so the oven heat can circulate all the way around the chicken, crisping the coating.

Cherry–Berry Endive Salad

Adding a few fresh ingredients to a purchased salad dressing really makes the flavor pop, and it tastes homemade.

1. In food processor or blender, combine vinaigrette, ⅓ cup raspberries, and lemon juice; process or blend until smooth. Cover and refrigerate.

2. In medium bowl, combine cherries, strawberries, and green onion. Drizzle with ¼ cup of the vinaigrette mixture, cover, and refrigerate up to 6 hours.

3. When ready to eat, combine endive and butter lettuce in serving bowl. Top with cherry mixture and toss gently. Sprinkle with remaining ⅔ cup raspberries and the hazelnuts. Drizzle with half the remaining vinaigrette and serve with the rest of the vinaigrette on the side.

SERVES 6

Calories: 129.68
Fat: 4.35 grams
Fat as % of calories: 30.2%
Carbohydrates: 17.63 grams
Fiber: 5.48 grams
Sodium: 100.35 mg
Vitamin A: 40% DV
Vitamin C: 60% DV
Calcium: 61.01 mg

INGREDIENTS
1 cup bottled raspberry vinaigrette
1 cup raspberries, divided
2 tablespoons lemon juice
2 cups pitted sweet cherries, halved
1 cup sliced strawberries
⅓ cup sliced green onion
6 cups chopped curly endive
2 cups butter lettuce, torn
⅓ cup chopped toasted hazelnuts

Christmas Salad

This red and green salad has a fabulous combination of flavors and textures. Serve it any time of the year!

1. Heat olive oil over medium heat in a medium saucepan. Add onion; cook and stir until tender, about 5 minutes. Remove from heat and let cool for 15 minutes.

2. Whisk in vinegar, sugar, salt, tarragon, and mustard; set aside.

3. In large serving bowl, combine remaining ingredients and toss gently to coat. Drizzle onion mixture over all; toss gently and serve immediately.

SERVES 8

Calories: 235.95
Fat: 7.58 grams
Fat as % of calories: 28.9%
Carbohydrates: 37.61 grams
Fiber: 7.23 grams
Sodium: 209.16 mg
Vitamin A: 45% DV
Vitamin C: 45% DV
Calcium: 49.61 mg

INGREDIENTS
2 tablespoons olive oil
1 red onion, chopped
5 tablespoons red wine vinegar
1 teaspoon sugar
½ teaspoon salt
1 teaspoon dried tarragon leaves
2 tablespoons Dijon mustard
1 Granny Smith apple, chopped
1 Red Delicious apple, chopped
1 cup dried cranberries
1 avocado, diced
4 cups baby spinach leaves
2 cups torn butter lettuce
2 cups chopped red cabbage

INGREDIENTS

2 pounds broccoli
4 tablespoons olive oil, divided
½ teaspoon salt
⅛ teaspoon white pepper
2 pomegranates
2 tablespoons Dijon mustard
2 tablespoons honey
½ teaspoon dried thyme leaves

Roasted Broccoli with Pomegranate Dressing

Not only is this dish made up of gorgeous colors, the flavor is divine. It's perfect for a holiday dinner.

1. Preheat oven to 400°F. Rinse broccoli and cut into florets. Place on large baking sheet; drizzle with 2 tablespoons olive oil and sprinkle with salt and pepper. Toss to coat. Roast for 20–25 minutes or until tender.

2. Meanwhile, squeeze the juice from one pomegranate and place in small bowl. Add remaining 2 tablespoons olive oil, mustard, honey, and thyme leaves and whisk until combined.

3. Cut remaining pomegranate in half. Using a spoon, beat the back of each half to release seeds.

4. When broccoli is done, remove to serving platter. Drizzle with dressing and sprinkle with pomegranate seeds. Serve immediately.

INGREDIENTS

1 tablespoon butter
1 onion, chopped
3 cloves garlic, minced
⅓ cup orange juice
½ teaspoon salt
⅛ teaspoon pepper
2 cups pitted tart cherries, chopped
1 jalapeño pepper, minced
½ cup dried cherries
2 tablespoons lemon juice
½ cup cherry jam

Cherry Salsa

Cherry salsa is a great condiment to have on hand for the holidays. It can be served as a dip, a sandwich spread, or as a side dish for meats.

1. Melt butter in a large saucepan over medium heat. Add onion and garlic; cook and stir until tender, about 6 minutes. Add orange juice, salt, pepper, tart cherries, jalapeño, dried cherries, and lemon juice; bring to a simmer.

2. Remove from heat and stir in cherry jam. Let cool for 30 minutes, then cover and refrigerate up to 3 days. Salsa can be frozen for up to 3 months.

Cherries

Cherries have wonderful antioxidant properties. In fact, several studies have shown that they can reduce inflammation just as well as aspirin. This can help arthritis sufferers, but it can also reduce the risk of heart disease for everyone. There are two types of cherries: tart and sweet. Tart cherries are mostly used in pies, while sweet cherries are perfect to eat out of hand.

Creamy Cranberry–Orange Salad

This colorful salad is a nice addition to any holiday buffet. Garnish it with fresh mint leaves and some fresh cranberries.

1. In small microwave-safe bowl, combine gelatin and orange juice; set aside. In another small bowl, combine cranberries and sugar; let stand for 10 minutes.

2. In large bowl, combine both kinds of cream cheese and beat until smooth. Add blue cheese, then beat in the cranberry sauce until mixed.

3. Microwave the gelatin mixture on 50 percent power for 1–2 minutes or until gelatin dissolves. Beat this mixture into the cream cheese mixture. Stir in the cranberry mixture and then add the chopped oranges.

4. Pour into a 6-cup mold, cover, and chill for 4–6 hours or until firm. Unmold salad onto serving plate and slice to serve.

SERVES 8

Calories: 209.31
Fat: 7.67 grams
Fat as % of calories: 32.9%
Carbohydrates: 28.65 grams
Fiber: 0.97 grams
Sodium: 273.56 mg
Vitamin A: 15% DV
Vitamin C: 35% DV
Calcium: 104.29 mg

INGREDIENTS

1 0.25-ounce envelope unflavored gelatin
½ cup orange juice
½ cup chopped cranberries
¼ cup sugar
1 8-ounce package low-fat cream cheese, softened
1 3-ounce package nonfat cream cheese, softened
½ cup crumbled blue cheese
1 cup whole-berry cranberry sauce
1 11-ounce can mandarin oranges, drained and chopped

Caramelized Onion Potato Gratin

Caramelized onions are very sweet and nutty tasting. Be sure to cook them until golden brown to get the correct flavor.

1. In large skillet, melt butter and olive oil over medium heat. Add onions; cook and stir until onions are light golden brown, about 20–30 minutes. Add garlic; cook and stir for 4 minutes longer. Remove from heat and sprinkle with salt and pepper.

2. In small saucepan, combine milk with sour cream and rosemary; bring just to a simmer, stirring well; remove from heat. Preheat oven to 350°F.

3. Spray a 13" x 9" baking dish with nonstick cooking spray. Layer potatoes, onion mixture, and cheese in dish. Pour milk mixture over all. Bake for 65–70 minutes or until potatoes are tender and top is golden brown.

SERVES 10

Calories: 231.77
Fat: 5.24 grams
Fat as % of calories: 20.3%
Carbohydrates: 38.95 grams
Fiber: 3.67 grams
Sodium: 356.63 mg
Vitamin A: 6% DV
Vitamin C: 30% DV
Calcium: 197.33 mg

INGREDIENTS

1 tablespoon butter
1 tablespoon olive oil
3 onions, chopped
5 cloves garlic, minced
1 teaspoon salt
⅛ teaspoon white pepper
1 13-ounce can nonfat evaporated milk
½ cup low-fat sour cream
1 tablespoon minced fresh rosemary
3 pounds russet potatoes, thinly sliced
⅓ cup grated Parmesan cheese

Calories: 464.86
Fat: 11.83 grams
Fat as % of calories: 22.9%
Carbohydrates: 64.87 grams
Fiber: 7.01 grams
Sodium: 480.02 mg
Vitamin A: 25% DV
Vitamin C: 50% DV
Calcium: 330.49 mg

INGREDIENTS

6 russet potatoes
1 tablespoon olive oil
2 tablespoons butter
1 onion, chopped
3 cloves garlic, minced
1 leek, chopped
3 carrots, sliced
3 tablespoons flour
½ teaspoon salt
⅛ teaspoon pepper
1 cup nonfat light cream
1 cup chicken broth
½ cup evaporated milk
1 cup shredded Swiss cheese
*1 tablespoon chopped fresh
    tarragon*
*1 6-ounce pouch salmon,
    drained and flaked*
½ pound cooked small shrimp
2 cups frozen baby peas
¼ cup grated Parmesan cheese

Seafood Potato Gratin

This delicious and beautiful casserole can be made ahead of time. Serve it with a fruit salad and Apricot Rice Pudding Tart (page 187) for dessert.

1. Slice potatoes thinly; set aside. In large saucepan, melt olive oil and butter over medium heat. Add onion, garlic, leek, and carrots; cook and stir until tender, about 6–7 minutes. Add flour, salt, and pepper; cook and stir until bubbly.

2. Add cream, broth, and milk; cook and stir until mixture thickens and starts to simmer. Remove from heat and stir in Swiss cheese and tarragon.

3. Spray a 13" x 9" baking dish with nonstick cooking spray. Place ⅓ of potatoes in the dish, then top with ⅓ of the salmon, shrimp, and baby peas. Pour ⅓ of the cheese sauce over all. Repeat layers. Sprinkle with Parmesan cheese.

4. The casserole can be refrigerated up to 24 hours before baking. When ready to eat, preheat oven to 350°F. Bake casserole, covered, for 40 minutes, then uncover and bake for 30–35 minutes longer or until potatoes are tender when pierced with a fork and top is bubbling and golden brown. Serve immediately.

Cheesy Vegetable Medley

*A creamy yet low-fat cheese sauce makes
a medley of vegetables truly delicious.*

1. Bring a large pot of water to a boil. Snap the ends off asparagus; cut the rest into 2-inch lengths. Add to water; boil for 2 minutes, drain and place in 3-quart casserole.

2. Melt butter over medium heat in a large saucepan. Add onion, garlic, and mushrooms; cook and stir until tender, about 6 minutes. Remove with slotted spoon to casserole with asparagus. Add leek and carrots to pan; cook and stir until crisp-tender, about 6–7 minutes. Remove with slotted spoon to casserole.

3. Add olive oil to pan. Add flour, salt, pepper, and thyme leaves; cook and stir until bubbly. Add broth and milk; cook and stir until mixture bubbles and thickens. Remove from heat and stir in Cheddar and Swiss cheeses. Pour over vegetables.

4. The casserole can be covered and refrigerated up to 8 hours before baking. When ready to eat, preheat oven to 375°F. Uncover casserole and sprinkle with Parmesan cheese. Bake for 30–40 minutes or until bubbly and hot, adding 10–15 minutes if casserole has been refrigerated.

SERVES 8

Calories: 180.68
Fat: 7.10 grams
Fat as % of calories: 35.3%
Carbohydrates: 17.16 grams
Fiber: 3.56 grams
Sodium: 415.12 mg
Vitamin A: 150% DV
Vitamin C: 25% DV
Calcium: 241.75 mg

INGREDIENTS

1½ pounds fresh asparagus
2 tablespoons butter
1 onion, chopped
3 cloves garlic, minced
1 8-ounce package sliced mushrooms
1 leek, chopped
4 carrots, sliced
1 tablespoon olive oil
4 tablespoons flour
½ teaspoon salt
⅛ teaspoon white pepper
½ teaspoon dried thyme leaves
1 cup vegetable broth
1 cup 1% milk
1 cup shredded extra-sharp low-fat Cheddar cheese
½ cup shredded low-fat Swiss cheese
¼ cup grated Parmesan cheese

SERVES 8

Calories: 286.84
Fat: 8.68 grams
Fat as % of calories: 27.2%
Carbohydrates: 42.24 grams
Fiber: 3.54 grams
Sodium: 181.61 mg
Vitamin A: 6% DV
Vitamin C: 40% DV
Calcium: 127.59 mg

INGREDIENTS

*1 8-ounce package low-fat
   cream cheese, softened
½ cup whole-berry cranberry
   sauce
¼ cup powdered sugar
1 teaspoon vanilla
8 Easy Sweet Crepes (page 198)
1 cup chopped strawberries
1 cup raspberries
½ cup Low-Fat Fudge Sauce
   (page 199)
2 tablespoons powdered sugar*

SERVES 10

Calories: 348.01
Fat: 11.11 grams
Fat as % of calories: 28.7%
Carbohydrates: 62.04 grams
Fiber: 4.00 grams
Sodium: 122.83 mg
Vitamin A: 5% DV
Vitamin C: 10% DV
Calcium: 39.40 mg

INGREDIENTS

*3 tablespoons cocoa
2 tablespoons butter, melted
¼ cup raspberry jam
2 cups raspberries
1½ cups sugar
½ cup raspberry juice
2 tablespoons lemon juice
¼ cup corn syrup
⅛ teaspoon cream of tartar
2 egg whites
1 Whole Wheat Pie Crust (page
   188), baked and cooled*

Sweet Berry Crepes

*These beautiful little crepes can be filled with any fresh fruit you'd
like. The gorgeous pink of the sweet cranberry spread contrasts warmly
with the fudge sauce.*

1. In small bowl, beat cream cheese until fluffy. Add cranberry sauce, powdered sugar, and vanilla and beat until smooth. Cover and refrigerate up to 24 hours.

2. When ready to serve, arrange Crepes on work surface. Gently spread each with some of the cream cheese mixture, then top with strawberries and raspberries. Roll up Crepes.

3. Place Crepes on serving platter. Place Fudge Sauce in small microwave-safe bowl or pitcher. Microwave on 50 percent power for 1½ minutes or until warm; stir. Drizzle the warm sauce over Crepes; sprinkle with powdered sugar and serve.

Fluffy Cocoa Raspberry Divinity Pie

Divinity is a fat-free candy.

1. In small bowl, combine cocoa and butter and mix well; set aside. In medium bowl, combine jam with raspberries; stir well and set aside.

2. In medium saucepan, combine sugar, raspberry juice, lemon juice, and corn syrup. Bring to a simmer over medium heat. Cover the pan and cook for 2 minutes. Uncover, reduce heat to low, and cook without stirring until the mixture reaches 246°F.

3. In medium bowl, combine cream of tartar and egg whites; beat until stiff peaks form. When the sugar mixture reaches 255°F, slowly pour in a thin stream over the egg whites, beating constantly, until mixture begins to lose its gloss. Fold cocoa mixture into egg white mixture. Place half in cooled Pie Crust and top with half of the raspberry mixture; repeat layers. Refrigerate for 4–6 hours.

Pumpkin Puff Pie

A chewy low-fat pie crust holds a fluffy pumpkin mousse filling in this delicious recipe.

SERVES 8

Calories: 282.08
Fat: 5.39 grams
Fat as % of calories: 17.2%
Carbohydrates: 55.87 grams
Fiber: 2.02 grams
Sodium: 225.80 mg
Vitamin A: 170% DV
Vitamin C: 5% DV
Calcium: 82.76 mg

1. Preheat oven to 375°F. Spray a 9-inch pie pan with nonstick baking spray that contains flour and set aside.

2. In medium bowl, beat egg white until soft peaks form. Gradually add sugar, beat until stiff peaks form. Fold in cracker crumbs and 1 teaspoon vanilla. Spread into the pie plate, pressing onto bottom and up sides. Bake for 12–15 minutes or until set. Cool completely.

3. For filling, in small bowl, combine gelatin with ¼ cup milk. In large saucepan, combine remaining milk with egg yolks, honey, brown sugar, salt, and pumpkin pie spice. Heat until steaming. Stir in gelatin, and cook over low heat until gelatin and sugar dissolve.

4. Stir in the pumpkin and remaining 1 teaspoon vanilla and beat well until smooth. Let cool for 45 minutes. Fold the whipped topping into the pumpkin mixture and spoon into pie shell. Cover and chill for 4–5 hours until firm. Sprinkle with toffee bits and serve.

INGREDIENTS

1 egg white
¼ cup sugar
1½ cups finely crushed graham crackers
2 teaspoons vanilla, divided
1 (0.25-ounce) package unflavored gelatin
1 cup 1% milk, divided
2 egg yolks
½ cup honey
¼ cup brown sugar
¼ teaspoon salt
1½ teaspoons pumpkin pie spice
1 15-ounce can solid pack pumpkin
1½ cups nonfat frozen whipped topping, thawed
⅓ cup toffee bits

SERVES 12

Calories: 270.14
Fat: 8.63 grams
Fat as % of calories: 28.7%
Carbohydrates: 42.53 grams
Fiber: 1.06 grams
Sodium: 242.47 mg
Vitamin A: 20% DV
Vitamin C: 9% DV
Calcium: 70.96 mg

INGREDIENTS

1 8-ounce package low-fat
   cream cheese, softened
1 8-ounce package nonfat cream
   cheese, softened
¾ cup sugar
1 egg
2 egg whites
¼ cup orange juice
1 teaspoon vanilla
2 tablespoons butter, melted
3 tablespoons honey
6 9" x 14" sheets frozen phyllo
   dough, thawed
¼ cup ground walnuts
1 15-ounce can apricot halves,
   drained
¾ cup apricot jam

Mini Baklava Apricot Cheesecakes

*Cheesecake is usually loaded with fat and calories.
A honey-laced phyllo crust and low-fat products make
this elegant dessert low in fat and calories.*

1. Preheat oven to 350°F. In large bowl, combine both kinds of cream cheese with sugar and beat until smooth. Add egg, egg whites, orange juice, and vanilla and beat until smooth and creamy. Set aside.

2. In small bowl, combine butter with honey and mix well. Arrange a sheet of phyllo dough on work surface and brush with butter mixture; sprinkle with 1 tablespoon of walnuts. Repeat layers, then top with another phyllo sheet.

3. Cut the phyllo stack into 6 squares by cutting in half to make two 4½" x 14" rectangles, then cutting each rectangle into thirds. Gently press into muffin cups. Repeat with remaining 3 sheets of phyllo dough, butter mixture, and walnuts.

4. Spoon cream cheese mixture into each lined muffin cup. Bake for 16–20 minutes or until filling is just set. Cool completely.

5. Drain apricot halves and coarsely chop. In medium bowl, combine with apricot jam. Top each cheesecake with this mixture and chill for 2–3 hours before serving.

Canned Fruits

Apricots and peaches are among the canned fruits with the most vitamins, but you could also use canned drained pineapple or cherries in this recipe. There are many new varieties and combinations of canned fruits on the market. Look in the produce aisle for exotic fruits like mangoes and other tropical fruits.

Gingersnaps

*These flavorful gingersnaps, using two kinds of ginger,
are tender and chewy.*

1. In large bowl, combine butter, honey, molasses, and brown sugar; beat until smooth. Add egg, orange juice, orange zest, and vanilla; beat until smooth.

2. Stir in all-purpose flour, whole wheat flour, baking soda, salt, ground ginger, cinnamon, and cardamom until blended. Work in the candied ginger. Cover and chill for 2–3 hours.

3. Preheat oven to 350°F. Roll dough into ¾-inch balls and roll in sugar. Place on cookie sheets. Bake for 9–13 minutes or until gingersnaps are just set. Cool on cookie sheets for 4 minutes, then remove to wire racks to cool completely.

Making Cookies

To make the best cookies, you must follow some rules. Measure flour correctly by spooning it lightly into a measuring cup and leveling it off with the back of a knife. Don't handle the dough too much, and make sure your oven temperature is accurate. Use shiny cookie sheets, not dark ones, and don't overbake the cookies.

YIELDS 3 DOZEN COOKIES

Calories: 55.54
Fat: 1.84 grams
Fat as % of calories: 29.8%
Carbohydrates: 9.07 grams
Fiber: 0.52 grams
Sodium: 40.44 mg
Vitamin A: 2% DV
Vitamin C: 2% DV
Calcium: 7.23 mg

INGREDIENTS

5 tablespoons butter, softened
2 tablespoons honey
2 tablespoons light molasses
⅓ cup brown sugar
1 egg
2 tablespoons orange juice
1 teaspoon grated orange zest
1 teaspoon vanilla
1 cup all-purpose flour
1 cup whole wheat pastry flour
½ teaspoon baking soda
⅛ teaspoon salt
1 teaspoon ground ginger
½ teaspoon ground cinnamon
⅛ teaspoon ground cardamom
¼ cup minced candied ginger

YIELDS 36 COOKIES

Calories: 162.23
Fat: 5.56 grams
Fat as % of calories: 30.8%
Carbohydrates: 25.89 grams
Fiber: 1.83 grams
Sodium: 51.16 mg
Vitamin A: 5% DV
Vitamin C: 5% DV
Calcium: 14.06 mg

INGREDIENTS

1 cup chopped dates
½ cup chopped dried cranberries
½ cup chopped dried blueberries
1 cup chopped walnuts
2 cups graham cracker crumbs
1 cup crisp rice flake cereal
¼ cup orange juice or rum
¼ cup butter
1 10-ounce package large marshmallows
8 ounces dark chocolate, chopped
½ cup milk chocolate chips

Glazed Fruitcake Balls

Instead of fruitcake stuffed full of candied fruits, this recipe uses healthy dried fruits to add flavor and color.

1. In medium bowl, combine dates, cranberries, blueberries, walnuts, cracker crumbs, and cereal and toss to mix. Set aside.

2. In large microwave-safe bowl, combine orange juice, butter, and marshmallows. Microwave on high power for 2 minutes, then remove and stir. Continue microwaving for 30-second intervals, stirring after each interval, until marshmallows are melted and mixture is smooth.

3. Add the cracker crumb mixture and mix with a wooden spoon until combined. Wet your hands and form mixture into 1-inch balls; set on waxed paper. Refrigerate until firm, about 1–2 hours.

4. Place dark chocolate in a microwave-safe measuring cup. Microwave on 50 percent power for 2 minutes, then remove and stir until smooth. Stir in milk chocolate chips; keep stirring until melted.

5. Dip balls into chocolate mixture, shaking off excess. Place on waxed paper and let stand until set. Store at room temperature in an airtight container.

Coconut Rum Balls

If you're making these for kids, omit the rum and use orange juice or apple juice instead. You can roll them in powdered sugar or ground nuts if you'd like.

1. Finely crush the graham crackers and combine in large bowl with hazelnuts, powdered sugar, and coconut.

2. In small bowl combine honey, rum, and butter and mix well. Add to graham cracker mixture and stir until combined. Press mixture into 1-inch balls and place on waxed paper. Let stand for 30 minutes to set, then store in an airtight container at room temperature.

YIELDS 24 BALLS

Calories: 79.37
Fat: 3.05 grams
Fat as % of calories: 34.6%
Carbohydrates: 12.31 grams
Fiber: 0.46 grams
Sodium: 56.72 mg
Vitamin A: 0% DV
Vitamin C: 2% DV
Calcium: 4.62 mg

INGREDIENTS

28 honey graham crackers
½ cup ground hazelnuts
½ cup powdered sugar
½ cup flaked coconut
¼ cup honey
2 tablespoons rum or orange juice
2 tablespoons butter, melted

Pomegranate Punch

Punches are usually fairly bland; not this one! Its gorgeous color and sweet-tart taste will have people coming back for more.

1. Cut pomegranates in half. Using a spoon, hit the back of two halves to remove seeds; place seeds in small dish, cover, and refrigerate. Squeeze the juice from the remaining pomegranate halves.

2. In large pitcher, combine freshly squeezed juice with 2 quarts pomegranate juice, orange juice, lime juice, and sugar; stir until sugar dissolves. Cover and refrigerate up to 8 hours.

3. When ready to serve, pour pomegranate juice mixture into punch bowl. Add the champagne or cider and stir gently. Sprinkle with pomegranate seeds and serve.

SERVES 8–10

Calories: 229.64
Fat: 0.55 grams
Fat as % of calories: 2.1%
Carbohydrates: 40.79 grams
Fiber: 0.95 grams
Sodium: 4.73 mg
Vitamin A: 5% DV
Vitamin C: 45% DV
Calcium: 10.05 mg

INGREDIENTS

3 pomegranates
2 quarts pomegranate juice
2 cups orange juice
¼ cup lime juice
½ cup sugar
2 750-ml bottles champagne or sparkling cider

SERVES 8

Calories: 307.54
Fat: 11.71 grams
Fat as % of calories: 34.3%
Carbohydrates: 50.41 grams
Fiber: 4.63 grams
Sodium: 101.91 mg
Vitamin A: 5% DV
Vitamin C: 10% DV
Calcium: 54.62 mg

INGREDIENTS

3 pears, peeled and chopped
½ cup white chocolate chips, chopped
½ cup dried cranberries
2 tablespoons lemon juice
¼ cup brown sugar
3 tablespoons butter, melted
3 tablespoons honey
10 9" x 14" sheets frozen phyllo dough, thawed
8 tablespoons ground almonds

Pear and Cranberry Strudel

This beautiful strudel has the perfect color for the holidays. You could also serve it as part of a dessert party on New Year's Eve.

1. In medium bowl, combine pears, chocolate chips, and cranberries. Sprinkle with lemon juice and brown sugar, stir gently, and set aside.

2. Preheat oven to 375°F. In small bowl, combine melted butter and honey; mix well. Place a sheet of phyllo dough on work surface. Brush with some of the butter mixture, then sprinkle with 1 tablespoon ground almonds. Repeat layers, using five sheets of phyllo dough.

3. Place half of the pear mixture 1 inch from the long side of the phyllo dough stack, making a rectangle 3 inches wide. Roll up phyllo dough, enclosing filling. Place seam side down on a parchment paper–lined cookie sheet. Brush with more butter mixture. Repeat with remaining dough, butter mixture, almonds, and filling.

4. Bake the strudels for 30–40 minutes or until pastry is golden brown and filling is bubbling. Let cool for 1 hour, then slice to serve.

Phyllo Dough

Phyllo dough (also known as filo or fillo) is a paper-thin dough that is very low in fat. It must be layered with some fat so it becomes flaky, but you can use cooking spray alternating with melted butter to reduce the total amount. Also think about combining butter with syrups to reduce fat.

Chapter 15

Make-It-Together Party Food

SERVES 6–8

Calories: 343.69
Fat: 11.95 grams
Fat as % of calories: 31.3%
Carbohydrates: 31.13 grams
Fiber: 5.08 grams
Sodium: 403.01 grams
Vitamin A: 230% DV
Vitamin C: 35% DV
Calcium: 420.72 mg

INGREDIENTS

1 pound 85% lean ground beef
1 onion, chopped
1 cup grated carrot
1 cup diced mushrooms
1 14.5-ounce can diced
    tomatoes, undrained
1 8-ounce can low-sodium
    tomato sauce
1 13-ounce can low-fat
    evaporated milk
2 tablespoons cornstarch
½ teaspoon dried Italian
    seasoning
1 cup shredded part-skim
    mozzarella cheese
1 cup shredded Cheddar cheese
12 whole wheat soft breadsticks
2 cups celery sticks
2 cups baby carrots
2 cups grape tomatoes

Cheeseburger–Veggie Fondue

*The kids will love this one! It's mild and cheesy,
and the vegetables are almost undetectable!*

1. In large saucepan, cook ground beef with onion until beef is browned, stirring to break up meat. Drain off any fat. Add carrot and mushrooms; cook and stir for 3–4 minutes until crisp-tender.

2. Add tomatoes, tomato sauce, milk, cornstarch, and Italian seasoning and bring just to a simmer. Add the cheeses; cook and stir constantly over low heat until cheese is melted and mixture is smooth.

3. Pour into a fondue pot and light the heating element. Serve immediately with remaining ingredients.

Healthier Cheese Fondue

Adding some mushrooms and onions to a classic fondue adds fiber and nutrients while enhancing the rich flavor.

1. In large saucepan, melt butter over medium heat. Add onion, garlic, and mushrooms; cook, stirring frequently, until vegetables are tender and liquid has evaporated.

2. Add wine to the pan and heat over low heat until bubbles begin to rise. Toss the cheeses with the cornstarch and add to the wine mixture, a handful at a time, stirring constantly over low heat.

3. Stir in the lemon juice. Cook and stir until mixture is smooth and blended. Pour into fondue pot, light the bottom heat source, and serve with remaining ingredients.

SERVES 6

Calories: 448.38
Fat: 16.12 grams
Fat as % of calories: 32.3%
Carbohydrates: 42.88 grams
Fiber: 6.64 grams
Sodium: 256.65 mg
Vitamin A: 220% DV
Vitamin C: 30% DV
Calcium: 684.52 mg

INGREDIENTS

2 tablespoons butter
1 onion, chopped
3 cloves garlic, minced
1 cup diced cremini mushrooms
2 cups dry white wine
2 cups grated low-fat Swiss cheese
2 cups grated Gruyère cheese
2 tablespoons cornstarch
1 tablespoon lemon juice
2 pears, sliced
3 apples, sliced
2 cups baby carrots

Perfect Pizza Sauce

Your own homemade pizza sauce is healthier than bottled.

1. In large skillet, heat olive oil over medium heat. Add onion and garlic; cook and stir for 5 minutes. Add carrot; cook and stir for 2 minutes longer. Add tomato paste and stir. Let cook for 5–6 minutes or until paste begins to brown.

2. Add the undrained tomatoes; cook, stirring to scrape the bottom of the pan. Let simmer for 5 minutes until thickened. Stir in remaining ingredients and remove from heat. Use as directed in recipes or cover and refrigerate up to 3 days.

Pizza and Health

Did you know that eating pizza may cut the risk of developing cancer? Classic Italian pizzas, with whole wheat crust, a good amount of tomato sauce, and minimal cheese and meat toppings are the focus of this health trend. The lycopene in the tomatoes is key.

**YIELDS 2 CUPS;
SERVING SIZE ¼ CUP**

Calories: 68.57
Fat: 2.19 grams
Fat as % of calories: 28.7%
Carbohydrates: 11.90 grams
Fiber: 2.62 grams
Sodium: 128.17 mg
Vitamin A: 35% DV
Vitamin C: 20% DV
Calcium: 31.00 mg

INGREDIENTS

1 tablespoon olive oil
1 onion, chopped
3 cloves garlic, minced
½ cup grated carrot
1 6-ounce can low-sodium
    tomato paste
1 14.5-ounce can diced
    tomatoes, undrained
3 tablespoons yellow mustard
1 tablespoon grainy mustard
1 teaspoon dried Italian
    seasoning
⅛ teaspoon pepper

INGREDIENTS

2 tablespoons butter
1 onion, chopped
3 cloves garlic, minced
2 tablespoons flour
¼ teaspoon salt
⅛ teaspoon white pepper
2 cups Healthy Chicken Stock
    (page 160)
1 cup 1% milk
1 8-ounce package low-fat
    cream cheese, cubed
1½ cups shredded Cheddar
    cheese
2 cups baby carrots
3 apples, sliced
2 green bell peppers, sliced
3 cups cubed Cracked Wheat
    French Bread (page 139)

Updated Cheddar Cheese Fondue

This fondue version is nonalcoholic, so kids can enjoy it too. You could also serve Healthy Meatballs (page 84) as a dipper.

1. In large saucepan, melt butter over medium heat. Add onion and garlic; cook and stir for 5 minutes. Sprinkle with flour, salt, and pepper and cook until bubbly.

2. Add stock and milk; cook and stir until mixture starts to thicken. Add cream cheese; cook and stir until melted and blended. Add Cheddar cheese; cook and stir until blended.

3. Pour into fondue pot and light the base. Serve immediately with remaining ingredients.

Homemade Stocks

Homemade stocks have much less sodium than even the low-sodium canned varieties. They are not difficult to make; they just take some time. Using your slow cooker is a great way to make stock with hardly any effort at all. It's best to freeze homemade stocks; make sure to leave headspace of about 1 inch in the container.

High-Fiber Pizza Crust

This pizza crust is crisp on the outside and chewy on the inside. The secret is to prebake the crust; that also lets you make it ahead of time.

1. In large bowl, combine yeast with ¼ cup warm water; let stand until bubbly, about 10 minutes. Add remaining water, orange juice, garlic, Italian seasoning, salt, and olive oil and mix well. Stir in whole wheat flour and beat for 2 minutes. Add wheat germ and flaxseed and beat again. Stir in enough bread flour to form a firm dough. Turn onto floured surface and knead for 10 minutes. Place in greased bowl, turning to grease top.

2. Cover and let rise for 1½ hours. Punch down dough, divide in half, place on floured surface, and let rest for 10 minutes. Preheat oven to 400°F.

3. For large pizzas, grease two cookie sheets and sprinkle with cornmeal. Roll out dough directly on the cookie sheets to almost cover; dough should be about ¼-inch thick. Let rise for 30 minutes, then bake for 10–12 minutes or until just set. Let cool and use in recipes.

4. For individual pizzas, divide into 12 balls. On floured surface, roll into 8" rounds. Place on cookie sheets and let rise for 20 minutes, then bake for 6–8 minutes until set. Let cool and use as directed in recipes.

YIELDS 2 CRUSTS; 12 SERVINGS

Calories: 163.91
Fat: 3.88 grams
Fat as % of calories: 21.3%
Carbohydrates: 27.65 grams
Fiber: 3.58 grams
Sodium: 99.19 mg
Vitamin A: 0% DV
Vitamin C: 4% DV
Calcium: 15.63 mg

INGREDIENTS

1 0.25-ounce package active dry yeast
1¼ cups warm water, divided
¼ cup orange juice
3 cloves garlic, minced
1 teaspoon dried Italian seasoning
½ teaspoon salt
2 tablespoons olive oil
1½ cups whole wheat flour
¼ cup wheat germ
3 tablespoons ground flaxseed
1½ cups bread flour
3 tablespoons yellow cornmeal

INGREDIENTS

1 tablespoon olive oil
1 onion, chopped
4 cloves garlic, minced
2 jalapeño peppers, minced
1 green bell pepper, chopped
1 15-ounce can vegetarian refried beans
1 15-ounce can black beans, drained
½ cup Perfect Pizza Sauce (page 237)
2 High-Fiber Pizza Crusts (page 239), prebaked
1 cup shredded part-skim mozzarella cheese
1 cup shredded Cheddar cheese
⅓ cup chopped green onions
1 cup chopped grape tomatoes
½ cup low-fat sour cream

Low-Fat Mexican Pizza

You could freeze half of the sauce if you want to make only one pizza. Thaw it in the refrigerator overnight, then all you have to do is assemble the pizza and bake it.

1. Preheat oven to 400°F. In large skillet, heat olive oil over medium heat. Add onions, garlic, and jalapeños and cook until crisp-tender, about 5 minutes. Add green bell pepper; cook and stir for 3 minutes longer. Add refried beans, black beans, and Pizza Sauce; simmer for 5 minutes.

2. Divide sauce among the prebaked Pizza Crusts. Sprinkle with cheeses. Bake for 20–25 minutes until cheeses are melted and brown.

3. Meanwhile, in small bowl, combine green onions, tomatoes, and sour cream. Use this mixture to top pizza after slicing it into squares.

Garlic

For a while, garlic was considered a miracle food, reducing cholesterol and preventing heart disease. The latest research shows that while it does help, it's not the magic bullet. It does not reduce LDL cholesterol as much as previously thought, but garlic does contain potent sulfur compounds that can help improve your health.

Chicken Veggie Tacos

This will surprise people who expect tacos to be made of beef. You could also substitute fish for the chicken for a California taco.

1. In large skillet, heat olive oil over medium heat. Add onion, garlic, green pepper, zucchini, and jalapeño pepper; cook and stir for 4 minutes. Add chicken and sprinkle with salt, pepper, and oregano. Cook and stir for 8–10 minutes until chicken is almost cooked.

2. Add lime juice and taco sauce; cook and stir for 3–4 minutes longer until chicken is tender. Remove from heat. Heat taco shells as directed on package. Make tacos with chicken mixture, lettuce, tomatoes, and cheese.

Stir-Frying

Stir-frying is a very healthy way to cook food. The quick cooking over high heat loses fewer vitamins than long simmering. All the ingredients have to be ready and prepared before cooking starts because the process is so quick. You can use your favorite vegetables in any stir-fry recipe.

SERVES 8

Calories: 242.30
Fat: 8.24 grams
Fat as % of calories: 30.6%
Carbohydrates: 23.13 grams
Fiber: 3.71 grams
Sodium: 410.20 mg
Vitamin A: 35% DV
Vitamin C: 110% DV
Calcium: 161.69 mg

INGREDIENTS

1 tablespoon olive oil
1 onion, chopped
3 cloves garlic, minced
2 green bell peppers, chopped
1 zucchini, sliced
1 jalapeño pepper, minced
1 pound boneless, skinless
  chicken breasts, cubed
½ teaspoon salt
⅛ teaspoon pepper
1 teaspoon dried oregano leaves
2 tablespoons lime juice
1 cup green taco sauce
8 crisp taco shells
2 cups shredded lettuce
2 tomatoes, chopped
1 cup shredded Monterey jack
  cheese

INGREDIENTS

1 pound 85% lean ground beef
2 onions, chopped
3 cloves garlic, minced
1 jalapeño pepper, minced
½ teaspoon salt
⅛ teaspoon cayenne pepper
1 15-ounce can vegetarian
    refried beans
½ cup taco sauce
8 crisp taco shells
¼ cup low-fat sour cream
½ cup Lighter Guacamole (page
    26)
1 cup Fresh Tomato Salsa (page
    25)
2 cups shredded lettuce
2 cups chopped tomatoes
1 cup shredded extra-sharp
    Cheddar cheese

Healthy Beef Tacos

This easy recipe stretches 1 pound of beef to easily feed eight people; that's a great way to reduce fat! Make the filling ahead of time and reheat when you want to eat.

1. In large skillet, brown ground beef with onions, garlic, and jalapeño pepper, stirring to break up meat. Drain thoroughly, then sprinkle with salt and pepper.

2. Stir in beans and taco sauce and bring to a simmer. At this point you can refrigerate this mixture; reheat in a saucepan before proceeding.

3. Heat taco shells as directed on package. In small bowl, combine sour cream, Guacamole, and Salsa. Make tacos with beef mixture, lettuce, tomatoes, cheese, and sour cream mixture.

Stretching Beef

Beef is one of the main sources of fat in the diet. Although it does contain complete protein and important vitamins and minerals, your recipes will be healthier if you limit it. The best way to do that is to make compound dishes like casseroles and tacos, using ingredients like meaty-tasting mushrooms and other vegetables to stretch the dish.

Vegetarian Tacos

For vegetarians, this version of taco filling is rich and satisfying. You could use other types of beans; chick peas and red beans would be delicious.

1. In large skillet, heat olive oil over medium heat. Add onion and jalapeño peppers; cook and stir for 6 minutes. Add black beans, corn, oregano, pepper, and chili powder; cook and stir until hot.

2. Remove from heat and stir in ricotta cheese. Heat taco shells as directed on package. Make tacos with filling, avocado, Salsa, Cheddar cheese, and Guacamole.

SERVES 8

Calories: 297.77
Fat: 11.73 grams
Fat as % of calories: 35.5%
Carbohydrates: 37.25 grams
Fiber: 9.33 grams
Sodium: 481.16 mg
Vitamin A: 25% DV
Vitamin C: 50% DV
Calcium: 167.89 mg

INGREDIENTS

1 tablespoon olive oil
1 onion, chopped
2 jalapeño peppers, minced
1 15-ounce can black beans, drained
2 cups frozen corn
½ teaspoon oregano leaves
⅛ teaspoon cayenne pepper
2 teaspoons chili powder
½ cup part-skim ricotta cheese
8 crisp taco shells
1 avocado, peeled and chopped
1 cup Fresh Tomato Salsa (page 25)
1 cup shredded low-fat Cheddar cheese
½ cup Lighter Guacamole (page 26)

Chopped Veggie Salad

You can add any fresh or frozen vegetables to this complex and colorful salad. Serve it on greens—baby spinach, curly endive, or butter lettuce—and top it with cooked shrimp, chicken, or ham.

1. In large bowl, combine peppers, onion, squash, mushrooms, green onion, cauliflower, and peas. Sprinkle with lemon juice, salt, and pepper, and toss gently; cover and refrigerate up to 2 hours.

2. When ready to eat, toss with salad dressing and serve with a combination of greens and other salad toppings.

SERVES 8

Calories: 99.55
Fat: 1.01 grams
Fat as % of calories: 10.1%
Carbohydrates: 20.51 grams
Fiber: 4.34 grams
Sodium: 264.46 mg
Vitamin A: 35% DV
Vitamin C: 170% DV
Calcium: 46.36 mg

INGREDIENTS

2 green bell peppers, chopped
1 red bell pepper, chopped
1 red sweet onion, chopped
1 yellow summer squash, sliced
1 8-ounce package sliced mushrooms
½ cup chopped green onions
2 cups chopped cauliflower florets
2 cups frozen baby peas, thawed
2 tablespoons lemon juice
½ teaspoon salt
¼ teaspoon pepper
1 cup nonfat ranch salad dressing

INGREDIENTS

6 cups baby spinach leaves
4 cups curly endive
4 cups butter lettuce
2 cups chopped tomatoes
2 green bell peppers, chopped
1 8-ounce package sliced
    mushrooms
½ cup sliced green onions
½ cup French Salad Dressing
    (page 163
½ cup Hundred Island Dressing
    (page 162)

INGREDIENTS

1 recipe Cracked Wheat French
    Bread (page 139)
3 tablespoons cornmeal
1 egg white
2 tablespoons sesame seeds

Make-Your-Own Salads

Add whatever toppings you'd like to this basic recipe. Cooked shrimp, chicken, chopped ham, chickpeas, lima beans, sliced roast beef, and more veggies are all good ideas.

Combine all ingredients except the salad dressings in a large serving bowl; toss to mix. Set up small bowls with the different Dressings and toppings around the big bowl, along with salad bowls, forks, and serving spoons.

Fresh Spinach

Fresh spinach, especially baby spinach, is sweet, tender, and delicious in salads. However, eating too much spinach can reduce the amount of calcium your body can absorb. It is a rich source of fiber and vitamins A and E, but it doesn't have the amount of iron that Popeye thought!

Cracked Wheat Hoagie Buns

Hoagie buns are like French bread but smaller, so they're easy to use for making sandwiches.

1. Prepare the Bread through Step 3. Let dough rise for 1 hour, then punch down, cover with a bowl, and let rest for 10 minutes. Divide dough into half; divide each half into thirds, then into thirds again, to make 18 balls.

2. Shape each into an oval. Grease baking sheets and sprinkle with cornmeal. Arrange dough on the cornmeal, then cover and let rise for 30–40 minutes until doubled. Carefully make two slashes into the top of each roll.

3. In small bowl, beat egg white until foamy. Carefully brush over the rolls; sprinkle with sesame seeds.

4. Preheat oven to 400°F. Bake rolls for 14–20 minutes or until golden brown and firm. Remove to wire racks to cool completely.

Easy Whole Wheat Crepes

Make two batches of crepes and a couple of fillings and have a crepe party! They're a low-stress dish for a brunch, and your guests will delight in the variety of choices.

1. In food processor, combine all ingredients except olive oil. Process just until batter is smooth. Cover and refrigerate for 3–4 hours.

2. If necessary, add more water to create a batter the consistency of pancake batter. Heat an 8-inch nonstick crepe pan or skillet and brush with some of the olive oil. Pour ¼ cup of the batter into the pan and swirl and tilt to coat bottom of pan.

3. Cook over medium heat for 2 minutes, then loosen edges of crepe and carefully flip over; cook for 50–60 seconds on second side. Flip out onto kitchen towel and let cool. Do not stack crepes. Fill with desired fillings.

YIELDS 16 CREPES

Calories: 90.09
Fat: 2.68 grams
Fat as % of calories: 26.8%
Carbohydrates: 12.64 grams
Fiber: 1.13 grams
Sodium: 75.45 mg
Vitamin A: 0% DV
Vitamin C: 3% DV
Calcium: 25.80 mg

INGREDIENTS

1 cup all-purpose flour
1 cup whole wheat flour
2 eggs
4 egg whites
1 cup buttermilk
¼ cup orange juice
½ cup water
¼ teaspoon salt
2 tablespoons olive oil

Best Low-Fat Beef Sandwich Spread

Beef is complemented by a curry-flavored cream cheese mixture and lots of fruits and vegetables for flavor and crunch.

1. In large bowl, beat cream cheese with sour cream and curry powder until smooth. Stir in celery, beef, apples, cranberries, and green onion. At this point the spread can be covered and refrigerated up to 2 days.

2. When ready to eat, spread the cut sides of the Buns with butter and toast under broiler. Make sandwiches with beef mixture and spinach leaves.

SERVES 8

Calories: 466.72
Fat: 17.29 grams
Fat as % of calories: 33.3%
Carbohydrates: 55.66 grams
Fiber: 6.41 grams
Sodium: 301.46 mg
Vitamin A: 25% DV
Vitamin C: 15% DV
Calcium: 74.59 mg

INGREDIENTS

1 3-ounce package low-fat cream cheese, softened
1 3-ounce package nonfat cream cheese, softened
½ cup low-fat sour cream
1 tablespoon curry powder
1 cup sliced celery
2 cups chopped deli roast beef
2 Granny Smith apples, chopped
½ cup dried cranberries
⅓ cup chopped green onion
8 Cracked Wheat Hoagie Buns (page 244), split
2 tablespoons butter, softened
2 cups baby spinach leaves

SERVES 8

Calories: 304.61
Fat: 10.46 grams
Fat as % of calories: 30.9%
Carbohydrates: 27.32 grams
Fiber: 2.43 grams
Sodium: 311.14 mg
Vitamin A: 50% DV
Vitamin C: 35% DV
Calcium: 294.32 mg

INGREDIENTS

2 tablespoons butter
1 onion, chopped
1 cup sliced carrots
1 green bell pepper, chopped
2 tablespoons flour
¼ teaspoon salt
⅛ teaspoon pepper
½ cup nonfat light cream
½ cup chicken stock
1 13-ounce can nonfat
    evaporated milk
¼ cup tomato paste
½ pound salmon fillet, cubed
1 cup raw medium shrimp
8 Easy Whole Wheat Crepes
    (page 245)
½ cup grated Havarti cheese
¼ cup grated Parmesan cheese

Seafood Crepes

*Now this is an elegant recipe! Make the sauce ahead of time and
assemble the crepes with your guests.*

1. Preheat oven to 375°F. In large saucepan, melt butter over medium heat. Add onion and carrots; cook and stir for 5 minutes. Add green bell pepper; cook and stir for 2–3 minutes longer until crisp-tender. Remove vegetables to bowl with slotted spoon.

2. Add flour, salt, and pepper to saucepan; cook and stir until bubbly. Add cream, stock, evaporated milk, and tomato paste; cook and stir until mixture thickens and bubbles. Remove 1½ cups of the sauce and set aside; add salmon and shrimp to remaining sauce and bring back to a simmer. Simmer for 5–6 minutes or until salmon and shrimp are just cooked. Return vegetables to sauce with the seafood.

3. Spray a 9" x 13" pan with nonstick cooking spray. Place Crepes on work surface. Place about 3 tablespoons shrimp mixture on each Crepe and roll up; place seam side down in pan. Pour remaining sauce over Crepes and top with cheeses.

4. Bake for 20–25 minutes until Crepes are hot and cheeses are melted and start to brown. Serve immediately.

Freezing Crepes

Crepes freeze very well, so they are great for entertaining. Cool them completely, then stack them with a piece of waxed paper or parchment paper between each one. Place them in a large resealable plastic freezer bag, label, and freeze for up to 3 months. To thaw, let stand at room temperature for 30–45 minutes until softened.

Veggie Cheese Crepes

This vegetarian crepe filling is full of vitamins and minerals, and it is delicious.

1. Preheat oven to 350°F. In large skillet, melt butter over medium heat. Add onion and garlic; cook and stir for 4 minutes. Add potato; cook and stir for 4 minutes. Add stock and bring to a simmer. Cover pan and simmer for 5 minutes or until potatoes are almost tender. Add carrot and peas to skillet; cook and stir until potatoes are tender and carrots are crisp-tender. Drain well if necessary.

2. In large bowl, combine sour cream, cream cheese, yogurt, dill weed, and Cheddar cheese; reserve ½ cup in small bowl. Stir vegetables into large bowl. Divide among Crepes and roll up. Spray 9" x 13" pan with nonstick cooking spray.

3. Place Crepes in pan, seam side down. Spread with remaining sour cream mixture. Bake for 20–25 minutes or until hot.

Spinach Pesto Pasta

Spinach adds color, fiber, and nutrition to pesto. You can make the sauce ahead of time, then toss it with the pasta and cooking water just before serving.

1. Bring a large pot of water to a boil. Meanwhile, in large saucepan heat olive oil over medium heat. Add onion and garlic; cook and stir for 6 minutes. Place mixture in food processor.

2. Drain spinach very well and add to food processor with both types of basil. Process until finely chopped. Add ricotta and Parmesan cheeses and process until blended; set aside.

3. Cook pasta in boiling water until al dente. Drain, reserving ⅓ cup pasta cooking water. Combine pasta and ricotta mixture in large saucepan; add enough cooking water to make a sauce. Cook and stir over low heat until cheese melts and mixture blends. Serve immediately.

SERVES 8

Calories: 260.85
Fat: 8.04 grams
Fat as % of calories: 27.7%
Carbohydrates: 31.31 grams
Fiber: 3.34 grams
Sodium: 346.71 mg
Vitamin A: 60% DV
Vitamin C: 25% DV
Calcium: 196.43 mg

INGREDIENTS

2 tablespoons butter
1 onion, chopped
3 cloves garlic, minced
1 potato, diced
½ cup vegetable stock
1 cup grated carrots
1 cup frozen baby peas
½ cup low-fat sour cream
3 ounces nonfat cream cheese
½ cup low-fat yogurt
½ teaspoon dried dill weed
1 cup shredded low-fat Cheddar cheese
8 Easy Whole Wheat Crepes (page 245)

SERVES 6

Calories: 449.43
Fat: 12.89 grams
Fat as % of calories: 25.8%
Carbohydrates: 65.86 grams
Fiber: 2.07 grams
Sodium: 198.92 mg
Vitamin A: 120% DV
Vitamin C: 25% DV
Calcium: 364.17 mg

INGREDIENTS

2 tablespoons olive oil
1 onion, chopped
3 cloves garlic, minced
1 10-ounce package frozen spinach, thawed
1 cup fresh basil leaves
1 teaspoon dried basil leaves
1 15-ounce container part-skim ricotta cheese
⅓ cup grated Parmesan cheese
1 16-ounce package whole wheat pasta

Calories: 202.29
Fat: 7.47 grams
Fat as % of calories: 33.2%
Carbohydrates: 18.63 grams
Fiber: 1.66 grams
Sodium: 312.24 mg
Vitamin A: 5% DV
Vitamin C: 10% DV
Calcium: 52.67 mg

INGREDIENTS

1 tablespoon butter
1 tablespoon olive oil
½ pound sirloin steak
½ teaspoon salt
⅛ teaspoon pepper
1 onion, chopped
4 cloves garlic, minced
1 cup diced portobello mushrooms
1 cup sliced mushrooms
1 cup low-sodium beef stock
½ teaspoon dried marjoram
    leaves
1 tablespoon lemon juice
2 tablespoons cornstarch
½ cup low-fat sour cream
8 Easy Whole Wheat Crepes
    (page 245)

Beef and Mushroom Crepes

Mushrooms taste meaty and are a great addition to this recipe. They also help keep the fat content down and add fiber and B vitamins.

1. Preheat oven to 350°F. In large saucepan, combine butter and olive oil over medium heat. Sprinkle steak with salt and pepper and add to saucepan. Cook for 4 minutes until steak turns easily. Turn and cook for 3–4 minutes on second side. Remove from pan and set aside.

2. Add onion and garlic to saucepan; cook and stir, scraping pan drippings. Add mushrooms to pan; cook and stir for 4 minutes. Add beef stock, marjoram, and lemon juice; bring to a simmer. Simmer for 5 minutes.

3. In small bowl, combine cornstarch and sour cream and mix well. Add to saucepan; cook and stir until sauce thickens and bubbles. Remove 1 cup of sauce to medium bowl. Slice steak across the grain into ¼-inch strips and add to sauce in bowl.

4. Spray 9" x 13" baking pan with nonstick cooking spray. Fill Crepes with beef mixture, roll up, and place seam side down in baking pan. Top with remaining sour cream sauce. Bake for 20–30 minutes or until thoroughly heated.

Caramelized Onion and Shrimp Penne

Make the caramelized onion mixture and store it in the refrigerator. When it's time for your party, heat it up slowly in a pan and proceed with the recipe.

1. In large skillet, melt butter and olive oil over medium-low heat. Add onions and sugar; cook and stir for 5 minutes. Reduce heat to low and cook onions, stirring frequently, for 20–25 minutes or until they are light golden brown. At this point the onions can be refrigerated up to 24 hours.

2. Reheat onions, if necessary. Add salt, pepper, and red bell peppers; cook and stir over medium heat for another 5 minutes.

3. Bring a large pot of water to a boil. Cook pasta according to package directions until al dente. Meanwhile, add shrimp, peas, and wine to the onion mixture; cook, stirring occasionally, until shrimp turn pink.

4. When pasta is al dente, drain, reserving ⅓ cup cooking water. Add pasta to skillet with onions along with enough water to make a sauce. Add cheeses and toss over medium heat until cheeses melt. Sprinkle with basil and serve immediately.

Caramelizing Onions

Onions have a high sugar content, which is overridden by the sharp sulfur compounds that give the vegetable its characteristic taste. Cooking helps reduce the sulfur compounds and develops the sugars. To caramelize onions, cook them slowly in a bit of butter or oil for about 30 minutes until they are golden brown.

SERVES 6

Calories: 388.25
Fat: 8.49 grams
Fat as % of calories: 19.9%
Carbohydrates: 56.33 grams
Fiber: 3.11 grams
Sodium: 442.16 mg
Vitamin A: 50% DV
Vitamin C: 150% DV
Calcium: 134.88 mg

INGREDIENTS

2 tablespoons butter
1 tablespoon olive oil
3 onions, chopped
1 teaspoon sugar
½ teaspoon salt
⅛ teaspoon pepper
2 red bell peppers, chopped
1 16-ounce package whole wheat penne pasta
1 pound medium raw shrimp, deveined
2 cups frozen baby peas
⅓ cup dry white wine
¼ cup crumbled feta cheese
¼ cup grated Romano cheese
½ cup chopped fresh basil leaves

SERVES 12

Calories: 217.04
Fat: 4.99 grams
Fat as % of calories: 20.1%
Carbohydrates: 35.69 grams
Fiber: 0.01 grams
Sodium: 176.18 mg
Vitamin A: 6% DV
Vitamin C: 2% DV
Calcium: 260.33 mg

INGREDIENTS

2 cups nonfat light cream
1 13-ounce can sweetened condensed milk
1 13-ounce can nonfat evaporated milk
2 egg yolks
¼ cup sugar
2 tablespoons cornstarch
⅛ teaspoon salt
1 tablespoon vanilla

Vanilla Ice Cream

For chocolate ice cream, stir 1 cup chopped good-quality chocolate into the custard mixture after it's cooked but before you begin to chill it. You could also add mashed strawberries, raspberries, or pears to create your own flavor.

1. In large saucepan, combine cream, condensed milk, and evaporated milk and mix until combined. Stir in egg yolks, sugar, cornstarch, and salt and beat well until blended.

2. Place pan over low heat and cook, stirring constantly, until mixture begins to thicken. Continue cooking until the custard coats the back of a spoon.

3. Strain custard into a large bowl and stir in the vanilla. Cover and chill for 4–6 hours in refrigerator. Freeze according to ice cream maker's instructions.

YIELDS 3 CUPS; SERVING SIZE ⅓ CUP

Calories: 92.79
Fat: 0.39 grams
Fat as % of calories: 3.9%
Carbohydrates: 23.48 grams
Fiber: 2.25 grams
Sodium: 18.95 mg
Vitamin A: 10% DV
Vitamin C: 80% DV
Calcium: 14.36 mg

INGREDIENTS

1 16-ounce jar sliced mangoes, drained
1 cup orange juice
¼ cup sugar
2 tablespoons lemon juice
1 teaspoon vanilla
Pinch salt
1½ cups chopped strawberries
1 cup blueberries
1 banana, sliced

Fruity Ice Cream Sauce

Use any fresh chopped fruits in this wonderful sauce. You could also make the base with canned peaches or nectarines.

1. Place drained mango slices in food processor. In small saucepan, combine orange juice, sugar, and lemon juice and bring to a simmer. Simmer, stirring frequently, until sugar is dissolved.

2. Add sugar mixture to mangoes and purée. Stir in vanilla and salt, then pour into a bowl, cover, and refrigerate until ready to eat.

3. Stir in remaining ingredients and serve over different flavors of ice cream.

Appendix A

Healthy Party Menus

Comfort Foods

Christmas Dinner

Boy's Birthday Party

Girl's Birthday Party

Job Promotion

Melted Cheese Rolls (page 136)
Rosemary Green Beans (page 145)
Apricot–Pear Angel Cake (page 191)

Milestone Birthday

Caramelized Onion Triangles (page 33)
Grilled Asparagus with Garlic (page 147)
Healthy and Rich Lasagna (page 80)
Simple Green Salad (page 162) with French Salad Dressing (page 163)
Gingerbread Carrot Cake (page 192)

Picnic at the Beach

Fruit Salsa (page 26)
Baked Spicy Tortilla Chips (page 35)
Light Ham and Grape Wraps (page 64)
Mom's Healthy Apple Coleslaw (page 166)
Potato Vegetable Salad (page 166)
Rocky Road Fruit Bark (page 174)

Teen Birthday Party

Mini Mexican Pizzas (page 28)
Light Oven-Fried Chicken (page 96)
Nutty Green Beans (page 210)
Oatmeal PBJ Cookies (page 182)
Orange and Lemon Olive Oil Cake (page 189)

Thanksgiving

Cranberry Punch (page 23)
Roasted Vegetable Tart (page 127)
Pumpkin-Stuffed Chicken Breasts (page 92)
Buffalo Smashed Potatoes (page 141)
Cheesy Vegetable Medley (page 227)
Fluffy Date Pie (page 186)

Romantic Dinner for Two

Cherry Salsa (page 224)
Light Cashew Rice Pilaf (page 149)
Baked Stuffed Shrimp (page 115)
Garlic Roasted Potatoes (page 141)
Simple Green Salad (page 162) with Raspberry Vinaigrette (page 161)
Low-Carb Truffles (page 174)

Teen Movie Night

Light Root Beer Floats (page 20)
Layered Taco Dip Without the Guilt (page 30)
Mini Turkey Meatloaves (page 206)
Pita Pizzas (page 210)
Healthy Norwegian Brownies (page 180)

Cook Together: Fondue Party

Healthy Salmon-Stuffed Mushrooms (page 32)
Simple Green Salad (page 162)
Cheeseburger–Veggie Fondue (page 236)
Healthier Cheese Fondue (page 237)
Updated Cheddar Cheese Fondue (page 238)
Cracked Wheat French Bread (page 139)
Peach and Blueberry Floating Islands (page 197)

Cook Together: Crepe Party

White Wine Sangria (page 21)
Cucumber–Orange Salad (page 164)
Easy Whole Wheat Crepes (page 245)
Seafood Crepes (page 246)
Veggie Cheese Crepes (page 247)
Beef and Mushroom Crepes (page 248)

Cook Together: Pizza Party

Layered Shrimp and Pesto Dip (page 27)
High-Fiber Pizza Crust (page 239)
Greek Pizza (page 132)
Low-Fat Mexican Pizza (page 240)
Perfect Pizza Sauce (page 237)
Soft Frosted Apricot Cookies (page 179)

Cook Together: Taco Night

Simple Green Salad (page 162) with Hundred Island Dressing (page 162)
Healthy Beef Tacos (page 242)
Chicken Veggie Tacos (page 241)
Vegetarian Tacos (page 243)
Mom's Lighter Apple Pie (page 184)

Cook Together: Sundae Bar

Vanilla Ice Cream (page 250)
Fruity Ice Cream Sauce (page 250)
Low-Fat Fudge Sauce (page 199)
Lemon Truffle Meringue Cookies (page 169)
Light Peanut Butter and Cherry Cookies (page 175)

Cook Together: Spaghetti Bar

Turkey Spring Rolls (page 65)
Sneaky Spaghetti Sauce (page 203)
Healthy Meatballs (page 84)
Spinach Pesto Pasta (page 247)
Caramelized Onion and Shrimp Penne (page 249)
Mini Strawberry Baked Alaska (page 191)

Cook Together: Sandwich Bar

Cracked Wheat Hoagie Buns (page 244)
Best Low-Fat Beef Sandwich Spread (page 245)
Grilled Tuna Salad Quesadillas (page 64)

Cook Together: Make Your Own Salads

Brunch for Weekend Guests

Easter Brunch

Fourth of July Picnic

Cozy Winter Dinner

Lunch on the Porch

Appetizer Party

Get-Together for Dessert

Dinner for the Boss

Grilled Asparagus with Garlic (page 147)
Strawberry Fudge Ice Cream Dessert (page 195)

Bridal Shower

Tomato–Egg Finger Sandwiches (page 29)
Guilt-Free Cranberry Scones (page 41)
Pistachio Tea Sandwiches (page 57)
Caribbean Shrimp Salad (page 114)
Chilled Pesto Gazpacho (page 155)
Low-Fat Brownie Pie (page 185)

Welcome Baby

Phyllo Berry Cups (page 50)
Parmesan Orzo Salad (page 57)
Pecan-Crusted Chicken Breasts (page 97)
Orange-Glazed Carrots (page 143)
Grilled Pear Angel Food Cake with Fruit Salsa (page 190)

Vegetarian Lunch

Cucumber–Orange Salad (page 164)
Stuffed Mushrooms in Phyllo (page 128)
Asparagus–Spinach Frittata (page 133)
Strawberry Fluff (page 197)

Appendix B
Resources

Books

Entertaining Light by Martha Shulman (New York, NY: William Morrow, 2000)
A selection of balanced and well-rounded entertaining menus, with an emphasis on low-fat foods like fish and vegetables.

Party Lights by Linda Rector-Page and Doug Vanderberg (Del Rey Oaks, CA: Healthy Healing Publications, 1994)
More than 500 recipes and seventy party menus will help you feed your guests healthy party food.

Celebrate! Healthy Entertaining for Any Occasion by the American Cancer Society (Atlanta, GA: American Cancer Society, 2001)
Twenty menus with easy flavorful recipes that are good for you.

Healthy Holidays: Total Health Entertaining All Year Round by Marilu Henner (New York, NY: Collins, 2002)
A new twist on entertaining, with menus and party ideas for everything from Earth Day to Bastille Day.

Party Food by Sharon Dalgleish (North Mankato, MN: Smart Apple Media, 2007)
Healthy food can be food for celebrating in this book that focuses on family gatherings.

Web Sites

Entertaining at About.com
www.entertaining.about.com
Menus, games, and party ideas for every occasion, including healthy foods and tips.

Nutrition at About.com
www.nutrition.about.com
Comprehensive information about nutrition, latest research, and healthy recipes, including tips for entertaining.

Family Fun: Parties
www.familyfun.go.com/parties
Focus on family parties and healthy, quick, and easy recipes and menus. Lots of ideas for children's parties.

Birthday Party Ideas
www.birthdaypartyideas.com
Large collection of birthday party ideas for kids, including a sweet sixteen party, scavenger hunt, and sleepover party. Parents offer tips and recipes.

Coolest Kid Birthday Party Ideas
www.coolest-kid-birthday-parties.com
Information about themes, costumes, and the best ideas for children's birthday parties.

Magazines and Newsletters

Cooking Light
This magazine focuses on healthy foods, especially recipes that use healthy fats and lots of fruits and vegetables. There are lots of party and holiday ideas.

Weight Watchers Magazine
Classic Weight Watchers' recipes and tips, including how to attend a party and still eat healthfully.

Women's Health
Focus on women's health, with easy recipes and some holiday and entertaining information.

Shape
Emphasis on fitness, nutrition, and beauty, with recipes and entertaining tips.

Child Magazine
Focus is on children up to age twelve, with information on nutrition, recipes, growth, and development.

INDEX

Standard U.S./Metric Measurement Conversions

VOLUME CONVERSIONS

U.S. Volume Measure	Metric Equivalent
⅛ teaspoon	0.5 milliliters
¼ teaspoon	1 milliliters
½ teaspoon	2 milliliters
1 teaspoon	5 milliliters
½ tablespoon	7 milliliters
1 tablespoon (3 teaspoons)	15 milliliters
2 tablespoons (1 fluid ounce)	30 milliliters
¼ cup (4 tablespoons)	60 milliliters
⅓ cup	90 milliliters
½ cup (4 fluid ounces)	125 milliliters
⅔ cup	160 milliliters
¾ cup (6 fluid ounces)	180 milliliters
1 cup (16 tablespoons)	250 milliliters
1 pint (2 cups)	500 milliliters
1 quart (4 cups)	1 liter (about)

WEIGHT CONVERSIONS

U.S. Weight Measure	Metric Equivalent
½ ounce	15 grams
1 ounce	30 grams
2 ounces	60 grams
3 ounces	85 grams
¼ pound (4 ounces)	115 grams
½ pound (8 ounces)	225 grams
¾ pound (12 ounces)	340 grams
1 pound (16 ounces)	454 grams

OVEN TEMPERATURE CONVERSIONS

Degrees Fahrenheit	Degrees Celsius
200 degrees F	100 degrees C
250 degrees F	120 degrees C
275 degrees F	140 degrees C
300 degrees F	150 degrees C
325 degrees F	160 degrees C
350 degrees F	180 degrees C
375 degrees F	190 degrees C
400 degrees F	200 degrees C
425 degrees F	220 degrees C
450 degrees F	230 degrees C

BAKING PAN SIZES

American	Metric
8 x 1½ inch round baking pan	20 x 4 cm cake tin
9 x 1½ inch round baking pan	23 x 3.5 cm cake tin
1 x 7 x 1½ inch baking pan	28 x 18 x 4 cm baking tin
113 x 9 x 2 inch baking pan	30 x 20 x 5 cm baking tin
2 quart rectangular baking dish	30 x 20 x 3 cm baking tin
15 x 10 x 2 inch baking pan	30 x 25 x 2 cm baking tin (Swiss roll tin)
9 inch pie plate	22 x 4 or 23 x 4 cm pie pl
7 or 8 inch springform pan	18 or 20 cm springform o loose bottom cake tin
9 x 5 x 3 inch loaf pan	23 x 13 x 7 cm or 2 lb narrow loaf or pate tin
1½ quart casserole	1.5 litre casserole
2 quart casserole	2 litre casserole